D1579414

David John Barrington Parsons was born in the UK and has travelled extensively, having lived for a short time in Germany, Spain and Africa. He has lived in the UK for many years, with his wife Sue, and his dog, a border-collie-bearded Collie cross. His hobbies include walking, writing and reading. He has a great interest in questions that puzzle mainstream science, which has led to several years researching a wide range of topics to find alternative solutions. The author has interest in sailing, having sailed his own boat from Cape Town to the UK and later sailed his own steel home-built yacht from the UK to Turkey with his family.

To my wife Susan, for her total support, and Jill for her boundless creativity.

David John Barrington Parsons

THE MATRIX OF THE MIND

AUSTIN MACAULEY PUBLISHERS™

LONDON * CAMBRIDGE * NEW YORK * SHARJAH

A CIP catalogue record for this title is available from the British Library.

ISBN 9781398426887 (Paperback)
ISBN 9781398426894 (ePub e-book)

www.austinmacauley.com

First Published 2023
Austin Macauley Publishers Ltd®
1 Canada Square
Canary Wharf
London
E14 5AA

Table of Contents

Preface

This book describes a quest to arrive at answers to several profound questions. Firstly, to understand the causes and sequence of events involved in the formation and evolution of the cosmos and eventually, the establishment of the planet Earth with its life-supporting environment.

Science currently views the start of the formation of the cosmos as being an event called the Big Bang, which was a vast outpouring of matter from a single point in space around 13.8 billion years ago. The original state of the universe before the Big Bang was a Great Void, which was a limitless expanse of nothingness.

The arising of matter from what was clearly a vast expanse of nothingness does pose a question as to how this could possibly come about. The Big Bang event saw the coming into being of matter and time.

The vast amount of matter resulting from this event enabled the formation of stars, galaxies, planets and ultimately the building-blocks for the entire universe. However, the world of science does not know what triggered the Big Bang event.

This book describes a completely new and revolutionary explanation for the evolution of the cosmos from the time of the Great Void through to the initiation of life on Earth. It also explains the evolution and diversification of the many species and the eventual establishment of humankind. The unique aspect of the human animal is their mind, which has demonstrated amazing capabilities of invention and creativity and original and even abstract thought.

Research into these aspects rapidly led to the assembly of a much wider list of questions regarding other phenomena that defied easy explanations. The expanded list of questions became:

I.   What triggered the Big Bang which seemed to spontaneously create matter from the Void, making "something" and "anti-something" out of seemingly, nothing-ness. Professor Hawking and others state an approximate date for the event, but there is no generally agreed explanation for how it came about.

II.   How did life start on Earth? Explanations seem to run back to a series of random chemical reactions forming amino acids and proteins, but as shall be demonstrated in this book, several scientists who are foremost in their fields, have calculated that this is a mathematical impossibility. A revolutionary new explanation will be described in this book.

III.   A general consideration of evolution from the first simplest living cell through to modern day man demonstrates that the progress and diversity of the species was not due to a series of *random* mutation/evolutionary steps but appears to be a long series of evolutionary and mutation events driven by teleological processes. This leads to the question; what is the evidence for existence of these processes, and what are the mechanisms?

IV.   Various research projects by Professor Sheldrake, Professor Sir R Peters from Oxford University, C Honiton and many others over several years has demonstrated conclusively that the phenomenon of telepathy exists, albeit in a fairly weak and inconsistent manner, requiring huge numbers of experiments and the application of meta-analysis to prove its existence. The phenomenon has been proven to exist beyond doubt. Some of these experiments will be described in chapter 8. But what is the mechanism? How can telepathy work when it would appear to contradict established laws of physics?

V.   More prosaically, how do eels manage to navigate from their place of birth in the Sargasso Sea to a specific river estuary in the UK where they were conceived? They do not swim by a direct route, but by using routes that provide the most favourable ocean currents, greatly reducing their travel time.

VI.   After having achieved this amazing feat, they then mate in the river estuary and eventually swim back to the Sargasso Sea, using different favourable ocean currents to minimise travel time. Having arrived back in the Sargasso, they produce their young hatchlings and die, completing the life cycle.

VII.   How do some migrating birds navigate from the UK to specific places in Africa by specific routes and return later in the year to the same locality in the UK from which they started. Even if they each had a built-in compass, they would know north and south, but that is not enough to navigate with such a high degree of accuracy. They also have to solve the navigational problems associated with magnetic variation.

VIII.   The Flatid Bug, as described by anthropologist L B S Leaky, is a flying insect which occurs in three colours: green, half coral/half pink and pink. A swarm of these bugs have the ability to organise themselves on a small branch, so that the swarm at rest resembles a flower with a green stem and a pink/coral flower.

IX.   If the swarm is disturbed, the bugs fly up, then eventually resettle on the twig, climbing over one another to arrange themselves once again to look like the flower. It is beyond the ability of any single bug within the swarm to have an "overview" that would allow the bugs to arrange themselves into the form of a flower. By disguising itself thus, it helps to avoid predators, but how the swarm achieves this feat is unknown.

X.   Professor Stephen Hawking states in his book "A Brief History of Time"[7] that there are certain fundamental numbers, like the charge on an electron, and the ratio of the masses of the electron and proton which, "seem to have been very finely adjusted to make possible the development of life."

XI.   If these numbers had been even slightly different in value from what they are, stars and planets could not have formed, super-nova would not have exploded seeding the cosmos with heavy elements essential for planet construction, and life could not have started. But how could those crucial numbers have been so finely adjusted, and by what mechanism?

This list contains several disparate subjects which seem to be entirely unrelated, but research described in the following chapters demonstrates that the answers are indeed related. They are explained by a completely new theory, Matrix Model Theory, which is presented here for the first time.

An Introduction to Matrix Model Theory

The background research required to answer these and other questions came from many sources including micro-biologists, psychologists, physicists, cosmologists and documents, books and research work from over fifty scientists and researchers. References to these sources have been provided: the relevant reference is indicated by a number attached to the text so that readers can find more details and see the source of the information described in the text.

Matrix Model Theory provides a completely new understanding of the evolution of the cosmos and how life on Earth started and how even the simplest life form can form, survive and thrive. The Matrix Model demonstrates that everything is interconnected and, in many ways, interdependent.

The Matrix Model itself evolved from the simplest format which existed just prior to the Big Bang which had only two domains, as will be described in detail in the chapters of this book. These acted as a catalyst to trigger the Big Bang and they also established the laws of science, which in turn lead to the establishment of the cosmos.

The Theory also describes the interactions between the domains which contributed to the eventual establishment of the Sun, the solar system and planet Earth with its life-supporting environment. The planet Earth has evolved by a series of remarkable and highly unlikely series of stages to eventually become a world with a moderate average temperature range and one with an -bearing atmosphere and a plentiful supply of water including the vast oceans, essential for the establishment of life. This made it an ideal environment for supporting wide and diverse forms of life and continues to do so.

Once the Earth environment had been established, the Matrix Model demonstrates that the evolution of a further crucial domain of the Matrix Model occurred which enabled the establishment of the first life form; the simplest living cell, capable of replication and surviving in the Earth environment.

Later evolutions of the Matrix Model had increasing numbers of domains, allowing the establishment of ever more complex life-forms, eventually arriving at the most complex of all, the Matrix Model associated with humans, Homo sapiens. The Homo sapiens Matrix Model has ten domains.

There is one unique Matrix Model for every species of life on Earth, with increasing levels of complexity as evolution proceeded. Matrix Model Theory also provides a new description of the structure of the "mind" of man, with logical extensions to other life-forms. It also explains how, even the simplest single-cell life-forms, can survive, replicate, and thrive even though they had no "brain", and were frequently having to cope with very hostile environments and had to be able to absorb energy sources from their environment.

First life

Before describing the formation of the first living cell, the structure of living entities in general will first be described. Even the simplest living cell is comprised of specific sets of amino acids arranged in a very particular way to form a specific protein. Many hundreds of these are specific but different proteins must be assembled in a unique way to establish this first simplest living cell.

Arguments persist as to how many proteins could constitute a cell which could truly be called "living", but Professor Morowitz[10] (Professor of molecular biophysics and biochemistry, Yale University) established that it would require a minimum of 239 proteins to form such a living cell which would have sufficient complexity to be called truly "living".

Further work by several researchers has established that such an assembly of proteins by a series of random chemical interaction events alone would have been impossible; a view shared by other prominent scientists. This research will be described, and Matrix Model Theory provides a feasible explanation.

Even the simplest cell would have to be able to carry a coded model of itself and be able to construct an identical model of itself from materials it would "find" from within its environment, or process within its structure, in order to reproduce, which is an essential characteristic of any living organism.

For this earliest living cell, it is thought that RNA, rather than DNA, would carry some of the genetic coding, but it would have to have been *given* or somehow acquired this initial coding. The great question relating to this is where did this coding come from in the case of the first living cell, since it would not have had any direct ancestors to inherit from? Matrix Model Theory provides an answer described in later chapters.

To continue to remain "alive," the cell would also have to absorb energy from its environment to sustain itself, whether in the form of chemicals or sugars, or other materials. Thus, even the simplest possible living cell had to have a high degree of sophistication to be regarded as truly "living". In spite of many years of research, no laboratory has ever produced a single cell which could be really regarded as *living* from combinations of chemicals alone. All living organisms are made from atoms and molecules, but they are not "just" atoms and molecules; there is the inherent capability for self-organisation[24].

When it comes to the critical subject of replication, it is not sufficient for life forms to have the *ability* to replicate, they must have some driving force that would compel them to do so. Replication is an energy consuming activity, even for a simple cell that replicates by cell splitting, where one cell becomes two in order to achieve reproduction.

Matrix Model Theory provides an explanation for the source of this *trigger* ensuring replication. It also explains how it was ensured that the cell sought and consumed the right chemicals and other materials from its environment to ensure its survival and ability to replicate.

Once the first living cell had been established, evolution and mutation together with natural selection enabled the appearance of other species of ever-increasing complexity, with each species having its own unique Matrix Model. This book describes the evidence for this, and how this earliest cell evolved with increasing sophistication to derive the vast number of different species we have today.

The natural evolution of new Matrix Models resulted in the evolution of new species. For each new species, the associated Matrix Model supported the new entity providing, along with the species' DNA, the coding which determined its form, function and behaviour. However, some of the essential coding continues to be retained within their associated Matrix Model domains, as is demonstrated by the missing heredity problem[17], which is described within these chapters.

The great majority of the ancestors of present-day species arrived and were first established during a relatively short period of time during the Cambrian period. In fact, so many new species appeared for the first time during this period, that it is called the "Cambrian Explosion".

Even Darwin had doubts that evolution alone could explain the arrival of so many new species in such a short time. The fact that the process is teleological, with the evolutions of many new Matrix Models supporting the many new and different species, provides the explanation. More detail and evidence for this explanation will be provided.

Matrix Model Theory also provides an explanation for a few of the so-called para-normal phenomena. One example is telepathy which is described in detail together with descriptions of the extensive research projects that establishes it as a real phenomenon. This field has been researched by credible researchers working within respected research institutions and have provided surprising results which are reviewed in this book and provide further strong evidence supporting Matrix Model Theory.

Having established that telepathy does exist, it is a weak and variable phenomenon and is not particularly useful. It does, however, provide a valuable insight into the functioning of the human mind. As professor J Jeans FRS[14] concluded, "telepathy does exist and has been proven."

Matrix Model Theory provides some of the missing elements that complete the understanding of a few other mysteries of nature, including the amazing organisation of bees, termites and ants, that seem to function as "super-organisms". It also explains the incredible navigational feats of the eel, the aerobatics capability of flocks of starlings flying in very tight formation in spectacular fashion.

It also provides an explanation for the migration of birds and their long-haul seasonal flights with staggeringly impressive navigational skills and the Flatid Bug's ability to arrange itself into a flower to fool predators, as described earlier.

With reference to the eel, there is no obvious way that the eel-hatchling could navigate as it does, even if it possessed a built-in compass, since such a compass would not be sufficient to enable the eel hatchling to cross oceans finding the favourable ocean currents and locate a specific river thousands of miles away from where they hatched.

Similarly, the eel could not navigate by the stars since it swims at depth and the stars alone would not provide the navigational accuracy to achieve this. The ability to ensure that it locates the beneficial currents, which the hatchling eel could not possibly know, since it would be its first journey across the ocean after hatching in the Sargasso Sea is amazing; there is no scope for learned behaviour.

The information is locked into its Matrix Model from the moment of birth; the domains of the eel's Matrix "learn" from the life experiences of countless millions of eels that have gone before and utilises this information to assist all members of that species of eels.

The mechanism providing this capability, is similar to that described by Professor C Jung,[20] when he detailed his theory relating to the existence of "instincts" within the collective unconscious relating to humankind. A similar domain of the unconscious, according to Matrix Model Theory, is also present in all animals, the content of which depends on the species.

As described earlier, Professor Hawking identified certain fundamental numbers associated with sub-atomic structure and states that if these constants had not been exactly as they are, supernova could not have formed or exploded. Supernova are exploding stars which seed the universe with all the heavier elements. These heavier elements are essential for the formation of rocky planets like Earth and for the start of life.

The supernova starts off as a huge star of lighter gasses which, as they grow and their gravitational force increases, drag in more hydrogen and helium. As the star's mass increases, it starts to heat up and the pressure in the core grows. Eventually, the temperature and pressure become so large that nuclear fusion starts, and the heavier elements are formed.

After a further period of time, the star becomes unstable and explodes with a massive explosion propelling the heavier elements into space in all directions. Since all life contains these heavier elements, from carbon, iron and oxygen, through to potassium and nitrogen, it can be seen how vital supernova were and are; its true to say that all planets and all life forms, including man, are ultimately made from star dust!

Matrix Model Theory provides part of the coding which, together with DNA, explains why offspring are very similar to their immediate ancestor. It also explains how the coding is supplied to enable, for example, a foetus to develop into an embryo and later into a child then progressing into an adult.

Each phase being different from the previous phase of its form, function and behaviour. As another example, it explains how an acorn develops into sapling and then into an oak tree and how new species evolve with ever more complex coding and sophistication.

There is also a phenomenon called "missing hereditability" as described by Professor Rupert Sheldrake[17]. He describes that large scale studies showed that genetics alone did not explain the inheritance of certain traits that would be expected to be inherited from parents.

For example, height, which statistics show is 90% heritable which means that 90% of the variation of height in a population can be shown to be inherited (tall parents tend to have tall children). However, as Sheldrake describes the genes in the parents were shown to have only small effects; they accounted for only about 5% of the height inheritance; the genes to define height "just aren't there."

Matrix Model Theory shows that there is another source of inherited coding lodged within the domains of the Matrix which not only adds to the coding within the DNA of an individual, but specifically helps define the form, function, and development of the individual throughout their life.

This domain is a compound of the corresponding domains from the Matrix Models of both parents, and thus solves the "missing hereditability" problem. This domain is unique for each individual and is a permanent domain within the individual's Matrix Model which continuously interacts with the individual from conception throughout life.

The Theory also describes the structure of the human mind and explains how the domains of the mind extend way beyond the "scull-encased physical brain" and include the domains of the unconscious and conscious.

Memory

There has long been a debate about human memory. It was thought that memories were formed by leaving chemical traces within the brain, and they were thus, accessible by some kind of retrieval system within the brain. However, as research has shown, no such memory traces have ever been located within the physical brain.

The reason is that long-term memory resides in the personal unconscious domain of the Matrix which was first proposed in the time of Jung and Freud over 100 years ago. This concept is extended in this book to propose that the personal unconscious, the content of which is unique to each individual, contains many of the memories of personal experiences relating to an individual.

The physical brain has access to the personal unconscious and its associated memories which explains why scientists have not been able to find memory traces within the physical brain; they just are not there[17]. These long-term memories exist solely in the personal unconscious, which "resides" in the non-physical domain.

This book starts from the time of the Big Bang and shows how the Matrix Model evolved from the earliest simplest version through to the establishment of Homo sapiens, with their far more complex Matrix Model, which includes the structure of the domains which provides a comprehensive model of the entire human mind.

To ensure that this book is readable and accessible to the general reader, the text provides descriptions which are as non-technical as possible but provides extensive references to the sources of information and research used. It also includes details of individual researchers and scientists, should any reader wish to explore these sources in more detail.

Chapter 1
In the Beginning; the Start of the Cosmos

Before the arrival of matter and energy in the universe, there was only a vast expanse of nothingness, a Great Void: an unbounded infinity of darkness and emptiness, without time. The most currently accepted theory among physicists and cosmologists is that the coming into existence of the physical universe started to occur about 13.8 billion years ago.

The word billion is the same as one thousand million. At this instant, at a single finite point in the cosmos, which scientists refer to as a singularity,[1] there was a vast out-flooding of matter in the form of sub-atomic particles at a temperature of billions of degrees centigrade.

This sphere of matter rapidly expanded and cooled. This event is called the "Big Bang". This was the event which described the coming into existence of matter and energy. It was also the start of time, since before the Big Bang, time did not exist[7].

Scientists define a singularity as a point in space where matter is incredibly dense and incredibly hot. What occurred at the singularity at the first instant of the event defies the currently understood laws of science; in fact, the laws seem to break down at that point. From this singularity, the ball of sub-atomic particles expanded in all directions.

The work of scientists, among them Professor Stephen Hawking,[2] often regarded as the most brilliant theoretical physicist since Einstein, together with George Ellis and Roger Penrose have calculated that the physical universe did have a specific beginning, as opposed to earlier theories that the universe had "always been there". They published research papers in 1968 and 1970 which confirmed that prior to the Big Bang there was no space-time, no matter or energy.

In terms of the Big Bang theory, the associated singularity can be regarded as the source of all matter, and the time at which it happened as the instant of the start of time, which is referred to as time-equals-zero. Initially, after 10^{-32} seconds (an incredibly short time) the universe was the size of a tiny ball, containing all the entire matter of the universe.

It was comprised purely of sub-atomic particles, some of which were called quarks and anti-quarks, which are the building blocks of all atomic nuclei. This tiny ball was rapidly expanding and cooling, but at that time, it was still too hot for the quarks to form atoms.

Professor Sheldrake[5] describes the initial state of the universe about one hundredth of a second after the Big Bang, where the universe had cooled to one hundred billion degrees, it consisted of an "undifferentiated soup of matter and radiation."

When quarks and anti-quarks run into one another, they can annihilate one another and leave behind electrons, another crucial building block for atoms. As the early universe expanded from the incredibly hot initial condition and cooled, more quarks survived and remained than anti-quarks so that although many quarks and anti-quarks would annihilate one another, the end point was that there was a vast number of quarks and a pool of free electrons.

These are the source materials for the formation of hydrogen and helium atoms. After just a few seconds, these quarks started to amalgamate into protons and neutrons, which are the nuclei, or building blocks of atoms. Just one second after the Big Bang, the temperature of the expanding matter was around 10 billion degrees Centigrade. This rapidly changing structure of our embryonic universe was cooling rapidly; just 100 seconds later, the estimated temperature had dropped to about one billion degrees.[55]

Less than 200 seconds later, following further cooling and expansion, the nuclei of hydrogen and helium, with a small amount of lithium, had formed, but it was still too hot for electrons to join these nuclei to form atoms. This started to occur after between 380,000-700,000 years as electrons started to orbit the established the protons and complete atoms of hydrogen and helium were eventually formed. The universe started to glow and emit light at this time due to cosmic radiation.

The establishment of hydrogen and helium gas enabled gas clouds to form and after more than 300 million years, gravity started to pull these clouds together to form stars and large numbers of these, in turn, later formed galaxies.

The starting point of all stars is the accumulation of vast clouds of hydrogen and helium, which, as they grow, generate an enormous gravitational field which then drags in yet more hydrogen and helium.

Eventually, the temperature and pressure at the centre are so great that the nuclear fusion process starts. This process forces lighter elements together to form heavier elements. These are the raw materials for planets, and everything associated with them. They are also the essential materials for life.

The "steady state" theory of the universe is the idea that the universe has always been there, unchanging, eternal. This was disputed by Edwin Hubble[3], one of the most important observational astronomers of the twentieth century, who showed that distant galaxies are moving rapidly away from us, regardless of which direction we look.

Also, the work of radio astronomers Penzias and Wilson[4] in 1964 to 1965 who, by measuring microwave background noise, showed that the universe had been much denser in the past, the implication being that it has been, and still is, expanding. This was further evidence to support the Big Bang Theory. The "steady-state" theory has now been abandoned.

If we know, as we do, that we have an expanding universe, and we know the approximate speed of the expansion, it is possible to extrapolate back to calculate when it started its expansion, and where the epicentre of this expansion, the singularity, originated.

By completing this work, the approximate age of the universe has been calculated, as previously described, as 13.8 billion years, the approximate instant of time of the start of the Big Bang. The sphere of matter at the Big Bang centre started to expand and has been expanding ever since.

Critical Rate of Expansion

Interestingly, the rate of expansion of the universe is very close to what is regarded as the "critical rate", that is to say that if it had expanded at a slightly faster rate, all matter in the cosmos at that time would have rapidly disappeared into the vast depths of the universe.

If, however, it had expanded slightly slower, gravity would have been sufficiently strong to pull all the matter eventually back towards the centre of the universe, and we would see an ever increasing contracting universe. This contraction of the universe back to its point of origin, should it have occurred, is called the "Big Crunch".

Professor Hawking indicates in his book "A Brief History of time[7]" that had the rate of expansion of the ball of matter just one second after the Big Bang been smaller by even one part in a hundred thousand million million, the ball of matter would have collapsed back to its point of origin and never would have reached its current size, and life could never have started.

He also wrote that if the Big-Bang Theory is correct, the parameters defining the initial state of the universe at the very start must have been "very carefully chosen". It is still expanding at close to the critical rate. This coming into being of matter, energy and time was the beginning of the physical cosmos.

Currently, theoretical physicists and cosmologists are continuing to work on alternative theories to explain the creation of matter and energy and hence our physical universe. Some are working on a quantum theory solution which they hope will not require a singularity. Some cosmologists are rather put out by singularities, since the laws of science as we currently understand them, appear to break down at that point. However, such an alternative theory does not yet exist.

Fundamental Numbers

Professor Stephen Hawking made an important observation. He indicated that in the world of science, there are several fundamental numbers, for example the size of the electric charge of an electron, or the mass of a proton as a ratio to that of an electron. These numbers appear to have been "very finely adjusted" with great care and precision to values that enabled stars to form and supernova to assemble and eventually explode.

This is important since without supernova, where hydrogen and helium are converted into many heavier elements by the process of nuclear fusion, the availability of key elements such as oxygen, carbon, iron, phosphorus and many others essential for planet formation, could not have occurred in sufficient quantities for the structure of the universe to be as it is. These heavier elements were also vital to enable the Earth environment to form and for life to start.

Most elements owe their existence to the nuclear fusion processes that fuel the stars which, if they are massive enough, eventually become supernova and explode. Basically, if the constants referred to by Hawking were not exactly as they are, and there is no known reason in physics why they should have "adopted" these values, our universe would not have formed as it has; rocky planets like Earth could not have formed and life as we know it would not have been possible.

This implies the need for some other solution which shall be covered in detail in later chapters. The concept that cosmos establishment is due to a most incredible series of extremely unlikely "random-chance" events is replaced by a completely new theory: Matrix Model Theory.

Theoretical physicists have continued to propose ever more complex theories to explain establishment and the start and evolution of the physical universe. Just to give one example, we have the "multiverse" or multiple-universe theory, whereby it is proposed that there are many parallel universes, one of which happens to be ours.

In order to get rid of the problem of the observed "critical numbers" described by Hawking, and the formation of the cosmos by any "purposeful" agency, many scientists are prepared to accept the concept of a vast (or even infinite) number of universes, all in some kind of parallel co-existence with our known universe, and each with different sets of critical parameters. We just happen to inhabit the one with the parameters which have these critical values which permit supernova to form, stars to evolve and life to begin. There is no empirical evidence for the multiverse theory whatsoever, yet the theory persists.

One of the more exotic theories was described by Julian Barbour in 1999 in a paper entitled "The end of time" proposes that time does not actually exist! Other theories will evolve, but they will all have to answer the fundamental question as to the origin of matter and energy and indeed, why they came into existence at all.

These theories may well be adapted and may change with the passage of time, and even the exponents of the "Big Bang" theory may themselves change their views in the light of more scientific data and with the formulation of new and more complex theories. Some of the current theories relating to the establishment of the universe are exotic to the extreme and border on the mystical. The Big Bang Theory is still the most widely accepted explanation for the establishment of matter and time.

However, matter and time came into existence and the physical universe was established and started the long and convoluted route to the formation of stars, galaxies, planets and ultimately, life.

This is a rather simplified overview of the start of the universe according to the current views of most scientists. It describes the Big Bang event and how critical the rate of expansion of the early universe was in forming the universe to be as it is which ultimately included our solar system and our planet Earth.

This was the cradle that allowed life, as we know it, to evolve. However, this explanation leaves a lot of unanswered questions, some of which will be addressed later in this book.

The Laws of Science

The laws of science define, in the broadest of terms, how matter and energy in their many forms, act and interact. There are many different laws and include the laws relating to the properties of gravity and those relating to electrostatics and electromagnetic forces, defining how they function.

Science currently recognises four fundamental forces at work in nature: gravity, electromagnetism, and "weak" and "strong" nuclear forces. Gravity relates to the fact that bodies which have mass attract or pull towards one another; gravity is a weak force which becomes effective with massive systems such as galaxies, stars, and planets.

For example, it ensures that the planets in our solar system orbit the Sun in specific and stable ways. The strong nuclear force holds quarks together to form the nuclei of hydrogen and helium atoms, and all other atoms, and is the basis of atomic structure enabling atoms to form and hold together.

Atoms are the building blocks of the elements and all matter. The weak nuclear force is responsible for radioactivity. The electromagnetic force enables particles with an electric charge to interact, either attracting or repelling one another.

At what point in time these laws that govern the physical world came into being is probably more of a philosophical question rather than a scientific one. Trying to argue that the laws have always existed is somewhat self-defeating since the laws define how the *physical* universe behaves; before the Big Bang, there was no matter or energy entities for the laws to apply to, and so the argument would have no testable answer but would perhaps, exercise the minds of cosmologists and philosophers.

The intriguing thing when considering the way matter and energy interacts is that it always interacts in a consistent manner. Matter always interacts with matter in the same way, and chemical reactions are largely predictable, and nuclear fusion is also a predictable process.

If this were not the case, cosmos formation as we know it would not have been possible and the formation of stars and galaxies would have been impossible and supernova, so essential for the formation of planets and life, could not have occurred, nor could eco-systems have formed.

The laws of science as we know them now, could have evolved from their initial form shortly after the time-equals-zero moment at the instant of the Big Bang, to meet the rapidly changing environmental conditions[17]. It is assumed that the laws of science always apply everywhere in the universe.

This gives rise to other philosophical questions such as, does this imply that these laws are "stored" somewhere in the universe as a universally accessible memory? The question arises[2] how, or why, were the laws of science chosen to be as they are. It could be explained by saying that interactions between elements of matter and energy have no alternatives but to interact as they do in all cases.

If interactions were not predictable and always the same, for example, when oxygen and hydrogen gasses interact, water is formed, the universe could not be as it is, and life would probably not have evolved. If the way elements of matter interact had been random, then there would have been no structure to the cosmos: it would have been a sea of chaos; interesting to observe, but mankind would not have been there to see it!

A knowledge of the laws of science contributes to our understanding of the physical universe and enable predictions to be made relating to the future possible states of physical systems, including how our solar system will look in the future.

As the universe expanded and cooled to the point where sub-atomic particles could form into atoms, new additional laws of science applied which would define how, for example, nuclear fusion would take place which allowed stars to form and super-nova behave and the formation of the different elements was able to happen, what specific characteristics these elements would have and how the countless other interactions between these elements would be governed.

These laws relate, not only to the micro scale, the sub-atomic level of the physical universe, but also the macro scale, the immense inter-galactic scale. For example, the way in which stars and galaxies exert a gravitational attraction on one another and the mechanism for nuclear fusion.

One of the most important elements to be produced by nuclear fusion was phosphorus, which became a crucial chemical in the eventual formation of DNA (deoxyribonucleic acid, a molecule carrying genetic information). The process of supernova explosions continues today, and without this series of cataclysmic explosions seeding the universe with heavier elements, planets could not have formed, and the evolution of life would have been impossible. These heavier elements are also vital in the making of all living structures, including man.

As matter and energy expanded away from the point of origin, some matter particles started to coalesce due to the attracting effects of electrostatic charge. Tiny particles can have an electrostatic charge, positive or negative, particles of opposite polarities attract one another. By this mechanism, larger "clumps" of matter were formed, and as they became larger, the effects of gravity then enabled them to form still larger pieces of space matter or space debris.

Gravity is one of the initial parameters which determines that particles of matter that have mass will be attracted towards one another and having come together, will form larger groups of matter with greater gravitational attraction. Gravity starts to become a significant force when matter combines to form larger and more massive structures.

This led eventually to giant spirals of matter and gas rotating and drawing in yet more matter. These spirals eventually started to coalesce and form millions of stars and galaxies. These stars occur in many sizes, but they are similar to our Sun. They then started to attract smaller spheres of matter and space debris by the effects of gravity and eventually captured them in orbit around themselves. Some of this debris coalesced to become planets, others became asteroids, comets and orbiting rocky debris.

The establishment of stars and planets is a continuing process; stars are formed, have a life span and then, in some cases, their mass and energy become so great that they become the centre of immense explosions in the form of supernova. Our Sun is too small to form a supernova, but eventually, it will run out of fuel and expand to form what is known as a red giant.

In doing so, it will consume the inner planets of the solar system, including planet Earth: but it will not happen any time soon. This process may start in about 5 billion years. The last stage in the life of our Sun, following its "red giant" phase, is that it will eventually shrink to become a white dwarf, a small high-density body.

For many billions of years, the universe developed as matter and energy in many forms combined to form stars, galaxies and planets as the universe continued to expand and cool. Much later, although in cosmological terms, recently, the first sparks of life appeared on Earth. This necessitated the preexistence of the laws that defined how biological entities that were to become the building blocks of life were to be formed. For example, to define how amino-acids and proteins would form, and how RNA (ribonucleic acid) and DNA (deoxyribonucleic acid) which are essential elements for life to form, would evolve.

Even the most basic and primitive life forms must be self-sustaining systems and be able to reproduce by making exact copies of themselves, and thereby multiply. They also had to be able to survive in their environment and indeed overcome changes to their environment.

It was also essential that the offspring they produced should be nearly identical to the parent. Otherwise, effective reproduction of species could not happen, and species replication would be chaotic. In general, every life form tends to have the same structure and behaviour as its immediate ancestor and to the other members of the same species.

The laws of science also relate to the way DNA, genes and chromosomes, function and contribute to the establishment and reproduction of living entities and contribute to their inherited characteristics. This is because they have, locked within them, part of the coding required to define the building of all the complex structures necessary for each life-form. But as will be described later, there is more to the defining of the structure of a life-form than "just" DNA.[24]

The structure of life forms seems to conform to some rules as to how they should be assembled and behave. Each species also has the same structure as its immediate ancestor, tends to have the same selection of food sources, respond the same way to changes in their environment and tend to reproduce in the same way.

These tendencies imply constructional and behavioural constants for every species which are defined by the coding locked within the genome and Matrix Model for each individual organism and which have evolved from ancestors of that particular species. The genome is the complete set of genetic material of an organism.

This ensures that the same structure and behavioural tendencies can be passed on to each successive generation. This is true for all living entities. Thus, form and function are species-specific constants and are passed from one generation to the next in the form of coded instructions contained within their genetic material and other sources which will be explained in later chapters.

The arrival of ever-more complex life necessitated the existence of, in part, corresponding more complex genetic structures with coding which would help define the form or physical architecture of the species and how this life form would sustain itself, procreate and adapt to its environment.

Both the original design and the implementation of the very first, and all subsequent life-forms, had to be such as to ensure they came into being as self-sustaining and self-organising systems right from the start. They also had to be able to consume energy from the environment, be able to reproduce extremely accurate copies of themselves and pass exact copies of their genetic material on to the next generation.

The arrival of the processes relating to evolution and mutation and natural selection were essential to the sustainability and development of life on Earth and the diversification of the species.

Some scientists have speculated on the reasons why the laws of science are as they are since, had they been even slightly different, we would be presiding (or perhaps not be presiding at all) over a completely different set of life-forms on Earth. Professor Rupert Sheldrake[5] has the view that there is no reason why the laws of science should be exactly as they are. However, had they not been exactly as they are, the universe would have been very different to what it is today.

One of the curious things about the laws of science is that they do not actually exist as entities in themselves; they cannot be seen or sensed. It is only because of the manner in which they influence the interaction of matter and energy which can be measured, and the laws thereby inferred, that we conclude that they exist.

Strange Denizens of the Universe

There are other denizens of the physical universe which exercise the minds of cosmologist and the theoretical physicists, such as black holes, which are places in space where the gravity is so extreme that even light cannot escape, so they appear to be black.

There are also white dwarfs which are the very dense cores of old dead stars. There are also red giants, which are luminous giant stars, representing the late phase of stellar evolution. Perhaps, dark matter and dark energy could be included, among others, which demonstrates the incredible diversity and complexity within the cosmos.

It is worth pointing out, however, that current understanding among cosmologists is that only about 5% of the content of the universe is matter and energy; the rest is referred to as dark matter and dark energy. Cosmologists have calculated that the expansion of the universe could not be as it is, and galaxies could not be held together as they are, without the existence of both dark matter and dark energy: there just is not enough "stuff" to make the cosmos act as it does.

According to some scientists, dark matter permeates the universe, but it cannot be seen: its existence is inferred from gravitational effects. Physicists are not sure of its form, and no one is sure about exactly what it is. It is invisible to electromagnetic radiation and has not yet been detected by current technology.

Dark matter is thought to act by exerting a gravitational pull within galaxies which enables them to avoid being flung apart, whereas dark energy, which is a kind of "antigravity" source, attempts to force the universe apart and is responsible for its continuing expansion.

Based on calculations, scientists require the universe to contain around 27% dark matter and 68% dark energy. Since the existence of dark matter, possibly some kind of sub-atomic particle, nor dark energy, have yet been proven, they remain at this time something of an act of faith among scientists.

A major experiment is currently being undertaken using deep underground detectors to try to detect and prove the existence of dark matter particles: none have yet been detected after several years but further work continues. Thus, the matter-energy content of 95% of the universe remains something of an unknown!

If dark matter and dark energy are found by further research not to exist, science will need a completely new theory to explain the accelerating expansion of the universe at close to the critical rate, and what it is that holds galaxies together. It is curious that even though there is a vast amount of dark matter in the universe it has proven, so far at least, impossible to isolate even one particle. However, the detection project continues.

The structure and function of supernova and their formation of the heavier elements that result from their fusion powered explosions have been described. It is notable that the greater the size and hence the energy of the super-nova, the heavier the elements that its nuclear-fusion process can produce.

A Russian Scientist, Mendeleev, (although some claim it was another scientist called Chancourtois) in 1869 grouped all the 60 known elements of the time into a table according to their atomic numbers. Different elements have different atomic numbers and different properties.

There were many gaps in his table, and these were gradually filled in over the years by other scientists to complete what has become known as the periodic table. Elements, ranging from the lightest, hydrogen which has an atomic number of 1, which was one of the earliest created elements present shortly after the Big Bang in vast amounts, through to uranium, the densest of the naturally occurring elements, with an atomic number of 92.

Above this number, elements are either very radioactive, like plutonium or are unstable and are synthesised, usually by forcing two lighter elements to collide at very high speed in a cyclotron or particle accelerator. The two lighter elements "fuse" together to form other heavyweight elements. Many of these synthesised heavy elements only last from a few hours to a few thousandth of a second before disintegrating.

Using a cyclotron to collide calcium with plutonium, they have managed to make element with an atomic weight of 118, oganesson, and it lasted a few seconds. It is difficult to see practical applications for these, but it is of great interest to science to further understand these interactions on the edge of physics, and applications may transpire, and may lead to a better understanding as to the structure of atoms. Element-blasting, in this way, could be regarded as a fascinating but expensive hobby. However, it may also lead to greater insights into the many structures that exist throughout of the cosmos.

Nature has used, and is still using stellar explosions, supernova to produce and distribute the heavier elements which are stable, and which are essential to seed the universe with these materials. The *distribution* effect of these monumental explosions is as important as the production of the heavier elements in the first place: the production of them would be pointless if they stayed located deep within the stars and did not spread throughout the universe.

Having established a universe with a wide distribution of the elements required to form the materials that make stars, planets, and the gasses which, in some cases, form the atmospheres associated with some of those planets, the next phase required to generate life had been started.

The formation of controlled energy sources in the form of stars and the formation of potential life-support platforms in the form of planets had been achieved. These processes continue and more stars, planets and elemental seeding of the universe provides the materials for the vast diversity of structures and forms in the universe. In the case of our solar system, these processes provided the materials to form the Earth and the extraordinarily complex Earth-environment, and the life forms which were eventually established.

The Solar System

Continuing the description of cosmos-building, the formation of our solar system was a vital milestone in the progress towards establishment of life as we know it. The solar system comprises the Sun and a series of planets which orbit around it.

The Sun not only forms the gravitational hub, keeping the planets in their respective orbits, but also provides a source of energy which warms and illuminates some of the planets. The Sun and solar system were established roughly 4.5 to 4.6 billion years before present (4.5-4.6 BBP). The massive amount of energy emitted from the Sun comes from a process of nuclear fusion within the Sun itself.

The solar system formed from a massive dust cloud known as the solar nebula. The rocky planets, Mercury, Venus, the Earth and Mars, grew from accretion of dust and rock clumps as these materials orbited the Sun.

The planets are organised in a series of circular or elliptical orbits with the Sun at the centre. The closest planet to the Sun is Mercury, which has a very hot surface temperature of around 180^0 Centigrade, and orbiting outside of this is Venus, with a dense atmosphere, high in carbon dioxide.

The Earth is the third planet from the Sun, with Mars's orbit further out making it the fourth planet. Next, there are the gas giants, so called because most of their content is gas rather than solid, although they do have solid cores. The giant Jupiter has about 79 moons, the largest being Ganymede which is larger than Mercury. Jupiter has a massive gravitational field due to its mass which is two and half times the mass of all the other planets in the solar system combined.

Saturn is next in line, which is also designated as an ice giant. It is distinctive because of its orbital rings of ice, it has up to 82 moons. Then there is Uranus, with up to 27 moons and Neptune, the furthest gas giant, sometimes designated as an ice giant, with around 14. Pluto is the furthest planet from the Sun, but has recently lost its planet status, since it is deemed too small: it has a surface temperature of minus 229^0 Centigrade. The "moon count" for these planets is approximate since new moons could be discovered at any time.

There is also a belt of asteroids, chunks of rock, some quite large, orbiting between Mars and Jupiter. Lastly, there are the comets, which although they orbit the Sun, they do so with huge elliptical orbits that make them usually remotely distant. They are mostly composed of rock, ice and dust, and if their orbit takes them close to the Sun, the ice starts to melt, and they leave behind their characteristic tail.

The Earth, because of its unique distance from the Sun, receives sufficient heat from the Sun to generate a moderate and normally stable temperature range, on average, across wide areas of the planet. This temperature range was, and is, suitable for a wide variety of life forms to be established.

The planets circle the Sun in stable orbits. Jupiter, due to its massive gravitational field, provides a degree of protection to the Earth from impact-threatening asteroids which was of crucial importance in enabling life on Earth to start and to survive.

The characteristics of each of the planets is widely differing and only Earth seems to have the ability to sustain any life-forms that we know of. That is not to exclude the possibility of life existing elsewhere in the solar system. For example, life may exist under the frozen sea surface of Europa, which is a moon of Jupiter, or possibly under the ice cap of Mars.

Europa is thought to have a frozen water surface, with the possibility of a liquid water ocean beneath its surface which could possibly be conducive to supporting life of some kind. There is also the possibility that life exists beneath the surface of other moons in the solar system.

The planets and the Sun have always had a mystical fascination for mankind of almost every culture and tradition: they have often been regarded as "gods", and for some, as sources of knowledge about the future or even as indicators as to human behaviour or characteristics as defined by the horoscope. Some of these superstitions are still prevalent even within the western society today.

In earlier times, and in some cultures, planets were given specific attributes and characteristics and observation of the planets were used by leaders, chiefs and kings, via their astrologers, wise men or advisors, who would use the position of planets and stars to "foretell the future" to decide on acts of war, peace and in some cases, the fate of nations. Therefore, the planets have had a significant cultural and religious relevance for mankind of many different cultures for thousands of years.

Formation of Planet Earth and the Moon

This, very simplistically, is how the physical universe was formed. It is still evolving and changing. From the viewpoint of the arrival of living organisms, the most important event was the establishment of our own solar system, with the Sun at its centre.

Between 4.6 and 4.5 billion years BP our own Earth was formed, from a swirling spiral of matter and debris which was captured in an orbit around the Sun. Initially, the Earth was a rocky sphere, which by about 4.4 billion years ago had cooled to form a hot, arid rocky surface structure, but with an atmosphere far removed from what it is today.

The Moon is thought to have resulted from some form of massive impact on the Earth by a planet-sized body at an early stage in the Earth's history, perhaps around 4.3-4.5 billion years BP. The impactor was a body about the size of Mars. It collided with Earth, and the impact blasted matter out of the Earth and into orbit around the Earth. That must have been a spectacular impact!

This debris eventually aggregated to form the Moon. Some scientists postulate that the evidence for this is that the Moon has the same oxygen isotope composition as the Earth whereas other rocks and materials from other parts of the solar system have a different composition. This impact would have increased the mass of the Earth.

The establishment of the Moon could, therefore, be regarded as an extremely freak event. The impact of the body striking the Earth would have had to be at just the right angle and at just the right velocity to have the energy to blast matter into orbit around the Earth in sufficient quantity to form the Moon, and at precisely the right distance from the Earth to coalesce in orbit around the Earth. This could be likened to an extremely accurate snooker shot!

Before the Moon was formed, the Earth's orbit was thought to have been "wobbly". The "wobble" is thought to have produced extreme weather such as violent hurricanes. The arrival of the Moon orbiting the Earth stabilised the Earth's orbit, making the weather less extreme and probably, making the establishment of life easier.

The formation of the Moon also provided much enhanced tidal ranges, another important factor in establishing life on Earth. When first formed, the Moon was much closer to Earth than it is today, which would have caused much greater tidal ranges than we are now familiar with. The Moon continues to move away from the Earth slowly; eventually it will probably leave its orbit altogether.

A current scientific view is that there was an event between 4.1 and 3.8 billion years BP, called the Late Heavy Bombardment when the Earth, along with the Moon and other planets, was impacted by a large number of asteroids and comets, some of which were tens of kilometres across. The source of these impactors is thought to be the Kuiper belt.

The Earth, prior to these impacts, was thought to have been only about 60% of its current mass, and the material from these impacts added greatly to the Earth's mass, bringing it to what it is today. It is not known for certain what caused this bombardment, but it was probably due to shifts in the orbits of Neptune, Jupiter and Saturn, where their combined gravity threw the asteroids and comets into the orbits of the other planets in the solar system.

The energy of these impacts could have caused a widespread "molten" state to prevail on Earth. Some of the impact craters have indicated that there were thousands of impacts with impactor diameter 20km, about 40 with a diameter of 40km, and several with a diameter of 5,000 km. These would have been massive impacts!

It is just possible, but highly unlikely, that any life could have survived this environment: certainly not on the surface, but it has been postulated that perhaps, some life could have survived beneath the surface. However, eventually the bombardment stopped, due to Jupiter and Saturn moving and adopting their current orbits, which lead to the giant planet Jupiter "mopping up" many of the potential impactors, protecting the Earth's surface and allowing the Earth to cool. Gradually, the Earth formed a solid crust across its entire surface.

The inner core of the Earth remains molten rock even today, with the outer crust having solidified and cooled to the point where it was mostly at a temperature which was conducive for the creation and support of life. The molten core contained within the outer hard crust is dynamic, and its movements cause the surface to shift and crack from time to time.

The hard surface plates move relative to one another, causing occasional earthquakes. The molten rock, called magma, can also force its way to the surface through weaknesses in the Earth's crust, which gives rise to volcanoes. This surface movement gives rise to continental drift, a gradual movement of the continents which has continued since the formation of the planet. The Earth is still structurally a dynamic ever-changing entity.

Like others of its kind, our Sun is a star and is a point of extremely high energy, releasing vast amounts of energy in the form of heat, light and other solar radiation in the process. However, other conditions were vital for the formation of life on Earth. The arrival of the oceans (which may have been around 3.8BBP) and the cooling of the Earth after the Late Heavy Bombardment to give a more amenable surface temperature range, were vital phases of development.

As the Earth cooled, with a lowering of the carbon dioxide levels in the atmosphere, oceans formed. How exactly they formed is not yet known for certain, and there are several theories. In part there was, over millions of years, an out-gassing of water from the Earth's interior, but it is thought that a significant proportion of the water forming the oceans came from extra-terrestrial sources, such as water-rich meteors and comets, or proto-planets, or possibly water-bearing impactors during the Late Heavy Bombardment.

The current most likely theory is that after the Earth had cooled, the impact, or near misses by these water-bearing bodies, over a long period of time, were then able to deliver water in copious amounts[8]. This is regarded as the most likely mechanism. Some water also formed due to volcanic action, where emissions condensed in the atmosphere as the Earth cooled.

At some time between 4.4 and 3.8 billion years BP, the Earth had most of the water required to form the oceans and enable the first steps towards the establishment of life. There would have also been the associated rivers and lakes and regular rainfall essential to irrigate the land and wash the atmosphere. The Earth had become a water planet.

Having a moderate temperature range and being cooler at the poles and warmer at the equator, a wide range of environmental temperatures evolved. The atmosphere on early Earth contained low oxygen levels but had high levels of carbon dioxide and other gasses. The earliest living cell is thought to have originally evolved in the oceans, which cover 70% of the Earth's surface.

The oceans were able to support life better than the terrestrial surface because high levels of ultra-violet radiation from the Sun were dangerous to all life forms on exposed land. The ozone layer had not yet been created, (not until around 600 million years ago) and its formation was essential since it forms a protective shield greatly lowering the levels of ultra-violet radiation reaching the Earth, thus allowing life to exist on the Earth's terrestrial surface.

The Earth at this stage was warmed and given energy by the Sun, had extensive oceans, rivers and rainfall, with a solid and increasingly stable land mass. It had almost, but not quite, arrived at an environment where life could start.

The first chapter of this book has provided a short overview of how the universe, the solar system and the Earth came into being according to current scientific thinking. It has been shown that it required a series of incredibly unlikely events to enable the universe to come into existence at all, let alone one with a planet such as Earth, configured as it is, with an environment capable of supporting a wide profusion of life.

The next chapter will describe certain key aspects of the Earth environment, how it evolved in ways that indicate strongly that it would have been almost impossible for either the environment or life to have evolved by pure random chance alone.

This leads to the conclusion that the existence of matter and the laws of science alone, are in themselves, insufficient to develop a solar system with an Earth that supports life and enable those life forms to be encoded with information that would enable them to function as self-sustaining living systems with the ability to reproduce copies of themselves.

Chapter 2
Making the Impossible Happen

Having covered the intriguing mechanisms involved in the formation of the cosmos according to current scientific theory, the mechanisms which enabled the processes for the formation of life on Earth will now be described. The mechanistic theory that life started by a series of random chance events will be compared with an alternative: that life started due to a series of teleological (purposeful) activities in nature.

The formation of the Earth and its biosphere, which is comprised of the sum of all eco systems within zone-of-life on Earth, and indeed life itself, were not only incredibly unlikely to form in the way they have, but they have shown life to be extremely resilient, and have survived several catastrophic events during Earth's history.

Further statistics that demonstrate that these factors and events could not possibly have occurred by random chance alone will also be presented.

The Statistics

Before venturing further into the realm of statistics, it may be useful to define how mathematicians write very large numbers in a convenient way. Writing 1,000 is easy enough but when we get to many millions, it can end up covering the page with clumps of zeros, which does not make for easy reading.

In the world of mathematicians, a thousand which can be written as 1,000 can also be written as 10^3 that is a 1 with three zeros after it. Similarly, a million, 1,000,000 is written as 10^6 and so on. The reason we need this easy-read format is because some of the numbers we will be dealing with here are very large indeed.

It is generally assumed in the world of probability that if an event has a probability of 1 in 2, it will occur on average once in every two attempts. One example would be the tossing of a coin. One would expect that, having completed a large number of coin tosses, there would be as many "heads" as "tails" so the probability of a head turning up would be stated as 1 in 2 if the coin was "fair", without any bias.

If an event can, on average, occur once in 100 attempts, it is said to have a probability of 1 in a 100, or 1 in 10^2.

Mathematicians often state that if an event has a probability of less than 1 in 10^{30} of occurring, that is 1 in a thousand billion billion billion (a billion is one thousand million), then it can be taken as being a mathematical impossibility. This means that any event which has greater that 1 in 10^{30} chance against it happening, means that in practice, it will never happen.

Proteins; One of the Building Blocks of Life

If we consider the nature of life as we know it, an essential prerequisite to form even the simplest living entity is the existence of proteins, the fundamental building blocks of life.

Amino acids are molecules made from atoms which include Carbon, Hydrogen, Oxygen and Nitrogen in various combinations. When amino acids join to form a chain, it is called a polypeptide chain. Proteins in turn consist of one or more polypeptide chains. Therefore, amino acids bond together in very specific ways to form these chains, and one or more of these polypeptide chains are needed to form a specific protein.

To arrive at a required protein, these amino acids have to be arranged in a biologically functional and very specific way in every case. It transpires, those proteins can fold up to adopt one out of a vast number of three-dimensional shapes, and it has been impossible, so far, to determine why a particular protein always folds in a particular way to adopt a particular 3D shape, in spite of the enormous number of alternatives.[17]

Protein folding enables the protein to be a biologically functional entity. The way in which they fold is thought to be defined by the amino acid chain that makes the protein. However, there is also a possibility that the folding could be directed by fields[5]. These could be psi-fields from the SFU family.

The protein folding process, according to Christian Anfinsen[52], a Nobel prize-winner for his work on proteins, appears "directed" to find its final required state in a very short time, even though there are many millions of alternatives. This structural aspect of proteins is of vital importance to the formation of stable proteins essential for life.

Several hundred proteins are required to form a simple basic living cell. If the protein fails to fold, it becomes dysfunctional. However, if it folds incorrectly, it can cause diseases like Alzheimer's, Parkinson's, cystic fibrosis among others.

Did Life Arise by Random Chance Alone?

Fred Hoyle[9] 1915-2001 was an eminent astronomer, and Plumian Professor of astronomy and experimental philosophy at Cambridge. He analysed the probability of life occurring on Earth by considering the chances of essential sets of proteins forming in nature by chance alone. Hoyle applied probability theory to the chances of proteins occurring to form a living cell. He deduced from the proposition that for life as we know it, a set of 2,000 basic proteins are required.

As previously described, the most basic building block of proteins are amino acids; there are many different types, but only 20 are used in building proteins for living cells. Some amino acids can be synthesised within an organism while others cannot. These must be absorbed from the environment.

To assemble the first living cell, as previously described, a specific set of amino acids had to combine and assemble in a specific order to form a specific protein. Having created one protein, the process needs to be repeated many times, with different combinations of amino acids in differing orders to create the many other required types of proteins to form an organism. These proteins then have to be assembled in a particular order to enable a living cell to arise.

If this is the case, Hoyle calculated that the statistical chance of even one protein occurring by chance is extremely low, and the probability of all 2,000 occurring such that they can interact with one another by *random chance alone* is 1 in $10^{40,000}$ which in real terms, since this number vastly exceeds the 1 in 10^{30} figure, means it could never have happened by random chance alone.

However, Hoyle's work has been criticised[27] on the grounds that the earliest and first life form would almost certainly have been much simpler than the 2000 protein model proposed above. This is certainly true and much simpler initial life assumptions have been made in research work by others, as detailed below.

As an atheist and a Darwinist, this statistical conclusion gave Hoyle a profound problem. Having demonstrated to his satisfaction that life could not have started by pure chance alone, he had to solve the problem as to how life started and developed. He spent time developing theories. He arrived at the theory that it must have come from a point in the universe where life started by some undefined process.

Life, having started there, could have spread out and thus, by some process of "seeding", the universe eventually spread to Earth, perhaps on meteorites or cosmic dust carrying living cells. But this is extremely unlikely since, during their journey through space, the living cells would have to survive cosmic radiation, extreme cold, perhaps below -200^{0}C followed by the extreme heat of entering the Earth's atmosphere, possibly as high as 2000-3000^0 C as the meteorite or dust particle sped through the Earth's atmosphere.

It is unlikely that life could have started before or during the Late Heavy bombardment, as described in Chapter 1, where the Earth was showered by a massive onslaught of meteors and comet-like bodies. This may have made much, if not all, of the Earth's surface into a molten, boiling surface which would probably not have sustained any form of life.

Since the Late Heavy Bombardment occurred sometime between 4.1-3.8 Billion years before present (4.1-3.8 BBP), this gives a time-window for the start of life, since it is likely to have been sometime after the end of the bombardment.

There is a theory that perhaps, basic life could have survived the bombardment by being located well below the Earth's surface, or in hydrothermal vents, although it is unclear that the oceans would not have become, at least partially, vaporised. Life surviving the bombardment is extremely unlikely, but the possibility remains.

Extrapolating from the Moon-cratering evidence to see what the possible effects could have been on the Earth, where weathering and other effects would have diminished or eliminated the evidence, researchers have established that the Late Heavy bombardment as described in Chapter 1 would have had a catastrophic effect on Earth.

It is also known that the earliest evidence of life discovered so far on Earth, is some fossilised micro-organisms, found in hydrothermal vent precipitate. These are the earliest evidence of life which date to around 3.7 Billion years ago (3.7BBP) and perhaps, as early as 4.28BBP. Other sources state that the earliest direct evidence of life is microorganisms dating from about 3.4-3.5BBP.

Some of these were found to be of a complex life structure, having cell walls protecting protein-producing DNA, which is a very complex molecule containing genetic information, and were therefore highly evolved. This indicates that the simplest cellular life must have started much earlier and progressed rapidly under the influence of mutation, evolution and natural selection.

If we assume that life on Earth could not have survived the Late Heavy Bombardment, this gives an incredibly short time window of approximately 100 to 400 million years for life to have started and to have evolved to the sophistication of the bacteria described above, with its DNA. This is the time between the end of the Late Heavy Bombardment and the age of the earliest micro-organism so far found.

Even if we assume that this early life-form pre-dated the Late Heavy Bombardment and survived these catastrophic events, this gives a maximum time window, from the time when water was first present on Earth, which is regarded as an essential prerequisite for life to start, to the date when we know the micro-organisms were present, of around 650-700 million years.

This is an extremely short time for the arrival of life starting from the materials available on Earth at these early times, which comprised a stock of non-living elements and chemicals. Either assumption gives far too little time for life to have started by a series of random chance events alone, as will be demonstrated later in this chapter.

However, elsewhere in the universe, there may be much older planets with life-friendly biospheres which are much older than Earth, giving life billions of years longer to have started. Life may have started there. If life started elsewhere in the cosmos, how it could have made its way to Earth is problematic.

An alternative to this theory, and versions of it, also postulate that life started by a steady flux of something akin to viruses arriving by comets or meteorites and having started, continued to evolve on Earth. The theory also allows for the possibility of further arrival of extra-terrestrial objects continuing to influence evolution.

The weakness of theorising that a virus as the first living entity to exist on Earth is that a virus is a very simple cell, which requires a living, more complex host, in order to replicate. Typically, it invades a host and injects some of the host's cells with its own genetic material.

This results in some of the cells in the host's internal structure making virus-copies, thus, the virus has solved the problem of replication. Clearly, there would not have been a living host if the virus were proposed to be the first living organism on Earth.

The concept of the arrival of life from extra-terrestrial sources is known as the "panspermia" theory, but it does not explain satisfactorily how the "life seed" could travel the cosmos, exposed to high levels of radiation, then enter the Earth's atmosphere, as described previously, without being exposed to very high temperature on entry.

However, bacteria with a high resistance to radiation are possible, and work on one meteorite has discovered traces of amino acids, but work continues, although this theory has little backing in the scientific community and is but one of several theories which are undergoing further research.

In terms of answering the question, "where does life come from and how did it start?" the panspermia theory merely pushes the frontier of the question to the unfathomable depths of space and therefore, into the realms of the unknown. An alternative is a theory known as "pseudo-panspermia" where life-building blocks originated in interstellar dust clouds has also been investigated, but this deals with "where" life started and not "how". None of these "extra-terrestrial" explanations for the start of life is widely accepted.

The discussion can be advanced further by agreeing with the idea that the earliest life form had a much simpler form than the 2000 protein model postulated by Hoyle. This level of complexity is common in modern highly evolved life. It is reasonable to assume that the very first living cell had a much less complex construction, with evolution, mutation and natural selection building complexity into this original life-form much later.

We know that even bacteria in the modern world are very highly evolved, and that earliest life would probably have been far more basic even than a modern bacterium, and the species representing the first living cell are probably extinct. Other simpler initial living organisms will be described later.

The Left-Hand Right-Hand Problem

Before continuing the development of this subject, it is necessary to cover another important issue. An additional and rather large problem for those that believe that life started from non-living chemicals and a random series of their reactions, lies with the fact that, however difficult it is to assemble the essential range and type of amino acids by random chance for life to start. they need to be the right type and arranged in exactly the right sequence. In addition, they also have to be the correct *chiral*, as shall now be explained.

As previously stated, there are over 500 types of amino acids, but only 20 are used for living things in current life forms. The atoms that make up each type of amino acid are assembled in two different modes known as 'left-handed' amino acids and 'right-handed' amino acids, each being a mirror image of the other, but identical in all other ways.

This left-hand right-hand characteristic is called their chirality. The left-hand and right-hand chirals in amino acids stand an equal statistical chance of being formed in nature, which means that, in the world of amino acid formation in nature, there would be about 50% left-handed and 50% right-handed for each type of amino acid.

However, all amino acids that make up living things are 100% left-handed, (with the exception of a few bacteria which have right-handed amino acid present within their envelopes). This is because it is thought that a mix of left-hand and right-hand amino acids could not form enzymes nor stable DNA molecules if even a single right-hand amino acid was present in the helix, since it would be unable to form its characteristic long chains. DNA constructed in this way would, therefore, not store much information, and not support life.

Therefore, for the first living cell to occur by random chance alone, not only would the right amino acids have to occur in the right numbers in the right place and at the right time, but it would imply a further requirement for large numbers of left-handed-only chirals of the amino acids to be co-located and to interact to form chains which in turn form proteins. Therefore, there had to be a mechanism for ensuring an environment with a large preponderance of left-handed amino acids.

Applying statistical probability to this, consider a simple protein, one that requires only 100 amino acids. This would represent an extremely simple protein, much simpler than that assumed by Hoyle, and which may or may not be viable in terms of contributing to the construction a living cell.

In an environment with 50% left-hand and 50% right hand amino acids, the odds of a protein forming with 100 left-handed *only* amino acids would be the same as flipping a coin and getting 100 heads in a row; that is 1 in 1.26×10^{30}, which, by the definition above, is a mathematical impossibility.

The first living cell, whatever that was, would have to have been assembled in an environment which was so naturally extremely rich in left-handed-only amino acids, that it could absorb 100% left-handed-only amino acids.

Research is continuing to try to explain how a preponderance of left-handed amino acids could occur in nature. Much research has been completed to find a mechanism that would achieve the goal of suppressing the right-hand chirals of amino acids and leave a large excess of left-handed chirals.

Researchers have looked at the effects of radiation, magnetic fields and ultra-violet radiation to investigate whether these environments have the effect of reducing right-hand amino acids relative to left hand. Other mechanisms have been investigated, including adding different reagents, catalysts, or forming amino acids on the surfaces of clay or crystals, and adding various solvents to the left hand, right hand amino acid mix to try to reduce the percentage of right-handed versions and allow more chance for the left-handed to predominate. So far, none of these mechanisms has succeeded in providing a high "left-hand" excess.

W C Harris[36] experimented with photons generated by spin-polarised electrons to measure whether, under specified environments, these might destroy more of the right-handed amino acids than the left-handed versions. This work met with little success. Further work gave, after analysis, a difference of 10,003 to 9997 over a total number of 20,000 measurements, which is far too small a difference. Also, as the paper states, in nature, it is not clear what would or could produce these spin-polarised electrons.

Other work by R Rosenburg,[37] experimented with irradiating large clouds of magnetised iron with X-rays. Slight excess of R-chirality was detected. The extremes researchers have gone to, in order to find a natural mechanism to provide a reliable excess of left-hand chirals, demonstrates how intriguing the chirality issue is. The paper goes on to propose that this environment might be achieved in nature in molecules stuck to magnetised particles in a dust cloud or comet. This again involves extra-terrestrial mechanisms.

Researchers have proposed that the rotation of the Earth (Coriolis affect) may have contributed to filtering out the right-handed chirals to leave a higher percentage of left-handed ones, but this is somewhat discounted now. Others, including M E Popselov, postulate that the Earth's magnetic field may have caused the preference for left-handed while others have proposed that perhaps, amino acids growing on certain surfaces may exhibit a preference for left handed, or that strings of left handed are perhaps, more stable and thus are more likely to survive, but so far no mechanism has really been found: work continues. It is currently a significant problem for those that support a purely random-chance explanation for the arrival of life on Earth!

As a final example, Professor Uwe Meierhenrich, professor of analytical and physical chemistry, researched the effect of circularly polarised light produced by light scattering in the atmosphere from neutron stars to investigate whether this would produce a change in chirality ratio.

This again demonstrated a very slight, but insufficient effect on chirality, but, as Professor Laurence Barron FRS[47] states after having reviewed a wide range of these various experiments, concluded that there are no clinchers, and that we may never know the answer to the chirality problem. None of the experiments analysed have provided a solution.

These experiments have produced little success and other solutions are sought but, currently, there seems to be no generally agreed explanation or solution in nature to this chirality problem. The mechanism would have to be such that a *significant* excess of left-handed amino acids would predominate to allow a sufficient quantity of left-hand-only amino acid polypeptide chains to form, link together and start the protein building process.

Once the first living cell had been formed, by whatever means, the coding within the cell, being all left-handed, may be able to ensure that its offspring would also be all left-handed in its amino-acid content since, perhaps, natural selection would apply.

As someone once said, "Give me a miracle, and I will explain the rest", which is another way of saying, give me the formation of the first living cell, and all subsequent life with all its diverse species can be explained by mutation, evolution and natural selection. A comforting but challengeable philosophy!

Chirality expert W A Bonner[11], in his book "Chirality and Life" considered a wide range of chance and deterministic abiotic mechanisms for the origin of chiral preference to explain the left-hand amino acid reality in the context of their potential viability on early Earth. He concludes that none of the mechanisms would be viable, and that the answer may be that the source of left-hand rich amino acids may have been extra-terrestrial. So, we are back to the extremely unlikely extra-terrestrial source again.

The First Life Form

Early life would have been relatively simple; however, no one really knows how such primordial life-forms were constructed. However, there is a limit to just how simple the first life-forms could have been. The first organism must have had sufficient complexity to enable it to reproduce and copy itself accurately and sustain itself from energy accumulated from its environment. This implies that there was a mechanism within even the first simple living cell that enabled the storage of genetic information.

In advanced living cells, this is achieved by DNA, that is deoxyribonucleic acid, which is a molecule that contains information and genetic instructions. The assumption is that DNA evolved later and was not available to support the first living cell. RNA, ribonucleic acid, although a complex molecule, is a much simpler molecule than DNA and could have provided the genetic information for the earliest cell.

The next obvious question is how did the first RNA come into being, and where did it get its coding from? Some scientists believe that RNA arose "spontaneously" others believe this to be extremely unlikely, since RNA is itself a complex molecule, making its spontaneous arising almost impossible.

Generally, in viruses, genetic information is carried in their RNA, so it is possible that the first living cell had some molecule that performed the same genetic code-carrying equivalent; that is, something storing genetic instructions, development, and hereditary information in some form of coding.

This genetic coding had to contain the information that enabled the correct assembly of the correct amino acids (all being left-handed chirals) and then from these building blocks, assemble the correct proteins; several hundred of these proteins would be required to form the first living cell.

Thus, to be regarded as "living", even the earliest living cell had to have a sufficiently complex structure to allow it to survive, reproduce, and pass on a copy of its structural coding to its offspring. But how would this original RNA (proto-RNA) get its coding in the first place?

This first cell also had to have a self-organising capability to enable it to arrange its internal structure to provide the functionality to enable it to survive. The answer is, according to Matrix Model Theory, the structure of the first life-form was based on coding provided by domains within the Matrix Model, which coded for left-hand-only amino acid chirals.

Subsequent offspring would then form from left-hand only chirals since the offspring would be exact copies of the structure of the original cell. The Matrix Model domains would also provide the initial self-organising capability.

For any living cell, passing on a true and exact copy of its own genetic blueprint to its offspring is crucial: without this requirement, life reproduction would tend to be random, and evolution would be arbitrary. Even the most basic version of the very first living cell had to have a cell wall of some kind to contain the proteins and genetic material.

It also had to have the ability to absorb and process materials gathered from outside its cell wall to meet its energy needs and to make the building blocks for constructing another version of itself. It also had to have the ability, as stated above, to manage its cell wall division and send the copy of itself into the outside world, if it is assumed that the simplest form of replication is by cell-splitting. Without these capabilities, it is not really "living".

Work has been done by Professor Harold Morowitz[10] of Yale university, who attempted to answer two crucial questions: "what would be the *simplest* free-living cell, capable of replication?" (That is the simplest possible life-form that could be capable of surviving and reproducing), and how many proteins would it require to have sufficient complexity to be able to achieve reproduction? His work concluded that it would require a minimum of 239 protein molecules. This is considerably simpler than that proposed by Hoyle.

Although this number is refuted in some quarters, it at least gives a starting point based on the analysis from a molecular biologist of high regard. Morowitz's work has since been confirmed by later research, as described below.

Taking this figure, it implies that if random chance alone were to be solely responsible for the coming into existence of this simplest possible living cell, "pure random chance" would have to arrange at least one complete set of 239 proteins, each with an average of 400 amino acids (his model assumption), all with exclusively left-handed amino acids, Morowitz has calculated that the odds of this happening by random chance alone, are 1 in 10^{123}, which makes it, again, a mathematical impossibility!

Morowitz's calculations have been criticised by a few sceptics on two main grounds. Firstly, that the very first and simplest living cell may have had far fewer than 239 proteins, and there may have been fewer than his assumed 400 amino acids per protein.

Let us assume that the critics have a point. If we arrange the calculations to be based on the number of amino acids per protein to be such that the chances of them then forming a protein were a billion-billion times greater (10^{18} times) and further, let us arrange that the actual number of proteins in this first living cell be reduced from 239 such as to make the formation of the first living cell to be a billion-billion times greater (also 10^{18} times) then the chances of our alternative simplest-simplest living cell then still remains 1 in 10^{87}; so still massively beyond mathematical definition of impossibility.

More recent research described in Science Daily in work entitled "Scientists find smallest number of genes for organisms survival" carried out at the University of California, headed by Dr C A Hutchison III, Professor of microbiology at UNC-CH school of medicine, The research concluded that the minimum number of proteins producing genes a single-celled organism needs to survive and reproduce in the laboratory is somewhere between 205 and 350. This research strongly supports Morowitz's work and calculations.

Professor Morowitz carried out research to find out how simple a cell could be, to really be capable of *living*. His calculations and assumptions to define what complexity this simple viable cell would have, is based on science. The sceptics of his work seem to be trying to "guess down" the structural complexity of the "first living cell" trying to get at all costs, the probability of random chance of its formation to a probability below the 1 in 10^{30} figure, where the remotest possibility of assembly by a series of random event could be entertained. So far, they have failed.

These figures differ from Hoyle's figures given above because it proposed a much simpler life form than Hoyle proposed and used other assumptions, since Morowitz assumes a cell could be viable (just) having far fewer amino acids and proteins.

Research work done by Professor Hubert P Yockey[42], a physicist and information theorist at Berkeley, University of California, will now be considered. He worked with Oppenheimer on the Manhattan project and his fields included molecular biology.

He analysed the microbiology mathematics associated with the construction of a single molecule of ISO-I-cytochrome c, which is a small and relatively simple protein common in both plants and animals.

His calculations concluded that the chances of formation of this molecule by random chance events alone, to be 1 in 10^{75} which is again, way beyond mathematical possibility (he also included in his calculations the effects of chirality).

To put this into context, in evolutionary terms, it has been calculated that if a random mutation of this molecule's ancestors had been provided every second from the birth of planet Earth, this protein molecule would now be only about 12.9% complete. For a truly living cell comprised of many proteins, the chances of this cell being formed by random chance alone could not have occurred.

Yockey concluded that life did not start in a primordial soup, as proposed by some, but that, *the origin of life is unsolvable as a scientific problem.*

These figures are representative of many similar calculations done by many scientists over many decades, and they are criticised by total-mechanists, (that is, scientists who will only accept a natural random-event explanation for the formation of the first living cell) on several grounds.

Firstly, that in spite of the astronomical chances against the first-life event happening by pure chance alone, they point out that in the oceans of the world at that time there would have been billions of chemical reactions occurring simultaneously, so there could have been billions more opportunities for the vital initial building blocks, the amino acids, to have occurred and interacted to make up the required proteins. However, this is offset by statistical distribution and time considerations.

As previously described, the relevant chemical interactions had to result in the right type and number of amino acids to come into existence. These would then have to be assembled correctly to create the initial living cell. For this to occur, the raw materials, amino acids, need to be co-located, which means they need to have come into existence within reaction-distance of one another.

This is true to enable the polypeptide chains to form, which then had to form close enough together to permit them to inter-react and string together to form the correct sets of proteins (this then has to be repeated between 205 and 350 times in order to arrive at the required set of proteins), which themselves would have to be within a short distance of one another so that they could inter-react and combine as required to assemble into the first living cell.

Given the vast size of the oceans, this proximity issue considerably offsets the argument that there are many billions of simultaneous chemical reactions that would naturally result in millions of co-located amino acids of the right type is extremely unlikely.

The question of time is also critical to the calculation. Even if the required proteins are formed by chance, and even if they are co-located, they need to also occur *at the same time*, or at least before the others they need to react with, dissipate. The process would not work if the second or subsequent amino acid or protein being established is formed just too late to interact with the first.

These place and time considerations would also tend to make the formation of the initial life-form by a series of random-chance events even less probable. This must be considered alongside the case that the chirality of the amino acids had to be exclusively left-hand.

A simpler life-form starting point was documented in the work done by Professor Bradley and Dr Thaxton[12] in their publication "Information theory and the origin of life". They used a different set of assumptions from Morowitz and Yockey, their work concludes that if a protein had only 100 amino acids, which would constitute an extremely simple cell, they calculated that the probability of getting a proper assembly to form their version of the simplest living cell would be only 1 in 4.9×10^{191}.

This cell would be a very basic, simple life-form and may be, in fact, too simple a structure to have the capability to be regarded as a true "living" cell. This is still an astronomical figure, representing a mathematical impossibility and continues to demonstrate, from a completely different perspective to that of Hoyle, Morowitz, or Yockey, the impossibility of random-chance life, even if we take the view that very early proteins would almost certainly have been very simple in structure.

Bradley and Thaxton, (Jan 1985) concluded that start of life from a pre-biotic soup from which the first cell arose, is a myth. They dismiss the idea that life could arise by chemical evolution entirely, using technical arguments from thermodynamics.

Note again, although if we are considering a molecule structure massively less complex than those that Morowitz, Yockey or Bradley and Thaxton considered, it has to be remembered that there is a minimum complexity of cell structure below which it would be unable to replicate, unable to absorb specific energy from the environment and therefore, could not be considered to be a living cell at all.

We do not know in detail what the initial environment conditions on the early aeons of the planet's existence were, nor is it known for sure what the construction of the earliest life forms would have been.

In fact, as Hoyle himself indicated in a lecture[13] that if one proceeded without the fear of incurring the wrath of scientific opinion, that biomaterials with their amazing measure of order and diversity of life, one has to arrive at the conclusion that they are the result of intelligent design.

Illya Prigogene[41] states in his "Thermodynamics of Evolution" that:

The idea of spontaneous genesis of life in its present form is therefore, improbable, even on the scale of billions of years.

And yet as we have shown, the timescale for the first emergence of life was considerably shorter than "billions of years", which makes it even more unlikely. Most critics also ignore the chirality problem and assume that somehow left hand chirals would occur in reasonable excess with respect to right hand on clay or crystal surfaces. Extensive research, as described before, has dismissed this and many other mechanisms (see conclusions of L Barron,[47] described earlier).

Dr Capra[24] noted that according to Darwinian Theory, to have a living organism formed by chance through random mutations and natural selection, the probability of even simple cells emerging in this way, within the known age of the Earth, is vanishingly small.

The conclusion from the work of some the scientific community as listed above is that the arrival of life on Earth is beyond explanation by current science[9, 42, 41].

The calculations presented above clearly demonstrate the massively high degree of improbability of life formation arising by random chance alone. The figures calculated by different scientists differ from one another because they used different assumptions and scenarios, but they all demonstrate that the probability of the cells they researched assembling by random chance alone is far greater than 1 in 10^{30} and are therefore, a mathematical impossibility.

Since life clearly did start somehow, the question of how it did so must now be addressed, which is the subject of the next chapter. But before moving on, there are just a few more factors which enabled life to start and to be sustained on Earth, which are worth covering.

It is generally believed that life started in the oceans because the early atmosphere had no ozone layer since there was too little oxygen in the atmosphere for ozone to form and so the surface of the Earth was unprotected. Ozone is formed by the interaction of sunlight with oxides of nitrogen and hydrocarbons. The presence of atmospheric oxygen, and hence oxides of nitrogen, was a prerequisite for the formation of the ozone layer.

The Earth's surface would have been subjected to dangerous levels of ultra-violet radiation. Life, as we know it, could probably not have started in such an environment, at least on the terrestrial surface; but life starting in sub-surface environments such as under the muds and clays, or in the oceans, is more probable.

It is far more probable, with current knowledge, that life started on Earth, by natural chemical and molecular interactions strongly influenced by teleological (purposeful) sequences, using mechanisms supported by Matrix Model Theory that will be described later in this book.

The formation of even the very simplest living cell depends, among other things, on the availability of information. These "instructions" caused a primitive version of proto-RNA to be assembled and provided with the coding to enable it to assemble the required chains of amino acids to form the first living cell.

The coding had to ensure that these amino acid chains were assembled correctly to form the required proteins which were, in turn, assembled to form the first living cell, which, in this book, is referred to as the protoid. The coding supplied by the protoid SFU[59] also answers the chirality problem; it supplied the proto-RNA with coding that specified only left-hand chirals of amino acids.

The protoid, with its proto-RNA suitably coded, was then able to pass on copies of that proto-RNA to its offspring, thus providing a mechanism for inheritance to pass on genetic material. The mechanisms that enabled proto-RNA to form and be supplied with the initial coding will be described in chapter 3.

The origin of life by purely random spontaneous series of chemical reactions has now largely been abandoned by an increasing number of scientists.

The Miller-Urey Experiment

To demonstrate that amino acids could have been created by natural means during the earliest periods of the Earth's existence, an experiment was conducted, which became famous in its time.

In the 1950's, an experiment was carried out by Miller and Professor Urey to try to generate amino acids from materials thought to have been present in Earth's atmosphere in the earliest times.

They had a sealed tank into which they put water-vapour, methane, ammonia and hydrogen gasses which do not react with one another normally. They then caused electrical discharge to pass through the mix simulating lightning acting in an Earth's environment assumed to exist at that time.

This process produced traces of around 20 different amino acids. It was assumed by the experimenters that the Earth's early atmosphere contained almost no oxygen. However, if it contained no oxygen, then there would have been no ozone layer in the Earth's atmosphere at that time, and therefore the ultra-violet radiation on the Earth's surface would probably have seriously damaged some of the amino acids so produced.

More recent work on the content of the Earth's early atmosphere indicates that it was not as assumed for the Miller-Urey experiment where they based their experiment on an atmosphere rich in hydrogen and low in oxygen. However, it is now believed to have had a higher oxygen content than was assumed for this experiment. Such an atmosphere would diminish both the amount and variety of the amino acids produced.

The "primordial soup" theory, which states that the mix of chemicals and minerals present in the early Earth's environment, such as hypothesised by Miller and Urey, also has certain problems in that such an environment would also produce substances that would tend to prevent them from forming longer chain molecules. This provides another conundrum as to how and in what environment the first living cell appeared.

Another problem is that if, by some means, the result of some mechanism had placed amino acids in the oceans, are the effects of hydrolysis. Water tends to break down or split apart some types of bonded molecules such as amino acids. Sea water does tend to destroy the peptide bond, which bonds amino acids together, but in some cases, this process can take a long time.

There is no doubt that amino acids can, and do form in nature, the problem is finding mechanisms that will enable the right types to be produced close enough together such that they can be assembled in the right order and last long enough to form the required proteins.

Crucially, as previously described, there is also the question as to where the information (coding) came from that defined the assembly-order of the amino acids and proteins and defined which amino acids should be assembled to form these specific proteins. Something has to organise these amino acids and assemble them correctly into proteins.

Although this is still an important experiment, since many traces of amino acids were produced, many scientists have now focused on deep sea vents, alkaline vents, and in some cases, outer space as sources of amino acids; but occurrence by natural means, on the Earth's surface and in the atmosphere, has also been proven.

This experiment would produce amino acids of both left and right-handed chiral types in roughly equal measure with the attendant issues described previously, that is, that life as we know it requires exclusively left-hand chiral amino acids, so we are back to the chirality problem.

In general, it is not sufficient to have all the ingredients available to enable the assembly of a life-form; there also has to be some degree of structure and organisation. The issue of where the "organisational influence" came from to enable the very first living cell to form and replicate to enable natural selection to be able to function has, currently, no generally agreed answer in mainstream science.

As Jonathan Wells[29], an American Molecular Biologist, University of Berkley, California was of the opinion that although the Miller-Urey experiment is often presented as proof that science has demonstrated the first step to explaining how life started on Earth, in fact, as he states, although it was an important experiment, it does no such thing.

It is notable that, so far, all experiments in laboratories have failed to produce a single living cell by naturalistic processes alone. As someone wrote "If I put a frog in a blender and push the button, I have all the ingredients for a frog, but I don't have a frog".

This is another way of saying, that even given all the right amino acids in the right place at the right time, in the right atmosphere, there has to be some kind of "instruction" to initialise the organisation of the building blocks in such a way that they form the right assemblies to enable even the most basic life form to be realised. In science, there is still no "agreed standard model" of the origin of life.

How Can Life Arise from Lifeless Matter?

There is also a more fundamental question here; how can life arise from non-living materials, given any degree of random interactions? The spontaneous arising of living cells from non-living material in known as abiogenesis. For abiogenesis to be satisfactorily explained, the process of self-replication has to be explained, and how self-assembly took place.

The emergence of membranes to enclose and protect the genetic material would also be an essential precondition for even the simplest living cell to have formed. The even more perplexing question is how highly sophisticated DNA/RNA information could ever be created and encoded without implying a naturally occurring intelligent entity at work. Even given the specific effects of natural selection, this continues to challenge current micro-biology. Proteins are incapable of assembling themselves or creating copies of themselves without the assistance of at least a prototype version of DNA or RNA.

The DNA contains the instructions as to how to construct a particular protein that is required to perform a particular function. It seems that DNA is required to assemble the required proteins and proteins are required to arrive at the right DNA (or equivalent) structure, an example of the "chicken and egg" paradox. As described above, it has been assumed here that an early form of proto-RNA was the initial code-carrier.

This poses the question as to how any combination of chemicals and molecules occurring naturally could interact with one another in such a way that they could end up programming proto-RNA building blocks with coding (information in a particular format) required to determine the assembly of amino acids to arrive at even the simplest and most basic life form.

Dr Werner Gitt[25], former Professor at the Institute of Physics and Technology wrote that, *information cannot arise by naturalistic processes.* His view is that there is no law of nature or process that can cause information to arise and originate from matter. He concluded that the incredible complexity of DNA, with its vast data-store capability, demonstrates that it could only have arisen from an extremely intelligent source.

Dr David Foster[19], a cybernetician (International conference, Imperial college London 1969) concluded that the arrival of life on Earth had to be shaped and guided by an intelligent and purposeful source. He concluded that from a cybernetics point of view, it is possible to consider the universe in terms of data and data processing; a kind of "Intelligent Universe" of coded information. He also believed that wherever there is life, it is likely to evolve into higher levels of intelligence.

Matrix Model Theory proposes that intelligence is inherent in nature; we live in an Intelligent Universe, which all living entities are part of.

There is an old saying that given an infinite number of monkeys with typewriters, statistically one of them would eventually type out a Shakespearean play. The statistics are such that it can be assumed that, in reality, this would never happen, although we may end up with a lot of broken typewriters!

To arrive at the Shakespearian play, it must also be assumed that there is an infinite amount of time in which the monkeys feverishly bash away on typewriters. There never has been an infinite amount of time: time has been very finite since the formation of Earth.

The question arises as to whether, even given that significant numbers of proteins were somehow produced, would that in itself enable self-replicating and self-sustaining life to have emerged? Based on the statistical arguments contained within these chapters, such spontaneous arising of a living cell could never have occurred and would have been a statistical impossibility. Alternative answers to these questions are described in later chapters, using Matrix Model Theory.

A few other crucial environment evolutions shall now be described, each extremely improbable, they actually occurred, and each phase was vital for life formation and sustainment.

The Essential Properties of Water

Water is essential for the formation and maintenance of life. It possesses physical properties which cannot be found in other materials and without which, life as we know it would not have been possible.

The mechanism that bonds water molecules together, the hydrogen bond, is critical to the properties of water. For example, if the strength of this bond were slightly stronger, water would be more of a solid, and have a glass-like property. If it were slightly weaker, then water would only exist as a gas and only become a solid at low temperatures. Thus, the characteristics of the hydrogen bond are another example of critical parameters having to be *exactly* as they are to enable life to form.

Water is the only substance that can simultaneously exist as a gas, (water-vapour), a solid (ice) and a liquid (liquid water) over a wide range of temperatures. Returning to the importance of the hydrogen bond, a vital by-product of the critical strength of the bond is the formation of DNA.

If the bond were only slightly weaker or stronger, DNA would not have formed its famous double helix, nor been able to have many of its essential life-critical properties. It would seem that the strength of the hydrogen bond has been "selected" with extreme care! This is another example of a teleological influence at work.

Another crucial characteristic that water exhibits is the phenomenon of surface tension. The effect of this can be seen when water slides down a surface, even when the surface bends in such a way as the water flow seems to be such, that gravity should cause it to fall, it appears to cling to the surface and continue its flow down the surface. It is what causes rain to form almost spherical droplets on many surfaces. It is due to the water surface's tending to shrink to the minimum surface area. This characteristic is essential for several biological functions.

The Unique Properties of the Carbon Atom

All life that we know on Earth is carbon-based, that is, all living cells contain carbon atoms.

Sir James Jeans[14] Fellow of Trinity college, Cambridge, and a Professor of mathematics at Princetown University, concluded that life was only possible because of the exceptional properties of the carbon atom.

Fred Hoyle also worked on a theory of stellar nucleosynthesis[15]. He observed the generation of carbon following one specific reaction where carbon is generated from helium. This required the carbon nucleus to have a very specific resonance-energy and spin for it to work.

This led to him to predict the energy levels which were later to be proven correct by laboratory experiment. It is essential for life as we know it, that carbon should be produced naturally in extremely large quantities. However, the energy levels in carbon are such that they are statistically extremely unlikely to occur in significant quantity by chance alone.

Hoyle wrote:

Some super calculating intellect must have designed the properties of the carbon atom, otherwise the chances of finding such an atom through the blind forces of nature are utterly miniscule.

He continued, *The numbers one calculates from the facts seem to me so overwhelming as to put this conclusion almost beyond question.*

The abundant existence of the carbon atom was another essential ingredient in the long path to creating life, although for it to have occurred naturally in such vast quantities was, according to Hoyle following his research, nearly impossible.

A few other key ingredients which, although improbable, had to be in place to enable life to start shall now be described.

The Importance of The Earth's Magnetic Field

The Earth was formed from an initial mass of swirling debris and gasses. These assembled into a ball of hot rock, which eventually cooled to form a firm temperate surface crust with a hot molten core.

Since this core is predominantly comprised of iron and nickel, the effect of the rotation of the Earth is to give the Earth a magnetic field with a magnetic north and south pole, effectively making the planet into a giant magnet. This magnetic field helps protects the Earth from the emissions of charged particles from the Sun, which the Sun disgorges at regular intervals during events called solar flares.

During the solar flare event, vast quantities of charged particles, electrons, protons, gamma rays, x-rays and ultra-violet radiate from the Sun in all directions and some stream towards the Earth's surface. The Earth's magnetic field deflects the great majority of this radiation so that it sweeps harmlessly past the Earth.

However, some high-energy particles make it through into the Magnetosphere, a region above the ionosphere, where they are trapped in regions called the Van Allen Belts, where they are rendered harmless. There are two of these belts, one more distant from the Earth's surface than the other.

Without the protection of the Earth's magnetic field, this solar radiation would strip away the upper atmosphere including the ionosphere, which would allow much larger levels of ultra-violet radiation to hit the Earth's surface with seriously damaging effect on life. Eventually, this could lead to the loss of the atmosphere and eventually, the loss of the oceans.

It has been calculated (source Luhmann, Johnson and Zhang, 1992), that the near total loss of atmosphere on Mars occurred since the magnetic field of Mars turned off due to Mars's molten core, which gave rise to its magnetic field, cooled and solidified.

The Earth's magnetic field is therefore another of the many essential ingredients which had to be in place, or had to occur, for the formation of sustainable life on Earth to be possible.

The Atmosphere

James Lovelock[16], a Scientist, Visiting Fellow, Oxford University, and Fellow of the Royal Society, wrote a book called "Gaia, a new look at life on Earth" in which he puts forward his idea that the Earth is a living, self-regulating organism. He proposed that the Earth, and life on Earth, advanced and evolved by forming interacting processes between life forms and the environment, which enabled the Earth to regulate its environment, and seemingly always act in a manner that would tend to support and protect life on Earth.

Lovelock ran into problems with his first book on Gaia, since it attracted considerable criticism from some fellow scientists that his hypothesis seemed to be too teleological or purposeful. That meant that his Gaia hypothesis could have been interpreted as implying the existence of a causal agent directing the life process.

He met "persistent, almost dogmatic, criticism" which caused him to write a revision to his book expounding Gaia theory from a more mainstream scientific standpoint; "sanitising" the text to eliminate any idea that Gaia might be a sentient entity acting with purpose. As Lovelock put it, the new science of Gaia, geo-physiology had to be rid of any references or thoughts of Gaia, as an "Earth mother".

The opposition to any such concept and the attitude of some among the science fraternity, at that time, caused this concept of Gaia-science to be twenty-six years in the "wilderness", that is, before the work was published. This was unjustified, since James Lovelock is a scientist of renown, his concepts were, and still are, highly valuable: but it shows the deep uncompromising stance of some of the scientific community to ideas which are not of a purely mechanistic kind. In their view, there can be no purpose or organising force in nature.

Among other fields of research, Lovelock also studied the Earth's atmosphere. His theory was that the analysis of a planetary atmosphere would confirm the presence or absence of life on those planets (work at NASA), which would be useful when investigating whether there was life on other planets elsewhere in the universe without having to visit them. This is based on the theory that the atmosphere was always part of a "biological ensemble" rather than a mere catalogue of gasses.

Since the Earth was formed, the surface temperature of the Earth has generally remained remarkably constant, even though the composition of the atmosphere and the heat radiated from the Sun may well have changed or fluctuated greatly (for example, Lovelock maintains that the Sun's output has increased by 25% during the past 3.5 billion years[16]). Also, the concentration of ammonia in the atmosphere has been maintained to neutralise naturally occurring acids, keeping the atmosphere to be close to neutral, that is, neither too acidic nor too alkaline.

Lovelock's experiments and research into the atmosphere confirmed that its composition was such a curious and incompatible mix of gases that it could not possibly have formed by chance alone. The composition seems to fundamentally defy the laws of chemistry. He points out though, that is spite of this, the atmosphere does maintain life-favourable conditions.

A further example is that the concentration of oxygen has been maintained at around 21% which is ideal to support life. At one time in the early evolution of the atmosphere, the oxygen level rose to a point where it became toxic to life; the evolution of a sequence of different types of bacteria, enabling the oxygen toxicity problem to be solved. The mechanisms will be described later.

The oxygen level has evolved to be low enough to avoid toxicity and conflagration that would occur if it exceeded about 25%, and high enough to support life.

Lovelock explains this by his "Gaia Hypothesis" which postulates that the biosphere actively maintains and controls the composition of the air around us to provide an optimum environment for terrestrial life.

Thus, we have a "purposeful" element to our environment that has an influence over many critical things, including the atmosphere; the *formation and maintenance* of which has a teleological aspect. There is no sound scientific reason for banning the idea of teleological processes in nature.

A more detailed description is provided in Chapter 5 which covers the formation of the Earth's atmosphere and how it owes its composition to an incredible series of events achieved by bacteria, blue-green bacteria and other agents.

The Carbon Dioxide (CO_2) Cycle

Lovelock's Gaia theory proposed that the Earth is a self-regulatory, self-sustaining system in which both living entities and non-living entities are not just existing within an environment, but they are both part of that environment and shape it to support life.

An example of this is the carbon dioxide (CO_2) cycle. Early in the Earth's development, volcanic action was producing vast amounts of CO_2, which was blasted into the atmosphere. This warmed the Earth since CO_2 is a greenhouse gas. If its presence had not been reduced, this could have caused the Earth to overheat, and it would have become too hot for the formation and sustaining of life.

However, some living entities absorb CO_2 and give off oxygen during the process of photosynthesis. The process of rock weathering is also crucial to controlling the CO_2 level. As rock weathers, it interacts with rainwater and carbon dioxide to form carbonates, including carbonic acid. This process effectively removes CO_2 from the atmosphere and transfers it to chemical solutions.

Lovelock and others discovered that this was helped by the presence of bacteria, which greatly increased the rates of rock weathering. These solutions then washed into the rivers and found their way into the seas where some species of marine life absorbed these carbonate solutions to form their shells. When these species die, they sink to the bottom of the seas, and form carpets of limestone.

If the Sun warms the atmosphere further, it stimulates rock weathering and the bacteria that assist the process, so more carbonate solutions enter the seas. This forms one natural mechanism for controlling CO_2 levels, within limits, and hence helps to control the temperature of the atmosphere.

Some of the limestone thus formed on the seabed is absorbed into the Earth's crust, possibly assisted by tectonic movements, and thence down into the Earth's molten core, which makes it eventually available for volcanic action to once more release some of it back into the atmosphere completing the cycle.

According to Lovelock, there are other similar feedback loops controlling the levels of other gasses in the atmosphere, including oxygen. There are also mechanisms that control the salinity of the oceans which in turn control much of the Earth's temperature and climate to ensure it is suitable for sustaining a wide range of life.

This, in part, is the basis of Lovelock's Gaia theory. Another example of living entities contributing to the production and removal of certain gasses in the atmosphere was researched by Lynn Margulis[23], a microbiologist who worked with Lovelock: she especially researched the myriads of bacteria in the Earth's soil and their effect on the environment and atmosphere.

The whole environment is comprised of a series of self-sustaining systems which are established and evolved under the influence of both living and non-living entities. Many of these system processes use feedback loops to adjust the system's effect on the environment.

The evolution of the early states on Earth resulted in an atmosphere capable of supporting life as we know it. It was a complex, convoluted process which also appears to have been teleological.

The differences in opinion between the traditional mechanistic viewpoint and those with alternative views could be resolved, in part, by adopting an "open table of judgement" concept. By this, it is meant that every theory, explanation, hunch or hypothesis should be allowed to exist on the table of judgment for further consideration, until such time as they have either been disproved by research, further discovery or a new and better version, in which case the idea is consigned to the dustbin.

If, on the other hand, some are eventually proven to be correct or at least, to provide a tool for not only explaining aspects of observable phenomena in the cosmos but also enable predictions of phenomena which can then be proven by experiment or further observation, they can then take their place in the library of accepted knowledge. This approach is the most positive and constructive approach to this entire issue and indeed to many other issues outside the scope of this book.

One should bear in mind a salutary lesson from history. The early astronomer Copernicus stated that the Earth orbited around the Sun, rather than the Sun orbited around the Earth. In those times, this view was not accepted by the priestly establishment who sited biblical evidence that the Earth was the centre, and the Sun orbited around it.

His views were regarded as heretical and could have resulted in him being burned at the stake! (in fact, he was placed under extended house arrest). These days, if a scientist should invoke the "intelligent intervention in nature" concept of events leading to the formation of life on Earth, he merely risks being castigated by fellow scientists. However, he would probably be spared the stake! It is reassuring that we live in such enlightened times.

But only just! Lovelock and Margulis, who collaborated on the Gaia work, at first found it impossible to publish their work on Gaia hypothesis. Much of the established academic journals refused to publish it because, as referenced earlier, it seemed too "teleological" in its treatment of the processes of environmental shaping.

The conclusion is that the whole sequence of amazingly unlikely events described above, took place due to teleological interventions within nature that led to sequences of events eventually leading to the formation of the platforms and building blocks for life and an environment that could enable life to start and sustain itself. The question is, what *forms* did the teleological influences take, and how did they function? There were, and are, several entities involved in these processes, as will be described in later chapters; these entities form the foundations for Matrix Model Theory. The wider structure of the cosmos included entities which shaped the Earth and the total environment enabling life to start and evolve sustainably.

The very first living cell, the protoid, was assuredly much simpler than any cell living today and is now almost certainly extinct. The arguments above do demonstrate with a high degree of probability that the first living cell came into being over a very short time-period following, not only the complex and amazing formation of a life-friendly environment, but also the assembly of complex strings of amino-acids and their assembly into a very specific set of proteins.

The formation of the cosmos, the Earth, the Earth's environment and ultimately, the protoid, as the first living cell, was in fact the result of a whole series of teleological events and interventions from domains of the unconscious which will be detailed in the next chapter.

These domains evolved and their structures formed the Matrix Model which enabled the unlikely series of environmental characteristics described previously to evolve, and indirectly provided the coding defining the form, assembly instructions and behavioural influences for the protoid. This coding was stored within the protoid's primordial proto-RNA which enabled it to replicate, and the genetic coding be copied into the proto-RNA of its offspring.

Chapter 3
Domains of the Conscious and Unconscious; an Overview

A Brief Review

As a brief review, Chapter 2 provided evidence that the formation of the life by random chance alone was impossible and yet it has obviously formed, so alternative answers are required. The research carried out by Professor H Morowitz, was described where he proposed, based on his research, the structure of simplest possible life form that could be viable.

He calculated that even this simplest possible living entity, the protoid, had only a 1 in 10^{123} chance of forming by random-chance events alone. Yockey calculated a 1 in 10^{75} chance of his simple cell, (which was different from Morowitz's model) being formed by random events. It is not certain that some of the cells considered as being the "simplest life form" would have sufficient complexity to have the functionality and capability to be called a truly living cell.

Others have made similar calculations and come to the same conclusions. However, the researchers demonstrated that the *random* formation of any such simple life-form was so unlikely as to be way beyond the threshold of mathematical possibility.

Hawking observed that the laws of science contain many fundamental numbers which seem to have been "very finely adjusted" to make possible the formation of the cosmos, the coming into existence of the heavier elements, as described earlier and the development of life.

Having had to dispense with the purely mechanistic view to explain the structures of the cosmos and the establishment of life, we are left with the conclusion that some organisational or formative forces are inherent in nature. Self-organisation, in particular, is the key requirement for the establishment of life.

These organisational and formative forces have been functioning within the cosmos and have been at work since the instant before the Big Bang. These natural mechanisms enabled the arrival of matter and the start of the formation of the cosmos and have determined its evolution since the Big Bang, and, much later, enabled life to be established and diversify.

An Introduction to the Personal Unconscious

The existence of the human personal unconscious has been accepted by science for many decades, based on the work of many in the field, including Professor Sigmund Freud, a neurologist and founder of psychoanalysis and Professor Carl Jung[20], thought by some to be the father of analytical psychology and psychotherapy.

The usual definition describes the content of the personal unconscious is memories that have been repressed from the consciousness of an individual. These may include memories of trauma or of unpleasant experiences. Matrix Model Theory expands this definition stating that none of the memories within the personal unconscious are ever lost but are stored as long-term memories; most memories of an individual's life-experiences, including those that have been repressed, are retained. Therefore, the content of the personal unconscious grows and expands throughout the life of each individual, providing long-term memory store of the key experiences and events of an individual's life.

The narrow definition of the "unconscious", at least in humankind, is that it is part of the mind containing memories, instincts, impulses, images and ideas that are not generally available to be readily made conscious; in other words, we cannot easily be aware of them. The exception to this is the personal unconscious, which forms, according to Matrix Model Theory, the only source of an individual's *long-term* memory store and is repeatedly accessed to bring memories back to consciousness.

An Introduction to the Collective Unconscious

The collective unconscious was first proposed by Carl Jung and applies to the experiences of the whole human species. It can be regarded as an inheritance from all past human memories, the whole heritage of mankind's evolution made *indirectly* available to all humans. According to Jung, the contents of the collective unconscious experiences are retained, not as direct memories, but have evolved to provide mankind with the faculties of instincts and archetypes.

These are representations of archaic memories from vast numbers of human ancestors from the past, which are inherited, and have content which influences every human, since all humans have indirect access to, and are influenced by the content of the collective unconscious.

The domains of the unconscious in humans, affect behaviour, emotions, prejudices and aspects of decision-making, perceptions and actions and many other aspects of life.

Some of the content of the domains of the unconscious include images, symbols complexes and many other aspects of "human characteristics". They are present in our "mind envelope", which can be very influential. The domains of the conscious and the unconscious are present in all higher animals and man. How they interact will be described in detail in the description of the Matrix Model; they are key elements of Matrix Model Theory.

Because the human brain with its matrix of interconnections can "network" with its conscious and unconscious domains, it has access to a vast network of interconnected domains which represent a huge number of potential information sources for every individual, which collectively form the structure of the human mind. These interconnections of domains form part of the structure of the Matrix Model.

Expanding the Definitions to the Domains of the Intelligent Universe

A domain, in this context, is defined as a sphere of activity or knowledge. This concept is contextualised from the viewpoint that we are part of an Intelligent Universe, and that this intelligence is distributed throughout the universe, particularly throughout the living species on Earth. The concept of an Intelligent Universe is not original. In various forms, it has been proposed by Dr D Foster[19], Dr Werner Gitt[25] Professor Hoyle[9] and Sir James Jean[14] among many others. This will be described in more detail throughout this book.

The definition of the domains of the unconscious shall now be extended by describing their functionality to act beyond the conventional definition, which is usually restricted to relate only to mankind and higher animals. However, since we live in an Intelligent Universe, the universal "mind" also has domains of the unconscious and this has profound implications.

The earliest form of Intelligent Universe comprised just one domain; the universal unconscious which could influence and define how non-living matter would be organised, form and function, since at the time just after the Big Bang, there was no life, only non-living matter.

The Universal Unconscious and the Intelligent Universe

The highest and most remote domain of the unconscious hierarchy in the Intelligent Universe is the universal unconscious, which is defined here as infinite, boundless, impersonal and the source of later evolutions of unconscious domains.

Information-flows originated in the universal unconscious domain and emanated, and continues to emanate, a series of concepts for form and structure of material and non-material entities and life in all its many forms. These emanations of designs are called Ideations. The universal unconscious is the original and first domain of the Intelligent Universe, and one of its key attributes is creativity.

Ideations are what could be said to be necessary but not sufficient conditions for the realisation of events and physical entities. They are an essential precursor to the coming into existence of the cosmos and the structures that form it; they are the design and the definition of form and function.

Although these Ideations contain form and function information, they do not in themselves "make" or assemble anything in the physical domain, in the same way that the blueprint or design of a house does not cause a house to be constructed.

The Ideations contain the information, or "coding" that enable the "builders" to know exactly what to build. These Ideations defined the critical parameters described by Hawking that enabled atoms to form, stars to come into being, supernova to explode and life to originate.

The Ideations are the source of the "super-calculating intellect" referred to by Hoyle. These entities ensured the critical rate of expansion of the universe after the Big Bang to ensure it was not too slow, which would have caused the expanding matter in the then-universe to collapse back into itself, nor too fast, which would cause the matter within the universe to vanish into the depths of space. The rate of expansion is exactly right for the cosmos to have the form as it currently has. A later chapter will elaborate on the structure of the Earth environment including the remarkable establishment of the complex Earth's atmosphere.

The universal unconscious was the original source for the design and form of the cosmos and was active before time equals zero. The first task for the universal unconscious was to evolve an entity which could function to cause the establishment of matter the Great Void, that is, to act as the catalyst for the Big Bang.

This evolution was the establishment of the primary formative unconscious (PFU). This domain was the first crucial step in the establishment of a vast and diverse cosmos of matter and energy; the triggering of the Big Bang. This primary formative unconscious was the critical interface between the non-physical domain and the physical domain of matter and energy.

However, having the design and the driving force of the PFU is, in itself, not sufficient; there has to be entities which take the design, coding and intention and realise them in the physical domain, or, continuing the analogy above, the design also needs the builders, which we shall introduce in the next chapter as "the Effectuators", which are a series of naturally occurring entities.

The Primary Formative Unconscious (PFU) Family

Having introduced the primary formative unconscious, its function shall now be described. The PFU was evolved out of the universal unconscious, as described above, and is a domain which had, and still has, the task of implementing the Ideations (designs) which defined the structure and content of the non-living elements of matter and energy within the cosmos. It is the second domain within the totality of the Intelligent Universe.

The first implementation by the PFU were the laws of science/nature, which, as we have said, determine how matter and energy interact, which is an essential pre-requisite for cosmos formation to take place in an organised manner.

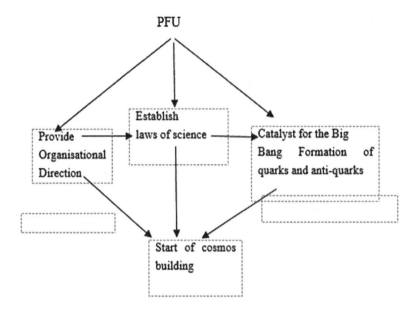

Fig 1. The Primary Formative Unconscious (PFU) provides the catalyst for the Big Bang, which caused the formation of quarks and anti-quarks which lead to the formation of matter as described in chapter 1. It also provided the establishment of the early laws of science and the organisational forces which determined the sequence and evolution directive for the form of the cosmos.

The PFU also ensured that the Big Bang occurred under the control of the early laws of science/nature. For the sake of simplicity, these shall now be referred to as the laws of science, although later evolutions were vital in determining how nature, biological systems and life functioned.

The Big Bang event was the implementation of the coming into being of matter, energy and time and the start of the formation of the cosmos. The laws of science included the establishment of the critical parameters at the precise values, as previously described, essential for the construction of the physical universe to be as it is.

The laws of science provided, and still provide, a high degree of order to the phases of universe building which continues. Without these laws, there would be chaos, as matter and energy would interact in a random and unpredictable manner.

Early in the formation of the cosmos, galaxies also formed. These are systems of millions or billions of stars, planets and space debris, together with gas and dust-clouds held together by gravity. The formation of the Sun, the Earth and the solar system have been described earlier.

The domains of the unconscious are both organisational and formative. By *organisational,* it is meant that they define how structures within the cosmos, and indeed life forms, are organised, where many different parts are coordinated to assemble into a structural whole. It is essential that all the separate elements function as a holistic system.

By *formative,* it is meant that they define how and under what influences the many distinctive non-living structures in the cosmos are formed from matter and energy, how they develop over time and how they adopt their distinctive shapes.

Having defined the universal unconscious and the primary formative unconscious, as the first two "founder members" of the unconscious domains within the Intelligent Universe, the first of the conscious domains in humans shall now be described.

Consciousness in Humans

One of the most controversial topics in science is the meaning and understanding of "consciousness" relating to humans and higher animals. It is defined simply enough, in the context of humans, as "the quality and state of being aware of external surroundings or something within oneself", or "having a sense of self".

Professor Max Velmans[6] and Susan Schneider are of the view that conscious experience is, at the same time familiar and at the same time mysterious. Anything that we become aware of is part of our consciousness. In other words, everything that we become aware of produces images within our brain and therefore, it is something that has been made conscious: we can "think" about it.

However, science does not have an agreed understanding as to how consciousness occurs, how it works or even what it is. Where it gets particularly interesting is when we consider non-human life forms. Higher animals like dogs or horses, clearly have a degree of consciousness: they have awareness of their environment, they run when approached by a predator or deliberately engage in activities to attract a mate, they tend to move away from what they perceive as unpleasant, potentially dangerous or uncomfortable, and towards areas where they reason that they are more likely to find food or shelter.

Higher animals also engage in sometimes complex rituals to attract a mate to enable them to replicate. Even a flower can turn its petals to face the Sun and track the Sun as it traverses the day sky. Is this evidence of a degree of rudimentary consciousness, or just an involuntary bio-chemical activity? At what point does "bio-chemical activity" become some primitive form of cognition or consciousness?

For the purposes of this book, consciousness shall be defined as anything that we, (or any animal), become aware of and can think about or "bring to mind," is present in its consciousness, however basic and elementary that may be.

The question arises as to whether consciousness can ever be explained by mechanistic processes; that is, entirely by the physical interactions of chemicals, some combination of molecules, DNA or some complex electrical or electro-chemical interconnections between neurons and other cells within the brain. Science is divided on its understanding of the real nature of consciousness and the definition of its properties.

The mechanistic view is based on the idea that all living things are quite like machines, programmed to react in certain ways under certain circumstances. In fact, science so far cannot explain how a collection of chemical reactions, physical interconnections or electrical signals humming through the brain can give rise to awareness, thinking processes, an awareness of "self" and original thought or even abstract thought.

Clearly, conscious thoughts in humans goes far beyond mere response to environmental stimuli and far beyond reacting to the five senses. Science currently finds difficulty in developing a generally accepted explanation of consciousness through strictly mechanistic or electro-chemical interactions.

How can this chemical and electrical activity within the brain, as those with a mechanistic world view believe, conjure original thought, creativity, the works of Bach or Mozart or the concepts of atomic theory, Einstein's relativity theory or quantum-mechanics and be capable of the most curious capability of creative abstract thought which is not an essential capability for survival?

How can such chemical and electrical activities make decisions, solve difficult problems, reason, think and evolve new ideas, or exhibit other of the many aspects of intelligence? The physical brain exhibits measurable electrical activity during its normal function which includes thought processes including creative or original thoughts. How can electrical activity which can be measured within the neurons of the brain be responsible for these thoughts and ideas?

Work done by Van Wedeen at the Martinos Centre for Biomedical Imaging[53] has shown that the brain is, in part, structured to include a grid of 100,000 miles of nerve fibres called white matter which interconnects the various domains of the brain. These areas of white matter give off radio waves. Brain-mapping has identified the areas associated with each of the senses and each stimulation affects the branches extending from the neurons.

It is proposed here that the chemical and electrical activity observed during brain scanning in humans and higher animals are the physical manifestation of "mind" activity, that is, resulting from interfacing with both the conscious and the unconscious domains and represent the brain acting as a communication "hub" between the domains of the conscious and the unconscious.

This electrical activity within the brain of an individual enables content to be made conscious or at least influence thoughts, ideas and perceptions for that individual. This electrical activity associated with each stimulation is the "language of the brain".

Some of this electrical activity is due to sources within the brain but other electrical activity is due to sources within the domains of the unconscious; the Matrix of the Mind, which do not exist solely within the brain, as will be described next.

The Psi-Domain

All elements of the unconscious for humans exist in the non-physical domain, which we define here as the psi-domain. The psi-domain can be regarded as a non-physical universe which roughly parallels our familiar physical universe. Every naturally occurring entity has both a physical aspect and a non-physical or psi, aspect; the latter exists in the psi-domain.

This domain also contains the psi-aspect of every star, galaxy, planet including the planet Earth. If we consider planet Earth, the psi-domain contains and reflects the psi-aspect of mountains, oceans, forests and the psi-aspect of every living thing and naturally occurring non-living thing on planet Earth. The totality of the cosmos is therefore, a combination of the physical domain together with the non-physical or psi-domain.

All naturally occurring entities within the physical domain were first established in the psi-domain, including all celestial bodies, stars and planets including planet Earth. All entities established within the physical domain have one thing in common: their physical existence is time limited, they will all "die" or cease to exist eventually. This is true of all stars, planets and even our planet Earth and all living organisms within it.

The two domains operate in tandem, and the physical existence of everything from the initial matter following the Big Bang through to life itself, depended and depends on the unconscious domains within the Intelligent Universe which functions in both the physical domain and the psi-domain.

The Ideations (design concepts) for Earth involved the establishment of life, but before that could be implemented, Earth had to evolve from its original form as a hot, rocky, arid, barren planet into an environment that was temperate, had oceans, an appropriate atmosphere and was conducive to elementary life. This involved, among other things, the Earth's orbit being established at the critical distance from the Sun.

As was described in Chapter 2 and shall be further detailed in Chapter 5, life establishment also involved a whole sequence of extremely complex events to take place before the first living cell could be established.

The Wider Primary Formative Unconscious Family

The requirement to establish the Earth's environment caused the original PFU to enable the evolution and establishment of other more specialised versions of the PFU to establish other essential non-living systems. These cover the contribution to the formation of the atmosphere, the oceans, the formation of crystals and many other non-living structures.

There is a wide family of PFU evolutions, each specialising in particular physical aspects of the environment. The entirety of the PFU family define the function of the many phenomena that characterise the totality of the dynamics of the non-living environment.

In the case of the atmosphere, the majority of the gasses that make up the gas-content is largely defined by bacteria, but there are other mechanisms, for example, the weathering of rock by carbonic acid from the atmosphere,[16] which removes carbon dioxide from the air; this is accelerated by bacterial action.

The PFU family is therefore, a part of the answer to several conundrums and is a fundamental element of Matrix Model Theory which explains:

I.   How the laws of science were established with a number of critical atomic parameters defined which allowed stars to form and supernova to explode, which seeded the universe with all the elements. They were established by the PFU; both the initial laws governing the Big Bang instant, and later, when these laws evolved to govern the matter and energy entities that we are familiar with today.

II.   How, at the Big Bang, something could be created out of nothing; The PFU acted as a catalyst effected to split "nothingness" into "something" and "anti-something" that is more specifically, quarks and anti-quarks.

III.   How, after the Big Bang, quarks combined in different ways to form protons and neutrons. Later, after further cooling of the cosmos, these protons and neutrons captured free electrons and formed vast quantities of atoms of hydrogen and helium and a small amount of lithium.

IV.   How the evolution of the cosmos continued over many billions of years and resulted in the formation of the Sun, stars, galaxies and supernova and the solar system. Much later, the PFU family had to evolve to solve the Earth environment problems. The environment had to rapidly evolve from being a hot, dry, arid, rocky barren planet to a cool water planet, with oceans, lakes rivers, a suitable atmosphere and rainfall essential to clean that atmosphere. The entire biosphere had to be such, that it could actively support life.

V.   This was done in many phases. The first being to establish the Earth's orbit at a critical distance from the Sun, establish a stable orbit, establish the formation of the Moon and establish oceans, an atmosphere, a crucial magnetic field and a terrestrial surface with a moderate temperature range. Each of these critical phases had to be completed before any form of life could start. They were all the result of highly complex processes.

The PFU family continues to determine the evolution and structure of the cosmos.

The Species Formative Unconscious (SFU)

The Primary Formative Unconscious had established a growing, expanding and evolving cosmos, together with a life-friendly (almost) environment on

Earth. Now, a new domain of the unconscious had to be established as a catalyst for the establishment of life.

Thus, the PFU evolved a more specialist level of the unconscious domain; the Species Formative Unconscious (SFU). The SFU can be regarded as an evolution of the PFU which has evolved to have the unique capability of providing the essential coding for the architecture of the first living cell on planet Earth: the protoid.

The first SFU was dedicated to the protoid species and the protoid proto-RNA defining the cell's form, function and behaviour which were essential requirement for the protoid to be established and survive. This organism had to function, consume energy and be capable of replication. It had to be able to construct exact copies of itself during the process of reproduction or it would have rapidly become extinct.

Whereas the PFU family was the catalyst for the formation of matter and the shaping of the cosmos, the SFU was, at a much later time, the catalyst for the formation of the first living cell.

In terms of timescales, the PFU initiated the Big-Bang at around 13.8 billion years before present time; the Earth was formed around 4.6 to 4.8 billion years BP, and the Earth's atmosphere and environment evolved to be life-supporting, also under the influence of the PFU. The first SFU, and hence the first protoid, was established around 3.8–4.2 billion years BP.

This vital part of the hierarchy of the unconscious domains is shown diagrammatically in Fig.2.

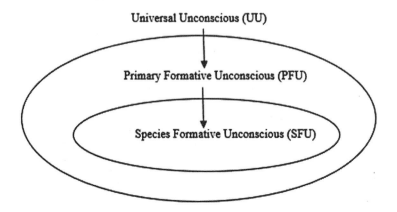

Universal Unconscious (UU)

Fig 2. The Universal Unconscious is boundless and the source of the Primary Formative Unconscious which was the catalyst for the establishment of the cosmos. It was the first link between the psi-domain and the physical domain. The Species Formative Unconscious was a much later evolution and was in turn the catalyst and code provider defining the form, function and behaviour for the first living cell, the protoid.

This SFU interacted with all members of the protoid species everywhere as they proliferated. Each individual organism was established as a self-organising, self-sustaining system. The SFU also ensured that the coding was in place within the protoid which defined its form and ensured that it could replicate. Once established, feedback from the protoid's form, function and behaviour was established, as shown in Fig 3.

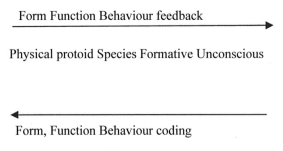

Form Function Behaviour feedback

Physical protoid Species Formative Unconscious

Form, Function Behaviour coding

Fig. 3

This initial state defining the form characteristics of the organism was stored in the SFU memory array. However, any changes to any of these characteristics of the cell would be fed back and also stored in the SFU memory array. The more protoids that formed, the greater the number of feedback messages were stored within the SFU and the more likely it was that the next protoid offspring would be exact copies of the parents since the coding would be reinforced by many generations of protoids.

Where there was a mutation (a change to the genetic build of the cell) within even one member of the protoid species, the feedback from that one cell to the SFU would change. For example, form may be slightly different. In this case, there was a finite possibility that new protoid offspring would copy the mutant form, since there was a finite probability that the coding from the SFU to define the next generation would carry the new coding.

In some cases, if the mutation carried benefits which gave the mutant version some survival advantage, the SFU may have suppressed the original version, and it would no longer be formed and the mutant version would become the next evolution of the species with only a small probability that the original version would form. Since the SFU functions with all members of the species, the change would be available to all members and their offspring would also be more likely to carry the beneficial mutation. This could be regarded as a form of natural selection.

As the species evolved and new species were established, more of the coding defining form, function and behaviour was embedded in the species' genome (the totality of the genetic information for the organism) and the total coding became a mix of coding from the SFU and from the species' genome.

As life evolved to have increasing degrees of complexity, greater degrees of cognition and intelligence were distributed among the species, especially among higher animals, particularly mankind. The faculty of intelligence requires a memory function. Thus, the domains of the unconscious have memory as they are part of the Intelligent Universe.

In higher animals, complex organs evolved, and many animals have also evolved a brain, whether rudimentary or highly complex. Planet Earth has also provided the environment that allows an extremely wide range of life-forms from the earliest life-forms, through to bacterium then through countless evolutions through to mankind.

The Hierarchical Family of the Domains of the Unconscious

There are crucial links between all the domains of the unconscious, both at the level of the Intelligent Universe and at the level of humankind.

The evolution of the first protoid-SFU and its essential role in establishing the protoid was the most crucial development in the history of life on Earth. This protoid-SFU was the first of a series of evolutions of further SFUs, each supporting a different species, and each one evolved from its immediate ancestor and designed to influence the form, function and behaviour of its associated species.

Each species has different form, function and behavioural traits and are designed in some cases to survive in different environments. Thus, each species has a unique and different SFU.

As previously described, proto-RNA is ribonucleic acid which carries genetic coding. The early version of proto-RNA ensured that the basic building blocks of the organism, the amino acid assembly and then protein assembly was correctly managed to form the protoid organism.

Living organisms obtain their coding from the genome passed on from their immediate ancestor but since the protoid was the first living entity, it did not have an immediate ancestor; the essential coding was wholly provided by its associated SFU.

Leslie Orgel [26] who collaborated with Francis Crick[56] in his work on DNA, was a proponent of the "RNA world theory", which proposes that before the evolution of DNA, which is far more complex than RNA, a form of RNA was the critical mechanism carrying the genetic coding for all early living cell construction.

Gradually, later evolutions of the RNA within later evolutions of living cells contained ever increasing quantities of this essential coding and was therefore, somewhat less dependent on coding supplied by the associated SFU. Therefore, this "enriched" RNA contributed more coding defining the form, function and behaviour of its associated life-form, although considerable coding continued to be contained within the SFU for each species as they evolved.

Each SFU has intelligence and memory and interacts continuously with a specific single species of life to ensure it can survive, within certain limits, and maximise the ability to replicate.

Species evolved and diversified as new evolutions of SFUs were established. Each evolved, in most cases, from its immediate ancestor which gave rise to a nested hierarchy of SFUs. Each later evolution nested within the envelope of its immediate ancestor as shown diagrammatically in Fig 4.

This shows the hierarchy of domains of the unconscious from the Universal Unconscious through to the PFU, thence the first life-forming domain of the unconscious, the SFU for the protoid. Later evolutions then led to the evolutions of later SFUs which support more complex living organisms, for example, bacteria and later, multicellular life.

As shall be described later, this leads to each subsequent evolution of a life form having not only the form function and behaviour of its own immediate SFU, but also weaker but noticeable influences from its ancestral SFUs. In practice, the full hierarchy of SFUs contains many thousands of SFUs, each supporting a different species, and later evolutions stacked within the SFUs of their predecessors. There were also forks and branches in the evolutionary model as species diverged, as will be described in chapters 5 and 6

Each SFU relates to a single species and its purpose, in conjunction with the RNA or DNA, is to provide the coding that provides the information, as described previously, to ensure the correct assembly of the series of amino acids in the correct order to form the correct proteins, and then assemble those proteins in the correct order to assemble the required living organism. The SFU, thus contributes extensively to define the physical architecture of its associated life form.

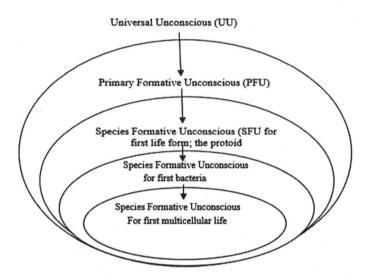

Fig 4. Showing later evolutions of the SFU from the PFU cosmos-builder through to the protoid SFU for the first living cell. This later evolved into more sophisticated SFUs, enabling the arrival of the more complex life-forms. This greatly simplified Figure shows the evolution of the first multicell SFU from the protoid, via the establishment of bacteria as an intermediate evolutionary life form. Note how the later SFUs are all nested within the earlier evolutions. The arrows indicate the direction of evolution. In practice, this is very much simplified; in reality, there would have been thousands of evolutionary steps and therefore, thousands of different species between the protoid SFU and the first multicell life form SFU.

When the protoid came into existence, it would have almost certainly have been incredibly vulnerable. It would have had to cope with the environment surrounding it. It would have had to be able to absorb energy from the environment in the form of chemicals found in the environment.

It would have to "know" what materials to collect and absorb to feed and sustain itself, and these materials possibly penetrated the cell's external membrane by some process akin to osmosis. Crucially, it also had to construct and contain within its envelope a blueprint of itself which entailed assembling a copy of its proto-RNA and its complete genome, since that is an essential prerequisite to enable it to replicate.

The SFU also had to provide the "trigger" which caused each protoid to carry out the processes essential to enable them to replicate. The protoid had to be able to create an identical version of itself and "release" it into the environment, to have replicated. No matter how simple the first living cell was, it had to be able to perform these highly complex functions or quickly become extinct. The provider of the sequence of these essential influences is its associated SFU as shown simplistically in Fig. 5.

There is no evidence that either RNA or DNA are in themselves a source of intelligence. Dr D Foster[19] concluded in a 1969 lecture at Imperial college London, that the intelligence to write code must be superior to the intelligence it is coding for. Thus, the SFU must always have a superior intelligence to the organism it is supporting. This also relates to the coding found in RNA and later, DNA.

The functions of the Species Formative Unconscious (SFU) for the protoid

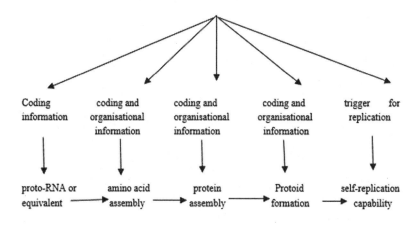

Fig.5 Showing the function of the first SFU for the Protoid. The SFU provides the initial coding for the proto-RNA which, in turn, provides the organisational instructions for the assembly of amino acids into proteins and the assembly of the proteins into the first living cell. This generates the first protoid as the first living cell. Also shown is the trigger ensuring that replication occurs. Thus, the protoid replicated and produced many offspring at this early-life stage, probably by cell-division.

The SFU for simple life-forms is also the source of the "borrowed mind", which enabled the entity to function and survive, even though the early very simple life-forms had no physical "brains" within their body structure and no inherent intelligence, but they did have a degree of cognition provided by their SFU.

Such mind-borrowing allows the provision of only the most basic functions essential for survival: feeding (absorbing energy in some form from the environment) and "knowing" what materials to consume, and how to assemble an exact copy of itself and thereby reproduce to ensure the species continues. Later evolutions enabled the more complex DNA and other genes to carry more of the instructions on body architecture, growth, function and reproduction for more complex species.

Having introduced the first living cell, evolution, mutation and natural selection processes were then able to progress the complexity and diversity of species rapidly. But as shall be described, the progress was in fits and starts and was not a smooth or linear process. Thus, the PFU itself evolved and established more and different SFUs and thus more and different species.

However, as the number and distribution of the species evolved, there were variations to the SFU of a particular species due to geographical isolation between members of a particular species or local environmental variations which led to evolution of local variations in the SFUs, and hence diversification and variations in the form, function and behaviour of elements of the species.

The Species Group Unconscious (SGU)

For some species, for example bees, termites and ants, their individuality and individual behaviour become somewhat fused as they have evolved the ability for each hive and nest to act almost as a single organism or big group (a super-organism) rather than as thousands of individuals. This was essential to enable the bees, ants and termites and some other species to survive.

The function of the SFUs in these cases was partially superseded by their Species Group Unconscious, the SGU. It enables the nest or hive to act with what appears to be a *group mind* to achieve common objectives, be that construction or repair of a nest or hive for example, foraging for food, feeding offspring or, at various stages, enabling sub-groups to leave the hive/nest and establish new colonies.

Starlings also have an SGU unique to each flock (murmuration) as an example, which arises on a temporary basis as they flock and perform amazing aerobatics in tight formation where they seem to be performing as though they had a "shared mind". After their group flight ends, they revert to behaving as individuals. Several more examples of the SGU function shall be described in chapter 4.

The Species Individual Unconscious (SIU)

There is one further domain which is mostly associated with "higher animals", which enables such animals to behave as individuals, with a high degree of autonomy, have the capability to make decision and develop thoughts unique to the individual. This is the Species Individual Unconscious (SIU). Each of the individuals within these groups have their own specific dedicated unique SIU.

The species which have individual SIUs includes man, all other mammals, reptiles and birds, which have been defined as "higher animals". Some other animals and insects have embryonic or extremely basic SIUs. The SIU includes the associated personal unconscious[20] as a sub-set. All the memories accrued by an individual during their life is stored here. The SIU affects the form, function and behaviour of every individual.

The SIU in each case is formed by a combination of the SIU from each parent (each parent providing 50% of the new SIU content) which is why, the form function and behaviour of offspring are usually similar, to a large degree, to those of the parents.

The SIU operates in conjunction with the individual's genome (which contains a complete set of genetic material for an individual) in this respect, but as shall be described, the genome model does not account for *all* the inherited characteristics: there is what is known as the "missing hereditary problem".

For some traits of offspring, for example in humans, as described earlier, height, the offspring has height inherited from the parents (tall parents have tall offspring) but this is not explained by the parental genes; for some traits, the genes to fully define height are "just not there". This is the missing heredity problem.

The SIU provides the "missing" heredity coding, solving the problem. More detail on this will be covered in later chapters. The totality of the coding from the genome and the SIU also determines, in part, how an individual develops later in life as their form and function changes as humans develop, then, as they age.

The SIU acts by providing a continuous flow of information (coding) to its associated individual by means psi-fields. There is a similar flow of information from the individual back to the associated SIU which constitute feedback loops.

Any changes to information relating to form, or physical aspect of the individual animal (including man) is fed back and stored within their associated SIU.

With higher animals, mutations tend to be regressive, but if there is a change, the SIU will store this and there will be a finite chance of the change being passed onto the next generation by the parents. If the change provides benefits (for example, the rapid increase in brain size during the evolution of mankind) the change will be passed from the SIU to the SFU, and thence become available to the entire species with increasing probability of that change dominating and occurring in future offspring for all members of the species.

Eventually, the SIU family may suppress the old version, and the mutant change will become the dominant version, with ever decreasing probability of the previous version being born. This is another form of natural selection: it is a teleological process.

In diagrammatic form, the hierarchy of the domains of the unconscious is:

Universal Unconscious: (UU*) Boundless domain and the source of the second domain of the Unconscious, the Primary Formative Unconscious.*

Primary Formative Unconscious: (PFU*) Established the laws of science, catalyst for the Big Bang,*

Species Formative Unconscious: (SFU) Provided coding for *the assembly of matter to form the first living cell from chemicals and elements available in the Earth environment.*

Species Group Unconscious (SGU) A later evolution spun off from the SFU

Species Individual Unconscious: (SIU) *Functions at the level of the individual in many animals including Man.*

Fig. 6. This shows the evolutionary flow from the UU through to the PFU and the evolutionary stages for the SFU family starting with the original SFU. This evolved to provide many SFUs, one for each species of life on Earth. The SGU is vital to group-animals like bees, ants and termites. The SIU for man and higher animals relates to individuals and provides a dominant input defining body architecture from the parents since the SIUs are a mix of the parental SIUs. All higher animals have the full SFU/SGU/SIU family influencing their form, function and behaviour.

In diagrammatical form, the structure of the SFU hierarchy.

Species Formative Unconscious (SFU*). Each* SFU *influences the form and behaviour of a particular species*

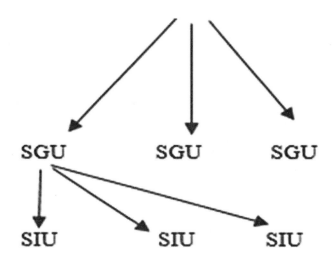

Fig.7. Overall structure of the SFU family. In the case of animals, the SGU has a vitally important role, especially for ants, termites, bees and others as described in the text. The SFU continues to function across the whole human species and contains instincts, based on the previous experiences of billions of Homo sapiens' that have lived and died since they first evolved. Each SIU is dedicated to a specific individual.

More on the Collective Unconscious

As previously described, this level of the unconscious was first proposed by Professor Carl Jung, (reference "Archetypes of the collective unconscious" by C G Jung)[20], published in 1959. Jung wrote most of his many papers during the early part of the 20th century.

Jung postulated, based on his extensive experience in the field of psychology, that the collective unconscious contains both instincts and archetypes. Instincts assist in determining our actions, whilst archetypes influence us in determining our understanding or perception of a situation. Jung worked at one time with Freud, and they fell out having disagreements as to the nature of the unconscious.

Jung concluded that although there was a "personal" aspect to the domains of the unconscious, there was also a deeper archive which was not personal but was derived from the experiences of thousands of generations of ancestors, and common to all men. Jung's conclusion was that the collective unconscious is a common psychic substrate in every human. Freud also accepted the existence of a collective mind.[5]

Jung was impressed by the fact that certain themes, symbols and motifs came to the consciousness of his patients during psychiatric treatment. These motifs and symbols did not seem to have any origin based on the personal experiences of the patient and were largely independent of the patient's culture, background and history.

After much research, he deduced that there seemed to be a common pool of experience, symbols, motifs and images which he called the archetypes, locked into the part of the unconscious which he later called the collective unconscious.

The collective unconscious was regarded by Jung as somehow hereditary. Since the archetypes appear to be common to all cultures, races and religions, their origin must be archaic, some of them dating back thousands of years to a time of common ancestry, pre-dating Homo sapiens' migration out of Africa, which occurred in several waves over many years between 50,000 and 200,000 years ago, and man's subsequent racial and geographical diversification.

Although Jung considered the archetypes to be inherited, he was unable to explain how this could occur. This has been explained by Matrix Model Theory, by the function of the Homo sapiens' SFU which contains the collective unconscious for the entire Homo sapiens species, the content of which evolved over thousands of years.

The collective unconscious is a part of the SFU for all Homo sapiens and is inherited and is indirectly accessible to *all* Homo sapiens. The archetypes are present as memories in the collective unconscious part of the SFU domain because the SFU has memory and it always has, and will continue to, interact with the species which it mentors. The SFU continues to gain more memories of the more powerful experiences from members of its species as they live and evolve.

Since the first Homo sapiens walked the Earth, believed to be in Southern Africa, memories of experiences, fears, disasters, heroic successes, symbols of importance, religious metaphors and many other memories have been stored in this collective unconscious memory which allows the resulting instincts and archetypes to be accessible to all men from all races; we are all probably descended from the same early stock.

This explains Jung's finding that certain images and symbols seemed common to many of his patients. They described during treatment, conscious images of symbols and shapes which were outside their personal experience, yet common to many of his patients, regardless of race or culture.

The "psyche" is defined as the whole of the conscious and unconscious. Jung describes the unconscious psyche as extremely old and is just as important in shaping man as his physical body.

Even with our modern knowledge of the human genome, which we understand to be one of the mechanisms for carrying inherited characteristics, there is no known mechanism by which the genome, or any other macro-molecule, can carry non-physical content, for example, thoughts, ideas, instincts, archetypes or any domain of the unconscious. These functions are performed by the domains of the unconscious family as external influencers in man and higher animals.

For humans, archetypes are innate unconscious modes of understanding which influence our perception. All mankind is influenced to some extent by the Homo sapiens' SFU, and its associated collective unconscious.

The link to the SFU and its collective unconscious also applies to higher animals and insects, particularly the instincts content, but this content is species-specific and will inevitably differ fundamentally from the content relating to Homo sapiens.

Instincts can determine, in some cases, actions, for example, the compulsion which causes birds to nest or some pigeons to home and explain many other animal behavioural aspects. With humans, the content of both instincts and the archetypes have a degree of commonality for all different races, although in some cases, with variations that have evolved over time for Homo sapiens, since they would have been influenced by many different cultures.

The earliest archetypes are of primal origin, and they occur in many forms. Because the archetypal images symbols and motifs are ever present although cannot be directly made conscious, they are just below consciousness. These images are frequently encountered and can be bought into consciousness in specific ways. They can influence behaviour.

Sometimes, the archetypal images can be made conscious during the dream-state where dreams make conscious those images residing in the unconscious. Similarly, deep meditation or altered states of consciousness can activate an archetype image.

The way in which the various domains of the unconscious network and interact, is best shown in the Matrix Model which is described in Chapter 7. Matrix Model Theory, therefore, encompasses Jung's collective unconscious, as a sub-set of the SFU.

A few of the archetypes most frequently encountered according to Jung will be described here. The subject is vast, but if a reader would like a more profound overview, Jung's "Archetypes and the collective unconscious" is one of the many publications that carry this subject much further.

A Brief Description of a Few Archetypes

According to Jung, archetypes are images symbols or motifs which are frequently "popping up" in myths, legends, religions, fairy tales, occult traditions and dreams. They are primitive mental images formed and as described earlier, inherited from all human ancestors and from every generation since, and are present in the collective unconscious. The content of the instincts and archetypes for Homo sapiens can influence thoughts, prejudices, actions, creative ideas and decisions.

Anima is only one archetype of many. This image is the soul-image for the male. She appears as a female typically a siren or a witch, a virgin or a sorceress, usually as a source of wisdom. She has been extensively represented in mythology which is where many of the archetypes are represented. Each archetype has both positive and negative attributes: none are either all good or all bad.

The anima has been defined as the archetype of life itself and includes such mythological figures as Venus and Helen of Troy among others. The relationship, in the world of the psychologist, between a man and his anima can be positive and constructive, or negative and destructive. Anima can be represented by a cave, bowl or chalice.

For women, the corresponding archetypal image is the animus often depicted as a heroic male figure, a male role model, or perhaps a priest-like figure. Jung states that the soul images in both cases are archetypal images from the collective unconscious but can be modified by the life-experiences of each individual. The animus can also be represented by a sword, tower or tree.

Another key archetype is the wise old man, sometimes depicted as the wizard or magician or teacher, as a sage or master. He symbolises the real meaning hidden in the depths and chaos of life. He represents the source of wisdom, the all-knowing ancestor.

This archetype is potentially the most powerful and potentially dangerous of the archetypes. It imparts a feeling of great wisdom, esoteric powers and gifts of healing, but it can also dominate all other aspects and become destructive. The wise old man is also the archetype of spirit.

This archetypal image pops up in many aspects of life as previously described in myths, fairy stories, plays, dreams and legends, for example, Merlin in the Arthurian legend.

A further, and perhaps most frequently encountered archetype is the "Great Mother", which is variously represented in mythology by Sophia, or from India, Kali, and from ancient Egypt, Isis. This archetype is frequently encountered in various religions, particularly more ancient religions where Earth goddess worship was common.

Some ancient burial mounds and centres of ritual use deep openings or caves in the Earth which represent the womb of mother-Earth. Entering such a cave would probably have been a kind of ritual activity, possibly performed by initiates.

The "Great Mother" archetype symbolises the life giver, protector, the one who provides and nourishes, also symbolises fertility and rebirth, identified as Gaia, the "Earth goddess", the spirit aspect of the physical Earth. Her negative qualities, according to Jung, include things secret, dark, the world of the dead.

This archetype also has attributes of nourishing and protecting emotionality. It is another almost universal archetype whose image occurs in folklore, pantomime (ugly sisters, fairy-godmother, good fairy, witch, for example), fairy tales and legend, one example being Guinevere, again in Arthurian legend. The Mother archetype can also be represented by the cup, well, spring, chalice motifs, among others. The Great mother and Mother archetypes are sometimes seen as opposites.

Archetypes can lead to the assistance of the archetypal forces to help, guide or influence the outcome of an issue on behalf of the subject. Archetypes, according to Jung, are "living psychic forces" and are thus, important influencers.

The archetypal images, such as the cross, the broken cross, the mother, child, the cup, or chalice are used extensively in both religion and in some traditions, so-called "magic" ritual. The symbols occur in the Kabbalah, in tarot cards, in religious ritual, initiation ceremonies and the symbols can be found frequently in churches, synagogues, temples and other religious centres.

The full set of archetypal images and symbols is available to all humans, whatever their race or culture, due to common ancestry, since we all have a common SFU which contains the collective unconscious. They can emerge as active entities influencing the ideas and perceptions of man as well as his actions.

Within the set of archetypes, there is one called the shadow. This is the "person behind the mask", the dark side of an individual which contains attributes which the individual would prefer to hide. The shadow is represented by the crone or devil motif. Since these forces cannot be changed, they have to be controlled or suppressed.

Another commonly encountered archetypal image is that of the child. This motif represents the potential future, the mediator and one that unites opposites. It also represents the healer or the one who makes whole. It is also represented by a circle or sphere.

For this reason, the child symbol or archetype is important in many religious traditions including Christianity. In fact, the Christian religion has frequently combined the child (Christ) image with the Great Mother (Mary) image, as two balancing archetypes. There are many paintings depicting this combination of archetypal images. This is a very brief look at a broad and deep subject and is included here because it is an inherent and important part of the SFU.

The Duad

The universe in total is a pairing of entities in the physical domain and the corresponding entities in the psi-domain. This scales up such that even the largest cosmic body has a physical and non-physical, or psi, aspect. This pairing is called a duad.

For example, the Sun, which is our closest star and the centre of our solar system, is a physical entity in the physical domain, and it has its psi counterpart in the psi-domain. The Sun together with the psi-aspect of Sun form the solar duad.

Every naturally occurring entity that is realised in the physical domain also has an existence in the psi-domain. The two parts of the duad continue to exist in parallel, each in its own domain; they have a high degree of independence from one another: they are not "in lock". This concept becomes important, particularly when we consider the duad of humans.

The physical-aspect and psi-aspect of an individual form a duad, including more than just the physical body and the brain (physical element). The psi-domain content for man includes all aspects of his unique SIU and shared SFU and SGU domains of the unconscious but also his higher conscious and the psi-aspect of his brain.

Each star and planet throughout our galaxy, and indeed throughout all galaxies in the universe, has a physical aspect and a non-physical aspect or psi aspect.

Currently, the only conscious awareness we have of the psi-domain is when we dream or engage in certain kinds of deep meditation or have a telepathic experience. We are influenced in our thoughts, ideas, memories and behaviour by the domains of the unconscious which reside in the psi-domain.

However, such effects are manifested in the brain-duad whereby, the psi-domain entities trigger electrical activity, which is measurable within the physical brain. This activity leads to thoughts and ideas and memories being made conscious.

There are various analogies to entities which we cannot see or observe directly but do exist. Besides the proposed existence of the unconscious, we could also include a thought or concept or abstract thought (and possibly, dark matter, until scientists are able to isolate a particle). These cannot be detected directly using our physical senses or indeed by current scientific measuring instruments.

We accept the fact that thoughts, concepts, instincts, perceptions and other abstract phenomena exist. We have an awareness of these as they arise. The mind embraces all domains of the unconscious and both levels of the conscious as well as the activities due to the brain reacting to the senses.

Thoughts and ideas exist as interactions between the mind-domains and are transferred to the domains of the conscious of an individual on a continuous basis.

The physical brain interacts with other aspects of the mind in its role as a communications hub, and how this interaction functions is an essential part of "holistic man," and indeed, all life forms with differing complexity, intelligence and cognition.

In the case of planet, Earth, the physical aspect we refer to as "Earth" and the non-physical or psi aspect, which in this book we have named "Gaia" which is the name of a Greek goddess. This word was used by Professor James Lovelock in his book "Gaia, a new look at life on Earth".

His usage of Gaia referred to the aspects of physical Earth that ensured that all the conditions of the environment on Earth have been *actively* made to be fit and comfortable by the presence of life itself. He viewed the Earth to be a vast self-regulating system.

In the context of this book, the Earth/Gaia duad is the physical and the psi-aspect of the totality of our planet.

Chapter 4
The Effectuators

The Function of the Effectuators

The essential requirement for the establishment of life on Earth was the availability of a series of entities in nature capable of providing the environments to support and evolve life. These entities are the Effectuators, which can be regarded as "Earth builders". There are eight Effectuators in all.

The Effectuators came into existence in a sequence according to the state of development of the cosmos. At the time of the Big Bang, only a few of the laws of science existed. These were the original set of laws that were limited to determine how matter would expand from the Big Bang singularity, and how sub-atomic particles would function to ensure atoms would form, as described in chapter 1.

Much later, the establishment of life with all its myriad of complexity necessitated the coming into existence of many more laws of science. For example, the arrival of life required the development of new laws relating to genetics, heredity, evolution and natural selection, among others.

The Primary Formative Unconscious, the PFU, evolved the other Effectuators, that will be described here, to interface with the physical domain and ensure the total environment developed to be life-friendly and capable of supporting a wide diversity of living, evolving organisms.

The PFU also acts to ensure that the Earth's biosphere could, and can, continually adapt to solve problems that arise with the oceans, atmosphere and the life-sustaining systems within the biosphere to ensure they were and are always maintained as life-sustaining environments. The PFU ensures, and always has ensured, that Earth-Gaia functions in such a way as to solve such problems and mitigate the threats as they arise; and there were a series of such major events.

As previously described, intelligence is not confined to the interior of an animal's skull, it is distributed and sourced in both the physical domain and the psi-domain throughout the Intelligent Universe. This allows even the simplest and most basic life form to have sufficient awareness of its immediate environment, take such actions as are required to sustain itself, be motivated to replicate, and take such actions required to endeavour to exist.

In order to do this, it must either be intelligent in itself or have access to some source of cognition or intelligence. Demonstrably, very simple cells such as bacteria, do not have a brain. Every species of bacteria achieves this capability, as previously described, by borrowing very basic but essential "mind" aspects from their associated species formative unconscious, its SFU.

This means that even the simplest cell must be comprised of, not just material "stuff", but also access to some kind of "mind capability" required to survive and replicate. The SFU associated with simple life-forms provides not only the coding required to define its structure but also the source of its borrowed mind, basic and elementary as it was and is.

Clearly, in the case of bacteria, to take one example, the associated SFU would provide only an elementary and primitive level of cognition, but just sufficient for the bacteria to survive and flourish; without this mentor, the cell would not have been able to form, nor would it have any degree of cognition, which is a fundamental requirement for all living entities.

Higher animals use their intelligence to think, adapt and problem-solve, learn from mistakes and memorise events. They receive some of this capability from their associated SFU/SGU/SIU family, which is collectively, an Effectuator, whilst some of this capability is vested within the animal itself.

Over millions of years, as more complex animals evolved, more function and intelligence became part of the animal's inherent capability, reflecting more coding being lodged within their embryonic genome and a greater level of intelligence lodged within their embryonic and developing minds, allowing them increasing levels of independence.

This meant that higher animals evolved greater degrees of intelligence, although they still had and have a degree of dependence on their associated SFU/SGU/SIU family for some elements of critical coding relating to their form, function, behaviour and development.

To provide a specific example, bees, among other species, as shall be described in more detail later in this chapter, function mostly as forms of collective organisms within each hive, each individual bee knowing its role and acting for the benefit of their hive or nest.

As individuals, they have the ability to problem-solve and perform other activities by using the very limited intelligence and memory they have within themselves, but they rely heavily on enhancing these capabilities by borrowing memory and problem solving from their associated SFU/SGUs families which together, has stored memories of the experiences of billions of bees of the same species that were ancestors of the present-day bees. The same is true of other insects, including ants and termites.

In the case of the bee, a typical problem it may have to solve might be which of several flowers it should access to yield the best nectar; it is thought that bees can "scent" flowers up to a mile away, but they have to "know" whether the journey would be worthwhile.

The collective memory within the bee's SFU/SGU "remembers" which is most likely to be the most beneficial flower to access, based on the accumulated experiences of many millions of bees that have gone before, and the correct decision is more likely to be made, even by a young bee on its first foraging expedition.

Each bee does not have to "re-learn" which flower to prioritise. This elementary degree of cognition is communicated to the bee via psi-fields from the associated SGU, whilst instincts are communicated from the bee SFU.

In terms of the more complex human, the myriad of thoughts, ideas, emotions, instincts, prejudice cannot be explained solely by the interactions of billions of electro-chemical events and signals within the brain, as previously described, nor by the content of their genome.

Many of these characteristics are not essential for life or survival but are highly sophisticated activities that have evolved over millions of years mostly within the more recent evolution of the higher conscious and the continuous interactions with the individuals' SIU, SFU and SGU family. On occasion, higher animals, including man, can "borrow" or be inspired by thoughts and ideas originating from these domains.

The Intelligent Universe concept indicates that intelligence and memory are distributed through many domains of the conscious and unconscious in the original Intelligent Universe, and in all living entities, and that all these domains evolve as the memory stores expand and the intelligence capability increases with time.

Interestingly, there would not appear to be any theoretical limit to how far this can progress. Technology, if that can be regarded as any kind of indicator, advances exponentially but without any kind of overall goal that we know of, and on many simultaneous fronts where progress is observed by a series of jumps across many different fields of knowledge functioning in parallel.

Sir James Jeans[14], who made important contributions to the fields of quantum theory and stellar evolution, had the view that there is a fundamental aspect to consciousness and that the physical universe is derived from consciousness. He also considered the universe to be closer to a "Pure Thought" than something mechanistic and that every individual's consciousness was like a brain cell in a Universal Mind.

Source (James Jeans, British Association 1934, Physics and Philosophy)

This concept provides one aspect of what is meant by an Intelligent Universe. Each of these Effectuators, will now be described, together with their roles and the sequence in which they became active.

First Effectuator: The Primary Formative Unconscious Family (PFU)

The Primary Formative Unconscious (PFU) family is the first Effectuator. The PFU, as previously described, pre-existed and was the catalyst for the Big Bang. The PFU had a lot of cosmos building to do before life could start. Included in the PFU family are the other domains of the unconscious, the SFU, SGU and the much later evolution of the SIU. Their functions have been described in chapter 3. Collectively, this family of domains form the first Effectuator.

The SFU Family Evolved Establishing Later Life Forms.

Following new Ideations, new SFUs evolved in the psi-domain to mentor new species. Evolution and mutation along with natural selection provided the tools in the physical domain to enable these new SFUs to establish these new species.

These evolutionary mechanisms enabled the establishment of early microorganisms and bacterial species and later, more complex multi-cellular species. Bacterial species can replicate rapidly, and thus are able to mutate and evolve rapidly.

This process of evolution was not linear: the overall hierarchy contains "branches" where different life forms, for example, plants, mammals, fish, insects and birds formed their own directions of SFU evolutionary hierarchy, where they diverged from the original evolutionary path over many millions of years.

As the SFUs evolve, they not only influence all members of the species they mentor but are themselves influenced by all members of their associated species. This influence is a two-way process. It has content part of which is locked within its memory which can be modified by experiential feedback from the population of that species. Over hundreds of thousands of generations, this represents a vast amount of information.

A storehouse of knowledge is therefore built up within the SFU for each species, based on the experiences of the species' ancestors over countless generations, as described previously. This storehouse gives rise to instincts which can also influence problem solving, the fight or flight decisions of an animal, what foods are good, and which are deadly, where food can be found, where possible dangers are recognised and many elements of behaviour.

For all animals, their SFUs contain the species collective unconscious which contains these instincts, which differs between each species as described in chapter 3. This indicates that a certain level of knowledge distribution across the entire species and is one of the fundamental properties of the SFU.

Living entities have one thing in common: a finite term of existence or life. In other words, eventually they die, and the constituent parts of their physicality and generally degrade into basic chemicals and elements. They cease to have a physical presence.

The gap between a non-living molecule and a living entity is vast; there is no "half-way house". The jump from non-living to living is such, that the establishment of a living entity from pure inorganic material has never been replicated in any laboratory, even using the most advanced facilities in the world and the most gifted micro-biologists.

This, given that the scientists can choose with great precision the environment and the substances which they can bring together to interact. In fact, scientists engaged in this research are able to act teleologically; they are effectively attempting to act like SFUs! The SFU family provided, and provides, a narrow, but teleological or purposeful influence in nature.

The incentive for scientists to achieve the creation of a living cell in a laboratory from chemicals is huge: Nobel prizes and world fame await the first to succeed. For this reason, the arrival of the first SFU in nature and its associated protoid was such an incredible and monumental step. It demonstrates how extremely complex even the simplest living cell is, and what is required to make a cell full of organic material and chemicals become "alive".

Many higher animals share certain aspects of body architecture: symmetry, a commonality of organ types and physical aspects; to give a few examples, eyes, legs, scent organs, arms, for some species wing protrusions and cardio-vascular systems have been built into many of the more advanced species.

These aspects have evolved from their ancestors, and natural selection enabled beneficial characteristics and traits to predominate for each species; they represent a tool kit for the evolution of new species.

The nesting of successive SFU's also explains why there tends to be a degree of similarity of form and behaviour among higher animal species and their ancestors. For example, apes and humans share some aspects of body architecture and the need for communal living, methods of eating, and they both have a survival-instinct decision capability. They share a common ancestor.

Psi-fields are the mechanism by which SFUs communicate with their associated species. These fields are active wherever any species exists, be it bacteria or humans; they are the medium of communication between all domains of the conscious and unconscious and the brain of animals, all living organisms and humankind.

In some cases, events or combinations of events, arise where a species cannot overcome threats that arise within its environment; perhaps climatic, or the arrival of a new predator or a disease pandemic. In some such cases, the associated SFU may be unable to cope with the new adjustment and ceases to be able to protect that species which will then become extinct.

In some cases, the extinction may be due to a new Ideation requiring the elimination of one species to make way for another. An SFU, however, once formed is eternal and carries on in its place nested within the hierarchy of SFU's in the psi-domain even after the species it was associated with has become extinct.

The implications of this are interesting: if scientists can succeed in using a DNA sample to in some way clone some extinct animal, for example, the woolly mammoth, its pre-existing SFU would already exist and re-activate to support it and regenerate its habits, instincts and behaviour.

How the cloned woolly mammoth would, in practice, cope in a modern environment would be interesting since its associated SFU would have stopped evolving many thousands of years ago with the demise of its associated species. Fortunately, it is rather unlikely that this experiment would be attempted even if scientists may have specimens of woolly mammoth DNA.

The SFU is a key influence on the way in which a species behaves, interacts with its environment and interacts with other members of its own species. More complex and sophisticated Ideations led to the evolution of more complex SFUs, which in turn enabled more complex and advanced species to evolve, equipped with increasing levels of intelligence.

To emphasise this, experimental work by William McDougall, Harvard University, will be described in detail in Chapter 7, where he trained rats to perform a specific task and he found that, initially, the rats were very slow to learn the specified task but eventually, became quite proficient.

He found that later generations of rats learned to perform those tasks much more quickly, even when the later generations of rats were not directly related, because they all had access to elements of the memory function of the SFU common to all rats of the same species.

These memory elements need not be made directly conscious by the rats, but work as instincts, influencing the rat's decision making and making it *more likely* that they would solve the task.

Thus, as generations of, for example, blackbirds are hatched, mate, age and die, their SFU retains memories of the key and important experiences of vast numbers of the most powerful experiences of those bird's millions of ancestors, and the subsequent generations become better at solving the commonly encountered problems. For example, perhaps problems associated with getting access to food, mating, nest building and caring for their young; the solutions are present in the form of instincts.

The SFUs of any species is unique to that species and has little or no interaction with other species. An evolution of SFUs for many species is the Species Group Unconscious or SGU, which relates to group behaviour associated with many animals, as described in the previous chapter. This relates to the group behaviour where a collective appears to act as a single entity or organism rather than a large number of individuals. A few specific examples of how the SGU explains certain characteristics of behaviour and capability in the natural world of animals shall now be described.

The Amazing Navigational Capability of the Eel.

All European eels are hatched in the Sargasso Sea, which is a large area of ocean in the Western Atlantic, off the east coast of North America. It is bounded by the Gulf Stream ocean-current to the west, the North Atlantic current to the north, the Canary current to the east and the North Equatorial current to the south.

The European Eel migrates to the Sargasso Sea from the rivers in Europe, and hatch their young there and, having completed their life cycle, they die there.

After hatching, the young eels make their way back to the river where their parents mated, obviously without their parents, which is typically a journey of over 3,700 miles and taking over three years. They do not use a direct route but deviate to use the most favourable ocean currents.

On arriving in Europe, they cross many barriers to reach the headwaters of the rivers, which can include crossing wet grasslands at night and even digging through wet sand. They undergo physical changes when moving from a sea water environment to a fresh-water environment where they find a mate. After some years, they leave their upper river environment to return to the Sargasso Sea to spawn. They again overcome many barriers to, once again, access the river that leads to the sea and complete the voyage back to the Sargasso Sea, again, not by the direct route, but by using the most favourable currents.

By the time they return to the sea in European waters, they have once again undergone physical changes. This includes their colouration, to make them less visible to predators. Also, their gut dissolves, making feeding impossible: they have to live from stored energy. Time is of the essence on this journey. Research has shown that they take between 140 and 180 days to reach the Sargasso Sea once more, where they have their hatchlings before dying.

The mechanisms that allow them to perform this feat of navigation, and indeed provide them with the *inclination* to do so in the first place, is a mystery to science: the knowledge of the routes outwards and back cannot be inherited, nor learned, their parents having died after giving birth in the Sargasso Sea as part of the eel's life cycle.

The navigational capability cannot be explained by some assumed sensitivity to the Earth's magnetic field, since magnetic north varies across the oceans (magnetic variation) and in any case, they have to find specific favourable ocean currents. A compass direction alone would be unable to provide the degree of navigational accuracy to locate a specific river on the other side of the ocean, nor would it give the eel a knowledge of where the favourable ocean currents are.

Since the eel swims in the depths of the oceans, it cannot use the Sun or stars as a navigational aid. In any case, to do this would require the eel to perform some complex calculations and have some accurate time knowledge, neither attribute is credible; just star gazing would, in any case, not provide the accuracy.

Migrating eels swimming from the UK back towards the Sargasso must use favourable ocean currents for speed, rather than the shortest direct route, since the currents give them extra speed and although the route may be longer, the journey is faster. This is particularly important as they swim back to the Sargasso to have their young, since they have to reach the Sargasso by April, the deadline for spawning.

These helpful currents head south from the west European coast, then west from the West African coast as part of the sub-tropical rotational ocean current system. Each eel, therefore, has to have access to *knowledge* that to get from the river in England to the Sargasso Sea, it must first head south from the English coast until it reaches the correct position off the West African coast, then change course to head west pushed by the favourable current that flows towards South America and the Sargasso.

Once its young are hatched in the Sargasso, these hatchlings in turn, must track the ocean currents to give them the fastest route back to the river in England where their parents mated. They use the Gulf stream, which is a north to north east-going current to speed them northwards until they reach a certain latitude, then they swim eastwards until they reach their target river. The "knowledge" to do this is provided by the eel's SFU/SGU family as strong instincts and is available to all eels of the European eel species.

To give an example of the difficulty of finding one's way at sea with nothing more than a compass, a sailor with just a compass starting from the Sargasso Sea, with no chart, sextant or satellite-navigation equipment would struggle to find a particular river in England.

Even with this lack of equipment, the sailor would still seem to have an advantage over the eel; he would have a rough idea of where to go based on his memory of geography; the eel has no such memory, never having seen a world map. The eels SFU/SGU, however, contains the information/coding for this navigational capability in the form of instincts, influences and instruction based on the key memory traces of countless billions of the eel's ancestors. The eel SFU/SGU, therefore, provides the directional guidance for the eels.

The ability to find and use the most advantageous currents is also incredible, considering that the young eel could not be "taught" this knowledge; it had to come from an external source and be accessible to all eels of that particular species.

Therefore, at this level, we see the SFU/SGU acting as part of the eel's shared "mind"; these domains provide the eels with both the *inclination* and the navigational instinct to make the journey. In general, as the eels swim on its journey, it acts with a high degree of independence swimming and feeding, but its SFU/SGU influences its general direction of swim, "lending" it knowledge of which direction to swim, acting as its navigator, and ensuring that it uses the ocean currents to speed its journey. This influence extends to all eels of the same species.

The Flatid Bug

Many animals in nature have evolved defensive capabilities which help them survive and resist predators. In a book by Robert Ardrey, called "African Genesis", he writes of an experience with an insect called the Flatid bug, which has a curious capability. Whilst walking with anthropologist L B S Leaky, they observed what looked like a pink and coral-coloured flower on a twig.

On reaching out to the flower, it dissolved into a swarm of flying insects. A little later, these insects once again settled onto the twig and, crawling around and over one another, they organised themselves into the shape of the pink and coral-coloured flower again. The insect was identified as the flatid bug, and it is a small flying insect that occurs in three colours. Some are green, some are pink and others are a deep coral colour.

Its method of survival is for a small swarm of these bugs to populate a branch or twig and arrange itself to look like a flower, which resembles something like a pink and coral lupin, with fleshy buds. This means that the bugs organise themselves in position according to their colour: the green ones organise themselves to look like the stem, whilst others arranged themselves to look like a flower with a pink/coral blossom. If the bugs are disturbed, they fly up and around before alighting once more on the branch and again crawling over one another again re-organising themselves to form the flower.

Clearly, it would not be possible for any individual bug to have an "overview" of the shape and colour distribution of the overall "flower", particularly since such a flower does not exist in nature: it is an "invented" flower-like creation unique to the flatid bug. Something needs to effectively "organise" the swarm, influencing the way the bugs arrange themselves to form the flower shape and colour distribution.

This capability is provided by the SGU of the flatid bug associated with that particular colony or swarm. This SGU contains the "design" of the flower and influences and organises the bugs so that each bug takes up the specific position required to provide the overall "flower" appearance. This increases its chances of being overlooked by predators and increasing the swarm's chances of survival.

The Flatid bug SGU provides an aspect of the collective overall "mind" of the bug swarm and influences the formation of the swarm to ensure that each of the bugs take up the correct position to form the appearance of the required flower. The exact shape of the flower-simulation depends on the shape of the branch that the swarm alights on.

It would clearly be impossible for any individual bug within the swarm to know where to move to without this influence. It is also impossible for this capability to be lodged in the coding of the bug's genome. The mechanism for information transfer between the swarm's SGU and the bugs within the swarm, is by psi-fields.

The Astounding Formation Flying of the Starling

A flock of starlings is known collectively as a murmuration. Generally, starlings behave much as any other bird; feeding, nesting and they sometimes gather in large flocks where they make a chirping cacophony, but they behave in many ways as a group of individuals.

Occasionally, however, they fly together as a tightly bunched group of many hundreds or even thousands of birds. They circle, swoop, soar and change form like a grey cloud of movement. They are often each barely the distance of a wingspan apart, yet never appear to come into contact with one another. The reaction times required to perform this feat has been researched and would require a faster reflex time than that measured for starlings.

Even if the reaction time of starlings flying next to one another was fast enough for them to respond to one another's flight direction-changes, it cannot explain what physiological mechanism allows direction change to happen almost simultaneously in birds separated by hundreds of feet and hundreds of other birds on the other side of the murmuration.

The uncanny synchronisation of the starling murmuration during their formation flying, makes it appear as though they are under the control of a single collective mind. An explanation to this phenomenon is unknown in the field of biology.

Research has shown that in murmuration-dynamics, each starling's flight is influenced by the movement of every other starling and vice versa, regardless of the size of the flocks (research covered flock sizes ranging from around 100 birds to over 4000). The research by Giorgi Parsi[40], a theoretical physicist from Rome University where attempts to explain the phenomena was made on the basis that the flock of starlings was a "critical system".

However, according to researchers, the starling flocks, during their aerobatics, seem to exhibit a near-instantaneous signal processing speed, but how they have such a strong correlation is a mystery. Their formation is sometimes in a single cloud, but can split into smaller clouds, sometimes linked, sometimes separating, then coming back together: an incredibly dynamic and creative display.

Edmund Selous[21], a naturalist who extensively researched flocks of birds over many years, observed that in order to explain the flock aerobatics, it must involve some kind of instant thought transference, which would almost indicate the involvement of telepathy or collective thinking.

The idea of invoking starling telepathy to explain the phenomena is doubtful, since which starling would "take charge", and how would it instantaneously dictate to all the starlings in the flock regarding details of the complex manoeuvres.

The overall flock would appear to be highly integrated during their formation flying manoeuvres. Even birds on opposite sides of the flock, often separated by a considerable distance, change direction almost instantaneously and do so without any collisions. This amazing synchronisation of not just flight, but of the aerial "dance", indicates strongly that for the duration of these flight patterns, they are under the control of a single mind. This phenomenon is known as "scale-free correlation" and, according to researchers, is beyond the field of conventional biology.

An understanding of the SGU provides an explanation. For the time of the flight, the starlings are all under the close control of the starling flock SGU; it acts during this period as the single collective but temporary "mind" for the whole starling flock, ensuring that they all receive the same pattern of thoughts directing the flight. This is because the SGU acts at flock level. It temporarily takes charge and all the starlings come under the influence of what is effectively a single temporary mind. This is shown simplistically in Fig. 8.

Different flocks will each have a different SGU. After the flight has ended, the starlings return to their higher degree of independence relating to their own SIUs: the SGU returns to the role of a secondary influencer, rather than an overall controller.

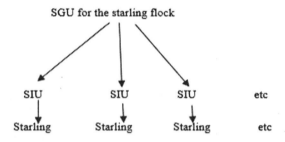

Fig. 8 Normal state of a starling flock; each bird operates as an individual under the influence of its own SIU

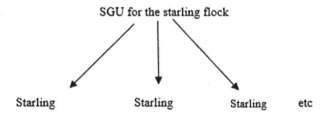

Temporary state of the starling flock. The flock SGU temporarily takes over from the many SIUs and influences the whole flock simultaneously, effectively forming a "group mind".

The Turtle Arribada

The Olive Ridley Sea Turtle has an intriguing method of ensuring they maximise their chances of survival. This species of turtle appears to co-ordinate its arrival on a particular stretch of beach on the Pacific side of Costa Rica known as Playa Ostinal. Such co-ordination results in a mass arrival of the turtles at about the same time. In addition, they all arrange the arrival time to be approximately 10 days before a new Moon, which means that there will be Neap tides, which means the tides will have a lower range between high tide and low tide.

At this time, they swim almost simultaneously to this beach, climb through the surf and up onto the beach to lay their eggs. This mass arrival is known as the Arribada. The numbers involved are between 50,000 and 100,000; the largest recorded is 500,000. This event takes place over two to five nights so that they all take advantage of the lower tidal range which are less likely to wash away the eggs from where the turtles have buried them in the sand at the top of the beach.

After around 50 days the eggs simultaneously hatch, and there is a mass movement of the hatchlings down the beach towards the sea. During this brief scramble, they are very vulnerable to predation. However, the sheer number of young ensure that they maximise the number that reach the sea; their sheer numbers overwhelm the ability of the predators to take too many of them.

The co-ordination of this event is amazing, since the turtles involved can be hundreds of miles apart before they all receive the "signal" to swim to that specific beach. This amazing coordination is due to the turtles' SFU/SGU domains to which they all have indirect access, ensuring a timely co-ordination and maximising the turtle's chances of survival.

The message from the turtles SFU/SGU to the turtles informs the turtles where to go and when to go there. Again, this co-ordination cannot be due to their individual turtle-genome, or any other part of the turtle's physical structure.

Migrating Birds

There is a proposition that migrating birds use the Earth's magnetic field for navigating, since they have traces of mineral deposits in their beaks or inner ears. However, if the birds relied exclusively on this, they would have navigational problems over long distances due to magnetic variation, which has the effect of changing magnetic north according to position on the Earth's surface.

The Earth's magnetic "north" varies and would affect directly in the bird's on-board compass. It also varies with time, slowly over many years. Near London, the variation is approximately zero, but as birds fly south, for example to over-winter in Southern Africa, they would fly across zones where the variation is as much as 10 degrees west and further south as much as 20 degrees west, approximately.

It is known that many British swallows, having spent the summer in Britain, migrate south from the UK and fly south over west France, Spain to Morocco (the latter's approximate longitude 5 degrees west) then across the Congo (longitude approximately 15 degrees east) then to South Africa (longitude approximately 25 degrees east).

There is, therefore, more to this navigation feat than just flying along a particular magnetic field-line: a degree of "knowledge" is required to journey across these countries as they do, and end up in Southern Africa in large numbers.

When they reach their destination, they congregate there in roosting flocks of many thousands, but many birds die along the route from starvation, exhaustion, predation and storms. They set off to return heading north to reach Britain in April/May.

There are three requirements to allow this annual migration to happen. One is that the birds must collectively have the *inclination and desire* to fly south and undertake the dangerous journey at about the same time, and secondly, they must have the *navigational ability* to fly to their wintering grounds, and thirdly, be able to *find their way back again* in the following year, again, all arriving at about the same time and often, at precisely the same place that they set off from.

Natural selection may have meant that over thousands of years, swallows that did migrate may have had a better chance of surviving than those that remained behind to face the winter, but it does not explain why large numbers of them seem to arrive at the same winter destination; nor does it explain the amazing navigational skills to achieve the two-way journey.

The swallow's SFU provides all swallows across the whole species with the instinct and desire to migrate at a specific time of year, since migration is a very energy consuming activity and the influence to make swallows migrate must be powerful. The swallow's SGU provide groups of swallows the directional influence to ensure sufficient accuracy for navigation for the outward and return journeys, different SGUs operating across different flocks of swallows.

This enables the swallows to migrate to Africa, and for each individual swallow to return to their original nesting grounds. It also allows the same SFU/SGU combination to ensure the swallows return in the summer, often to the same area in Britain from which they departed in the autumn.

European swallows migrate to a different destination but, accordingly, they have different SGUs providing different navigational information.

Migrating birds put on weight before migrating; they store the required energy before departure. It has been noted that even caged birds of the same species become agitated, and also put on weight as though they too would be migrating, even to the extent of repeatedly flying in the correct direction as far as their cage allows. The "call" to migrate is, therefore, very strongly communicated across the whole species.

An Experiment with Termites

Termites are fascinating creatures in many respects. Each nest contains thousands of termites which appear to be highly organised, and they create nests which can rise several feet in the air. The nest of one species *Eutermes* contains many chambers, all interconnected by many passages where they deposit chewed wood to feed fungus which they need to eat.

These passages are built by worker termites from small pellets of earth and saliva. How the worker termites know where to put each pellet in order to achieve the overall construction objective is, as Sheldrake comments[5], a mystery to science.

In a typical termite nest, it requires thousands of termites to be able to communicate with one another and somehow work to an overall "blueprint" of the nest. This is especially difficult, since the termites are blind and communication by some form of chemical means, sense of smell or vibration would be inadequate to transfer sufficient details to construct the nest which can be many feet across and contain many thousands of termites.

In some cases, where termites build vertical columns near one another, each construction team will bend their columns towards the other until they meet. Sheldrake writes about observations carried out by Eugene Marais[45], a South African naturalist where he noted that, when repairing damage to the nest, for example, a large breach in the nest wall, the termite workers start the rebuilding in a co-ordinate manner, from all sides simultaneously and the rebuilt parts join up correctly, in spite of termites being blind.

Marais then carried out an experiment; he inserted a steel sheet through the centre of the termite's nest, much wider and higher than the termite nest mound, effectively dividing the nest into two separate parts. The termites on each side had no way of communicating with one another and yet, Marais observed, that they built similar towers on each side of the plate independently, such that when the plate was removed, the arches matched perfectly once the narrow cut had been repaired.

Marais thought that the queen termite acted with an overall plan of the state and architecture of the nest, but how she could communicate with thousands of termites in parts of the nest that she could not see or be aware of, makes that most unlikely, and how could she carry a blueprint of the entire nest or be aware of the repairs required?

The termite SGU (there is a different termite SGU for each nest) however, provides the answer: it contains both the *intention* to build a nest and the *inclination* to do so and the *influence* to ensure that all termites act for the common objective, as though under the control of a single "mind". The SGU also contains a flexible and ever-changing nest "blueprint", acting strongly to influence how each termite behaves, enabling each individual construction to be coordinated with the others.

The termite SGU for each nest communicates with the termites within that nest through the associated psi-fields, directing the blind termites to a common purpose. It is the nest-SGU which is specific to a particular nest which co-ordinates the termite's activities. This is another example where the animal "borrows" complex mind functions from their SGU (as part of the SFU family) to perform activities which they would otherwise be unable to perform.

Bees and Their Hives

Bees form highly organised colonies and are social creatures. Generally, as far as honeybees are concerned, the hive consists of a single queen, thousands of workers and a few male drones. The workers make cells for the larva from a wax secretion from their abdomens.

The workers place pollen and nectar in the cells to enable the larvae to feed. The bee colony is sometimes described as a "super-organism" because of the way they appear to operate as a united entity collectively working together to support the colony.

As Capra[24] notes, insects such as bees cannot survive as individuals, but when they are together in large numbers, they seem to act as a single collective organism with a collective intelligence. The hive as a whole, has collective capability far superior to that of any individual bee.

At a particular point in time, a new queen hatches and she has to leave the hive and start a new colony. The workers stop feeding the new queen, possibly to ensure she did not get over-heavy for the forthcoming flight. Groups of bees are, in some way, allocated to the new queen. Scout bees, the oldest and most experienced foragers, are sent out to identify a nearby spot for the swarm to gather until an intermediate place can be found.

The swarm, comprising the new queen and many hundreds of workers, leave the hive and land on their initial resting place, clustering around the queen to protect her. They then send 20-50 scout bees to identify a better place for the swarm to move to. The queen is mated in flight. Having moved to this second base, they then take a few days to seek out and identify the final hive location, using scout bees, and almost "taking a vote" on which is the best site according to the degree of enthusiasm of the returning scout bees.

How the colonies can exhibit such close organisation where every bee "knows" its role, acts in the common interest of the colony and at swarm time, organise themselves to start a new colony with the new queen and again form the same highly organised colony is something of a mystery.

It is as though a single mind controls and influences each bee within the hive and ensures that they all operate according to a single "plan", even though each bee also functions with a degree of individuality, due to its associated SIU.

The "single mind" is the role of the bee-SGU, which provides the overview and organisational structure for beehive colonies, and works for all bee colonies, with each colony or hive, having its own unique SGU. It also ensures that the relative number of queens, workers and drones is in line with the efficient operation of the hive.

The original hive SGU splits to form a new SGU when a new swarm with a new queen is formed. In terms of generating the new swarm, the new SGU then causes the new queen and its attendant workers and scout bees to move out and set about starting a new hive. This process is therefore a vital part of the bee replication and distribution process. A wide distribution of hives increases the chances for survival for the species.

The existence of the new SGU accounts for the ability of the new queen and her attendant workers and drones to "know" how to swarm, how to protect their new queen and details the right number of experienced scout bees to find the new hive-site, even though they would not have carried out this process previously.

The bees are also sufficiently well-organised to ensure that every bee "knows" its role. Collectively, the bees have the ability to construct and "manage" a hive. In the case of a bee swarm formation, they would not have been able to "learn" the capability, since it would have been the first time they had swarmed intending to set up a new hive. The bee SFU/SGU has, over thousands of years, evolved the capability to carry the information required as instincts to establish and manage a hive, based on the collective and evolving experiences of billions of the bee's ancestors.

The bee SGU also enables them to act collectively rather than as individuals, although the bee has a basic SIU and is therefore, capable of a degree of individual decision making and independent action. We shall return to the bee again in Chapter 7, Fig 11 which shows how the complete bee Matrix Model is structured.

The Social Order of Ants

Ants similarly form highly complex, well-ordered nests, with a hierarchy where all ants have specific roles within the nest, with castes of workers and soldiers, most being wingless females. The ant nest is another example of a super-organism. They also have a few fertile males and a fertile female which is, as with bees, called a queen.

They have a basic level of communication and have an ability to collectively solve complex problems. They protect aphids, which they milk as a food source. Some species of ants also "farm" caterpillars, since certain caterpillars excrete honeydew from their segments so to take advantage of this, the ants take the caterpillars to their feeding grounds during the day and take them into their nests at night for protection. They optimise the numbers of foragers according to food supply. The operational role of an ant is decided at birth and remains the same during the life of each ant inside a strong social order.

The organisational influence is not provided by any individual ant, not even the queen, since she would not have the ability to communicate with each individual ant and instruct each activity for thousands of ants within the nest to coordinate activities.

The nest SGU, however, contains the information for the overall nest structure and organisation and influences each ant to act according to its designated role by means of the SGU psi-field which permeates the entire nest. Again, the nest SGU acts as a kind of collective "borrowed mind" influencing all the ants within the nest.

The Second Effectuator: The Laws of Science

This series of laws, which collectively form the second of the Effectuators, is also the most wide-ranging of all the Effectuators in the physical domain.

As previously described, these laws were instigated to enable the physical universe to come into existence. The "critical values" of parameters within atomic structure were also defined to allow the physical interactions to be defined, to ensure that stars and galaxies formed, supernova exploded, and planets had the materials essential for their formation, as described in Chapter 1.

At the time of the Big Bang, these laws defined how particles of matter would interact, resulting in the formation of atomic nuclei from the combining of quarks due to one of the four fundamental forces at work during this formative period: the strong nuclear force. This "glued" the quarks together to form the atomic nuclei: protons and neutrons.

Electromagnetic force came into play to ensure the electrons were captured in orbit around these nuclei, converting them into atoms. The laws of science increased in scope as the cosmos evolved to include laws that would define how larger molecules could form.

They defined, for example, how amino acids would bond together to form polypeptide chains and several of these in turn bond together to form proteins; these were, and are, key processes to enable living organisms to form.

Third Effectuator: The Sun

The third Effectuator operating in the solar system is the Sun. The Sun's gravity attracted and captured the matter which came to form the planets and moons of our solar system. The Sun holds the solar system together due to its enormous gravitational field and provides the essential energy, predominantly in the form of light and heat, which is vital to the formation of life on Earth.

The complex physics of the Sun maintains a stable, level energy supply to the Earth. The Sun itself is a huge physical sphere of matter, including hydrogen and other elements, powered by a massive nuclear fusion engine.

The Sun's gravity also contributes, although to a lesser extent than the Moon, to the Earth's tidal systems. It is also sufficiently stable to ensure that the environment on Earth is stable, at least within certain limits. Ice ages have been experienced on Earth, but they passed, the ice retreated, and life, in one form or another has always been able to continue.

The Sun also provides the energy to power photosynthesis, which was crucial in helping to define the Earth's atmosphere by enabling the green plants and grasses and trees to come into being and be successful in forming a vital part of the food chains. These "green life" species were, in turn, essential as they formed the food chains for many other species, and were essential for all higher life forms, including man, to evolve and survive. No higher life forms could exist had there not been a "green evolution".

Fourth Effectuator: The Earth

The fourth Effectuator is planet Earth itself. It was formed with an orbit that is at a critical distance from the Sun: a few percent closer and life would struggle to initiate, since the environment would be too hot: a few percent further away and the environment would be too cold.

Some of the mass of the Earth, as described previously, is probably due to the impact of a planet-size body which created the Moon, and also the late heavy bombardment event, where Earth was subjected to a mass of impactors which slammed into the Earth, probably sterilising the surface with molten rock pools, as described in chapter 1.

The formation of the Earth, and the highly complex series of processes that led to a life-friendly environment, were the result of a series of teleological influences.

The Earth is a water planet: it is the Effectuator supporting and sustaining life in the physical world, allowing species to be formed, providing food, light conversion to energy by photosynthesis, and all the complex bio-systems essential to the formation and support of life.[16]

The atmosphere evolved a shield to protect terrestrial life by the creation of the ozone layer, which was an important event, since it provided protection for the Earth's surface by greatly reducing the amount of ultra-violet radiation impacting the Earth's surface, and thus enabled life to exist and flourish on the terrestrial surface.

The Earth's magnetic field also provides an essential protection from destructive cosmic radiation, locking the heavier particles in the Van Allen belts where they cannot do any damage, and diverting other particles past the Earth's atmosphere, as described previously.

In order to establish, create and support life, it was first essential to Ideate and bring into being an appropriate Earth environment, which took time to evolve, and went through many phases. Effectuator Earth provided, and continues to provide, the environments required to start and support the wide diversity of life as we currently know it.

James Lovelock in his book "Gaia"[16] wrote:

The old Gaia was an entity that kept herself and all who lived with her comfortable throughout time and season. She worked so that the air, the oceans and the soil were always fit for life.

He later developed what he called the "Gaia Hypothesis" as described in Chapter 2, which postulates that the physical and chemical condition of the surface of the Earth, of the atmosphere and of the oceans evolved to be fit and suitable for life by the presence of life itself.

The Earth itself can be regarded as a huge multi-faceted group of self-organising, self-sustaining systems, enabling a wide range of life forms to exist. In fact, it is essential to the survival of a species to be a part of, and contribute to, the biosphere of Earth. They must also function as self-sustaining systems within themselves, contributing to and benefiting from the greater biosphere.

Fifth Effectuator: The Moon

The fifth Effectuator is the Moon, which has played a key role in creating and sustaining life on Earth. The Moon is mostly responsible for the ocean's tides, which created ever-changing, sub-littoral zones where some life forms are thought to have started out and where life forms which were created in the Earth's oceans, were able to access land, and evolve to adapt to life on land.

Sixth Effectuator: The Planets

The planets of the solar system collectively form the sixth Effectuator. The planets also played a role in the development of the physical world and contributed to Homo sapiens cultures, religions and traditions. The planets orbit around the Sun, together with a belt of asteroids which mostly lie between Mars and Jupiter.

The importance of Jupiter in the formation and shaping of planet Earth cannot be over-emphasised. It protects Earth's future: without Jupiter, there may not have been any advanced life on Earth.

The Galileo space probe launched by NASA orbited Jupiter gathering data, the probe was then sent towards the surface. They found that the environment is one of ferocious winds and massive surface pressure. The atmosphere is approximately 90% hydrogen with an upper atmosphere temperature of over 150°C, becoming much hotter at the surface estimated at around 6000°C and great pressure.

At these temperatures and pressures, hydrogen becomes a molten metal, and this is the probable nature of the core. Galileo vaporised before getting to the surface. Jupiter's huge size and gravitational pull ensured that it had, and continues to have, a huge influence within the solar system.

Very early in the formation of the solar system, Jupiter formed from the debris left over from the formation of the Sun, and being the first planet to form, absorbed much of the matter around at that time before the other planets started to form, which is probably why it became the biggest. As it absorbed yet more matter, it became larger, and its gravity increased still further.

The eventual orbit, following a large correction to Jupiter's orbit to where it is today, greatly reducing the intensity of the meteorite bombardment and instead of causing meteorites to be flung towards Earth, which caused the Late Heavy Bombardment, as described in chapter 1, Jupiter started to act as a meteor shield, protecting Earth.

By 3.8 Billion BP, Jupiter's orbit had settled, and the Late Heavy Bombardment of Earth had ceased. The frequency of bodies impacting the Earth continues to be influenced by Jupiter, which due to its size and consequential massive gravity, catapults some of the meteors and asteroids out of the solar system and gives the Earth some protection from an excessive number of impacts.

Occasionally, however, it is also responsible for pulling a body towards Earth with the possibility of impact, and this could possibly have been the case with the water-providing close miss by a comet in Earth's early history.

Proof that at least some of the water came from a comet was provided by the Max Planck institute for solar system research, by analysing the deuterium-to-hydrogen ratio in our oceans and in comets. This is a kind of "finger-print" which indicates the source of water.

The water analysis of comet Hartley 2, for example, the deuterium to hydrogen ratio is the same as in our oceans; it is, therefore, a possible source of at least some of the Earth's water.

When there is a massive impact event, it has been calculated that it can take the Earth around one million years to recover and rebuild its life-sustaining systems. Therefore, if impacts were too frequent, Earth would not be able to sustain life as we know it.

Professor Stephen Hawking concluded that higher life forms and even higher plants would be wiped out by any impactor greater than two kilometres in diameter striking the Earth! As described earlier, the Late Heavy Bombardment involved impactors many times that size.

There are, however, many small impacts. It has been calculated that if Jupiter had a mass of only 20% of its current mass, comet impacts on the Earth's surface would be much more frequent, and life on Earth would not have been possible.

If Jupiter had the reduced mass, instead of the Earth being impacted by a significant meteor or asteroid about every many millions of years, as is the case now, impacts would occur about every few hundred years and life on Earth would not have developed as it has, if at all. Thus, Jupiter could also be regarded as one of the pre-requisites enabling life to get established on Earth.

The last mass extinction of life on Earth was due to a large meteor impact that occurred 65 million years ago and lead to a mass extinction of a significant percentage of life on Earth, including a major contributing factor to the extinction of the dinosaurs. The known "massive" impacts have occurred several times during Earth's history and there is a degree of certainty that they will occur again.

It is probable that astrology-belief is buried deep in the collective-unconscious element of the SFU for the species Homo Sapiens, harking back to the very earliest civilisations. The symbols associated with astrology possibly form a series of archetypes residing within Homo sapiens' collective unconscious within their SFU. For these reasons, the planets collectively are regarded as Effectuators.

Seventh Effectuator: Evolution

According to Darwin, evolution took place gradually, mostly with a smooth transition from one species to the next, with small changes and no sudden steps. However, there are many examples in the fossil record of sudden new arrivals. An example of this would be the evolution of the giraffe with its uniquely long neck and long legs.

There are very few known examples in the fossil record of a succession of evolutionary steps leading to evidence of ancestors of the giraffe, in the form of animals with ever increasing neck length, from the short-necked giraffe ancestor to the modern-day giraffe.

The giraffe ancestors evolved around 20-25 million years BP, although they lacked the long neck and are thought to have looked more like deer. About 6-8 million years BP, giraffe ancestors with longer necks began to evolve. The previously held belief that giraffes evolved their long necks to enable them to browse on higher branches giving them a competitive advantage is now doubted, since giraffes also consume lower growing shrubs and grasses which are available even in the dry season and even when there are easily accessible higher browsing trees. The giraffe, as it is today with its long legs and uniquely long neck, evolved about one million years ago.

One explanation for the sudden appearance of the long neck is that the evolution of long legs meant that the long neck had to evolve to enable the animal to drink. However, this and other explanations are generally regarded as highly speculative. The long-necked giraffe appears to have suddenly appeared as a unique species and has happily survived ever since.

It was the result of the appearance of a new SFU following a "Giraffe Ideation", with the long neck and long legs evolving simultaneously. There are many examples of the rapid arrival of new species during the Cambrian period.

According to Dr D Foster,[19] a cybernetician, the universe can be regarded as a system defined by data and data processing. He reasoned that the programming (encoding) of DNA must involve an intelligence, and that intelligence must be far greater than that of our human intelligence.

This leads to the deduction that evolution is not accidental nor random but, as proposed earlier, has strong teleological processes driven by domains within the Intelligent Universe.

It is thought in some circles that all life forms descend from a single ancient ancestor, which has been called in this book, the protoid, which was established and existed around 4.2–3.8 BBP. It is estimated that there are now approximately 12 million species on Earth.

Once the first living entity had been established with its associated SFU, a mixture of natural selection, evolution and mutation resulted in both adaptations of existing species and the arrival of new species, following the evolution of their associated SFUs.

In each case, once the new-species or adapted species SFU had been formed, the Effectuators evolution and mutation came into play to implement the physical realisation of the Ideation for the new or adapted species.

It was essential that early living organisms could survive and develop to cope with changes in the environment and to evolve towards the more complex and higher life-forms in line with the successive Ideations.

Without evolution and natural selection applying to life forms, species diversification and adaptation to changes in their local environment would not have occurred. These were essential tools in being able to implement the successive Ideations and to make existing species more robust.

Once life forms started to exist on Earth, Effectuator evolution was already up and running as a catalyst for change and species diversification. Life forms have always had to contend with surviving the challenges of natural disaster or changes to their environments by evolving.

Higher life forms have evolved in such a way that they are comprised of groups of specialised cells and organs, each contributing to the whole survival and wellbeing of the whole entity. The whole is also greater than the sum of the parts, by which is meant that analysis of a particular cell or even a particular organ within a life form would not give any understanding of how that life form functions, and how it behaves under any set of environmental conditions. To understand that, one would have to consider the entity from a holistic viewpoint.

Evolution is a key Effectuator, functioning in both the psi-domain and the physical domain, evolving new SFUs from existing SFUs in the psi-domain, which in turn enables new species descended from their direct ancestors to become established in the physical domain. The fact that Ideations provide the design defining new SFUs as evolutions of existing SFUs or as completely new SFUs, shows how there can be "step changes" in evolution.

Evolution has rarely been a smooth and seamless process. The fossil record indicates that it can be irregular, with large groups of new species appearing over a relatively short time, for example, during the Cambrian period, which shall be covered in more detail in chapter 6.

There have been long periods in Earth's history, where there has been very little genetic variation; a sort of "stasis", punctuated by sudden and dramatic transitions. This is not predicted by Darwinism and is known as "punctuated equilibria". Natural selection is a key mechanism of evolution that favours the survival of life forms that are better adapted to their environment. They tend to survive in higher numbers and have more offspring.

Eighth Effectuator: Mutation

The eighth Effectuator is mutation, which is defined as the entity which causes a permanent change to the genome, DNA or other genetic material of an organism, which may then be transmitted to subsequent generations. It is sometimes due to damage to the DNA, perhaps due to chemical contamination, ultra-violet or other means.

This leads to errors in replication, leading to observable changes in the characteristics of the offspring. Mutation can, therefore, lead to changes which can lead to new species. They can also lead to disease and is often damaging, and to counter the negative effects of this, organisms have DNA repair mechanisms which can revert the damaged/ mutated sequence back to the original and reverse the damage/ mutation in some cases. In other cases, the change may be permanent, either giving positive or negative outcomes.

Mutation which is not damaging can thus lead to variations which are not corrected, and natural selection can then operate on the changed organism. Mutation is regarded as the most important source of genetic variation in species. In most cases, mutation will result in negative or regressive changes, but in other rarer cases, it will result in positive and advantageous changes.

Mutation probably works most effectively as a mechanism for change on those species that reproduce very rapidly, for example, bacteria. The negative or detrimental mutations would result in those life-forms would die out quickly, whereas the positive changes would result in continuity with the life-forms carrying the beneficial genetic changes multiplying and passing the benefits of quickly to later generations by natural selection following changes to the SFU. Very soon, all surviving members of the species would have the beneficial changes.

Chapter 5
Life Within the Intelligent Universe

Defining Life

When an attempt is made to define the term "life", it proves difficult. There are certain basic characteristics that seem common to all living entities which can be used as a guide. However, Lovelock's[16] view is that life has such variety and comprises so many different entities that an agreed definition of what life is has not yet been achieved.

The gulf between non-living matter, for example, elements, atoms, chemical compounds which are, in themselves, devoid of life, and a living cell, even of the most primitive type, is huge. This is the case even though all living and non-living entities are composed of molecules and chemical compounds and these in turn are composed of atoms.

Earlier chapters have demonstrated that it is the sheer complexity of the molecules that comprise a living cell that significantly differentiates a non-living entity from a living one. The living entity is far more than a complex collection of atoms and molecules, more than RNA, DNA, proteins and genes.

Even though these macro-molecules are extremely complex, how they interact, form self-organising, self-sustaining systems and can respond and interact with their environment is vitally important.

Also, the inextricable interaction between a genome (its complete set of genetic material, including its DNA) and its associated SFU family is also crucial. The SFU family provides the genome with some parts of the key elements of the coding which determines, in part, its form, function and behaviour, and the ability for an organism to survive and thrive.

There is a theory that biological evolution followed chemical evolution. However, as argued previously in this book, in spite of much research, no laboratory has yet managed to synthesise even the simplest living cell using nonbiological or chemical compounds, although for several decades, some scientists have claimed that such synthesis was "imminent."

Inanimate matter cannot generate life spontaneously, even given trillions of parallel chemical interactions. So far, all experiments in the twentieth century to create a living cell have ended in failure. It has not yet been possible, even in the most advanced laboratories in the world, with the experiments carried out by the foremost scientists in their fields making conscious efforts to do so.

Every new discovery shows that life, even the most rudimentary conceivable cell, was just too complex. Evolutionist Leslie Orgel[26] a chemist and research professor at California who is well known for his theories on the origin of life stated, after examining the structure of RNA, DNA and proteins, that life could not have arisen by chemical means alone.

Dr Fritjof Capra[24] concluded that there is something common to all living things, beyond just atoms and molecules; there also has to be a pattern of organisation, which is a non-material aspect. According to Humberto Maturana[54] living systems are cognitive systems: cognition is the process of life allowing all living systems to interact with their environments, whether they have a nervous system or not.

The holistic structure of the mind of man and animals will be described in Chapter 7, when the Matrix Model, and Matrix Model Theory, will be explained in more detail.

To define something as "living," the entity must have sufficient complexity to be able to contain, or in some way have access to, in some form or another, a plan of its own structure as has been stated in previous chapters. This can, in part, be in the form of coding within its genome, or in some other format. Without a plan of its own structure, it will not be able to self-replicate.

This assumes that the genome, DNA or in the case of the earliest living cells, their proto-RNA or equivalent, contains *all* the information required to define a living cell, and how it will develop, feed and self-replicate and provide its "instinctive behaviour". This assumption seems increasingly unlikely and is being called into question[17]. The critical additional component is the living entity's interaction with its SFU family.

With the very first living organism, the protoid, it may have had a simple version of proto-RNA, as explained in the previous chapter, but even this would have had to have been complex enough to be able to absorb and store the coding provided by its associated SFU that would fully define the entire form, function and behaviour of the organism and the information that would define how it would develop.

It must, however, be able to reproduce by gathering materials from the immediate environment and processing them to form the building blocks for its progeny. This whole process requires not just a plan, but an *intention:* the process has to be teleological. This aspect in a simple cell is provided by its associated SFU; it cannot be explained entirely by a genome or by a series of chemical reactions.

There is also general agreement that to be classified as a living entity, the cell must be carbon-based; that is, it must be organic. This does not preclude other life-forms elsewhere in the universe being based on some other element; we just currently have no knowledge of them.

The living entity must also be able to sustain itself by absorbing energy, in some form, from its environment. This may be, for example, in the form of chemicals, sugars or by photosynthesising. This enables it to continue as a self-sustaining system. During its earliest development and through its life, it must have a high degree of organisation, and also generally, contain critical sub-systems which in themselves must be self-organising.

As M Riddle, a mathematician, concluded that anyone hypothesising that life started with random interactions of chemicals would have to explain how the massive amount of information, essential to establish this first life-form with all its incredible complexity was formed, and how this information was encoded into its genome.

Even the simplest and most basic living entity must have a mechanism to be able to expel waste materials which are by-products of its living processes; these waste materials then become part of the evolving environment; all living organisms take from and contribute to the totality of the environment.

The other and obvious common characteristic of living entities is that their physical existence is time limited; by one means or another, they die. Even broader than that, is the fact that every entity, living and non-living, whether a living cell, star or planet or even galaxy, is time-limited in its existence in the physical domain and will ultimately cease to exist.

One of the differences between living and non-living entities is that the time for the existence of living entities is generally very much shorter than for non-living entities. Defining exactly what is a "living" entity is controversial and there is no common agreement.

Equally importantly, as described in Chapter 3, all living entities must have a mechanism that triggers the process of self-replication. This is a more difficult concept. In order to ensure that replication takes place, it requires intention, motivation and the will to make it happen. The materials must also be available from the environment, or the entity must have the capability to process materials to make the required building blocks.

This means that it is not sufficient for a life-form to be able to self-replicate, there must be a mechanism to ensure that it does, since reproduction is a process that uses energy, and living-entities usually try to conserve energy. The mechanism must influence the organism to make self-replication happen.

As simple animals evolved more complexity, more of the coding for body structure and development was evolved from their SFU into their genomes.

As described earlier, the coding and architecture contained within the acorn, seed, or embryo and its associated SFU family has to include the architecture of form and how that form develops *for each stage*, up to and including the final outcome. There is clearly a massive difference between the structure of, for example, an acorn and an oak tree or an embryo and an adult human.

The full description of any species therefore has to take into account a combination of its SFU family which contains not only the coding for its initial state (for example, in the case of the oak tree, the acorn form) but also the developmental coding which determines how the entity will develop and change its form over time.

For example, from acorn to seedling to sapling through to a great oak tree and provide a mechanism for the entity to develop from one stage to the next, including the stages leading to the point where the tree becomes reproductively active.

This implies that the content of the coding must include information defining *form* for each stage, a fact that, even for the simplest seed which develops into seedling, then into a flower provokes some amazement. As a human embryo, for example, which starts as a zygote, develops then to a foetus, then a baby, then an infant, then a child and then years later, into a mature adult. The adult then ages, with continuing changes in form, function and behaviour. Each stage differs in both form, function and behaviour and degree of dependency.

Another common and fundamentally important attribute of living organisms is their ability to repair or regenerate. In the case of humans, wounds heal, broken bones reunite, and some organs can replace damaged areas. Elsewhere in nature, some animals can regenerate even from massive damage; Sheldrake,[5] for example, cites the flatworm which can fully regenerate itself even after having been cut into segments. Complete plants can grow from cuttings.

Efficient Replication

Various bacteria species provide good examples of efficient self-replication. They reproduce by cell division, where cells divide rapidly; one becomes two, then two become four. If the division rate in a single bacterium takes place every 20 minutes, then over a 24-hour period, there would be 2^{72} bacteria ($4.7x10^{21}$ bacteria) which is a vast number.

Also, each unit of the offspring must contain an exact copy of its parental DNA, which in conjunction with its SFU, provides the coding for the design plan containing the information allowing each one to survive, feed and continue to self-replicate.

The replication process, therefore, has to be extremely accurate. This represents a massive difference from the establishment of the purely material, non-living environment which is mostly comprised of a mix of chemical compounds and elements.

Modern species of bacteria are highly evolved: the protoid would have been very much simpler in structure and function. It is, therefore, extremely unlikely that we shall ever know for certain what the protoid structure was, but Professor Morowitz has made, what is probably a "best estimate" of the simplest possible living cell, as described in chapter 2 that would be capable of being regarded as truly "living."

The Establishment of Self-Organising and Self-Regulating Systems

Self-organising systems are realised in many forms in biology, from organisms to eco-systems. More specifically, they can be observed in, among other phenomena, morphogenesis, which is the generation of form. To enable a living entity to become established, a high degree of organisation of its internal building blocks, processes and systems is essential. More specifically, self-organising systems are essential for living entities to establish the functionality required to survive.

An example of internal self-organisation would be the development of the various stages of a protein from the organised assembly of amino acids and the assembly of the resulting proteins to form a biologically functional organism, as described earlier.

A vital part in the sequence of establishing the correct biologically functional building blocks is not just creating the correct proteins, but ensuring they fold in the correct manner; if they don't fold, they have no functionality; if they fold incorrectly, they can cause malfunctions within the organism; for example, Parkinson's disease in humans. It is thought that the amino acid chains define how the proteins will fold, but how and why they fold in a specific way for each protein remains somewhat of a mystery, although progress is being made in predicting the folding using artificial intelligence systems.

Where groups of living entities are concerned, self-organisation can be detected by observing many facets in nature both external to the organism and internal to it. This includes the social behaviour in bees, insects and termites and mammals, flocking behaviour of birds, and shoaling of fish. Self-organising systems are present, in some form or another, in all living species, and is fundamental to their existence.

Those who support vitalism assert that some non-physical agency, force or field must be added to physics and chemistry to understand life; how it starts and how it behaves. Many biologists refute this. This moves beyond the question of "what are living things made of" because they are made of atoms which are built into molecules, sometimes of exceptional complexity.

This answer tells us nothing about function or behaviour. To understand a living entity, it is essential to understand its organisational system, as concluded by R Rosenburg.[37] Self-organisation includes, in living things, some means of defining how the life-building blocks are to be arranged to a precise design, and how the different elements within the entity interact to enable it to "function as intended" and perhaps, what defines this intention.

Self-regulating systems are also part of living entities; they can control and regulate the flow of materials required for them to sustain themselves, regulate their internal temperature, regulate their respiration where appropriate and many other critical functions. Higher life forms may have many self-organisational and self-regulatory systems.

For example, a human has systems that control body temperature and cardio-vascular systems that regulate blood flow according to demand by feedback systems within the brain, ensures that a state of equilibrium exists within the body and control many life-critical functions. These life-support systems are operative over a wide range of external conditions. In general, the animal is unaware, consciously, of the operation of these regulatory systems.

For any organism at any level to be able to survive on Earth, it must be a self-sustaining system or contain several self-sustaining systems. A system can be thought of as self-sustaining if it can continue to exist independent of external physical assistance, other than having critical materials available from the environment to supply its energy and replication requirements.

It does, however, continue to have a degree of dependency on its associated SFU, which, from a systems point of view, can be regarded as an integral and critical part of the organism. The complete system for any life-form includes the immediate environment, the atmosphere, the Sun and usually some form of water source.

The organism is changed by the environment and, as it functions, also changes its environment by absorbing some materials and emitting other materials, which then become part of the environment. As has been described with the evolution of the atmosphere, the subtle changes in the environment caused by one living entity can have fundamental effects on other living entities by changing the composition of the atmosphere and the content of the materials in the environment. Such changes can, and indeed did, determine which life forms can exist in the Earth's environment.

Daisyworld; an Example of Environmental Self-Regulation

One of the vital self-regulatory systems which had to be installed on Earth for life to start and be able to continue, was temperature control. This means that the temperature extremes for most of the planet had to be controlled within rather narrow limits, since extremes of temperature range would tend to seriously limit species diversification and where on the planet life could flourish.

There was a classic computer-model experiment by Professor James Lovelock[16,24] called "Daisyworld". In this model, Lovelock and his team designed a project and programmed the computer with a model representing a greatly simplified world, which was populated by only two species: black daisies and white daisies.

This idealised world was warmed by a heat source representing the Sun. In the model, the program controlled the radiated heat from the Sun which started with a radiated power that gave a very low surface temperature on Daisyworld, which gradually increased with time.

A pre-condition put into the program was that seeds from these two species are "scattered" throughout the model of the model planet evenly, with the constraint that the daisies could only survive within a certain temperature range. The question the team was trying to answer was, 'would the Daisyworld ecosystem lead to the self-regulation of its climate?'.

The results were interesting. Starting from a surface temperature at zero, and gradually increasing it, the model eventually showed a ring of black daisies around the equator, since the surface temperature had reached a level that enabled black daisies to spring into life.

Since the black daisies absorb more heat from the radiant heat-source than white and can therefore, live and stay alive at lower ambient temperature than the white daisies, initially, there were no white daisies.

As the model increased the Sun's heat emission, the surface temperature in the model increased, the black daisies moved to the middle latitudes, since the equator became too hot for them, but the white daisies took over at the equator, since their white petals reflected more of the Sun's energy keeping them cooler. Eventually, as the temperature increased, all daisy life became extinct at the equator and the white daisies moved to the middle latitudes with black daisies at the poles.

The final state with further increases in temperature showed no daisies in the middle latitudes and only white daisies at the poles. Further increase in temperature lead to daisy extinction.

The temperature on the surface of Daisyworld showed a fairly steady range throughout the experiment, once the daisies started to blossom, breaking down only when the Sun's temperature became too great for either. This was because when daisy world was cool, the black daisies warmed themselves and their environment, whilst the arrival of the white daisies reflected the Sun's energy, cooling themselves and their environment. Thus, the daisy world worked to stabilise the temperature for the benefit of all daisies, but to some extent, controlled by the daisies.

This experiment demonstrated that Daisyworld regulated its own temperature over a wide range of heat radiation, without any apparent sentient capability or external intervention. This is only partly true since James Lovelock and his team programmed the computer, set up Daisyworld, and devised the mathematical model that set the experiment in motion; they even defined how the seeds would be distributed. Lovelock had in fact acted as the *Ideator*, (initiator and designer of Daisyworld) and his team of programmers acted as *Effectuators* in that they implemented the design and made it happen.

In particular, the software team acted as an SFU equivalent, realising the Ideations in the form of algorithms and coding of software which defined the form and function and behaviour of Daisyworld. There was a slight difference in the software content for the black daises and the white ones, since the two species of daisies have different form, in this case different colour, and interacted differently with the environment: each had a slightly different model-daisy "SFU".

Once the Effectuators had done their work, the system was set in motion and continued, sustaining its model world from initiation through to extinction. Lovelock and his team had (unintentionally) created a model of the Ideation and Effectuation of a new self-sustaining system which started and "existed", albeit in model form, until extreme environmental conditions overwhelmed the model daisy's ability to survive, and this made them extinct.

Throughout the evolution of planet Earth and the diverse life-forms upon it, we see that once chemical reactions, bio-systems or eco-systems are set up, and are operating, they can continue interacting with their environment and their SFUs, changing according to the Sun's heat, the composition of the atmosphere or the interaction with other entities in the environment.

They require the design information from the Ideation and work by the Effectuators, and the establishment of associated SFUs to start them off but can then continue with little further intervention, other than continuing influence from their SFUs.

The Daisyworld experiment represents a simplistic model having no atmosphere and no other life forms to interfere with the process, and simple rules governing life and death and propagation in daisy-world. Although there cannot, therefore, be a direct comparison with what occurs in the real world, it did provide a useful exercise in computer-modelling a simple living system.

One conclusion was that the biosphere, together with living entities, act to regulate the climate making it habitable over a wide range of solar luminosity. Many other regulatory systems have been found to operate in practice on the "real Earth".

The Mysteries of Coding: The Transfer of Information

DNA contains information which can be *transcribed* into RNA molecules and then the RNA *translates* this information into a sequence of amino acids to make proteins. This DNA information is coded such that it can act as part of the system that performs these actions.

Eugene Koonin,[22] biologist and senior investigator at the National Centre for Information Biotechnology, has the view that the origin of transcription and translation, essential for DNA and RNA to function to enable proteins to be assembled, is unknown.

Although the answer may be that life started with a type of simple proto-RNA performing the function, but so far, this concept does not provide an adequate explanation. This is because the question remains as to what provided this first proto-RNA with its essential coding to enable it to construct the correct set of proteins from the correct sets of amino acids in the first place, as described earlier.

We could call this observation by Koonin, "the question of the missing link" between the coming into being of RNA and how it got its initial coding. This "missing link" is the associated SFU.

The RNA coding, or plan, is vital. If we consider basic chemical reactions, they will occur spontaneously wherever two or more chemicals are placed within a distance close enough for them to react with one another. They will react and produce the results of those reactions without any requirement for a trigger, motivation or "intention" whatsoever. However, in the case of a life-form replicating, it is not a series of chemical reactions alone.

In all cases, basic organisms like bacteria have to construct some form of membrane to enclose this new assembly to protect the contents of the cell and then ensure cell division takes place. Only then has one organism become two and the amazing feat of replication has occurred. Once established, evolution and natural selection could start to function. Therefore, it had to have been able to access information from its SFU to obtain these instructions.

Once RNA had formed in the physical domain, DNA, which is far more complex, could then occur by a mixture of evolution, natural selection and the establishment of ever more complex SFU's. DNA is found in nearly all living organisms in modern times.

By the mechanisms explained above, the seemingly unbridgeable gap between non-living chemicals and compounds and the first simple living cell can be explained. Certainly, the first living cells are formed by complex combinations of chemicals woven into massively complex macro-molecules, but it has always been a question of how this complex combination occurred, not once, but many times over.

Dr Capra[24] concludes that although biologists have extensively analysed and know the structure of a number of genes, the way they function and communicate together to form an organism is largely unknown.

The Bacteria Ideation

Bacteria are single cell microorganisms. They do not have a nucleus but they contain DNA. They have a cell membrane to keep their material together and protected, and they have a cell wall. A considerable number of evolutionary steps would have taken place between the establishment of a Protoid and DNA-bearing Bacteria.

Bacteria is currently thought to have come into existence on Earth around 3.4-3.7 BBP in the oceans and lakes, and later in the surfaces of soil and the wet mud and sediments. The many species of bacteria could have descended from the protoid. As was described earlier, fossilised mats of cyanobacteria called stromatolites have been found dating from somewhere between 3.0-2.1Billion years ago.

Bacteria are incredibly resilient and adaptable life forms. Some bacteria can even exist in radio-active waste or in the incredible pressures of the deepest oceans. They also live in symbiotic or parasitic relationships with plants and animals which, in some cases, would not be able to live without them. They are vital in recycling nutrients, and they convert dissolved compounds, such as hydrogen-sulphide and methane, into energy.

The earliest bacteria survived in a very harsh environment which was undergoing dramatic change and was, in some places, hostile to life of any kind. They were originally inhabitants of the oceans and lakes, mud and wetlands because life on the land surface was almost impossible due to, among other things, the very high levels of ultra-violet radiation. There was no protective layer of ozone at these earliest times.

Rapid mutation and evolution of bacterial SFUs led to a rapid evolution of many bacterial species and they inhabit all environments. They have survived several mass extinction events; they have been, and are, probably the most successful life form ever to evolve.

Reactive Behaviour

Bacteria were thus able to develop a degree of ability to respond to certain features present in their environment, meaning having some degree of awareness of the environment, even though bacteria do not have a "brain". Being under the influence of their shared SFU, they "learned", for example, to move towards "sugar" and away from "acid". They could also move towards or away from light or perhaps, towards warm and away from cold as is the case for all living organisms; they have a degree of cognition.

This basic level of reactive behaviour in response to their environment assisted them in their bid for survival elementary as it was. These memories and rudimentary capabilities were "stored" in the bacterial SFU, but increasingly over time, evolution ensured increasing degrees of cognition was stored in their physical structure.

The Bacterial Contribution to the Formation of the Atmosphere

Since bacteria reproduce at great speed they can evolve rapidly and can therefore, adapt to a wide range of environmental changes quickly. Very early after the arrival of water on Earth, some bacteria evolved the ability to absorb energy from chemicals in the water and sea and lake beds by the process of fermentation.

This process gave these bacteria the ability to convert sugars into energy-carrying molecules which form the energy sources for many life forms. Bacteria were, therefore, able to survive by generating energy from basic chemicals in the environment, giving off carbon dioxide into the atmosphere in the process.

This meant that they became one of the engines driving the evolution of the complex content of the atmosphere. These bacteria were thus, not only living in the environment, but they were also actively changing it, and were functionally part of it. This was another vital step in establishing the right environment for higher life-forms.

Carbon dioxide is a greenhouse gas, and its presence in the atmosphere contributed to warming the atmosphere, which was essential early on, since the Sun had considerably less luminosity, and less ability to radiate heat, in the early aeons of the Earth.

Later, a new SFU evolved supporting a new species of bacteria which had the ability to absorb nitrogen directly from the atmosphere, a process known as nitrogen fixing, which is a difficult process. Nitrogen is essential for all living organisms to build proteins, another key ingredient for all living cells.

Some organisms (cyanobacteria for example) evolved the ability to photosynthesise, which enabled them to convert light from the Sun into usable energy. Early versions of bacteria with this capability used hydrogen sulphide from the atmosphere as a source of hydrogen, plenty being available from the activities of volcanoes which were far more active than they are today.

This gave Earth-Gaia another mechanism for cleaning up and rebalancing the atmosphere, since an atmosphere high in sulphides is undesirable for most life-forms. This hydrogen was then used by the bacteria to form organic compounds after chemical reactions with the carbon dioxide in the air and by the action of sunlight.

The arrival of the ability to photosynthesise, thus solved another potentially major problem. Photosynthesis is also the fundamental source of energy supply for plant life, the basis of the Earth's food chains. These bacteria were, therefore, gradually changing the atmosphere, evolving it towards what it is today.

The capability of some organisms to photosynthesise also solved another problem. During this period, there was free hydrogen in the atmosphere which cannot, in the long term be retained, being too light for the Earth's gravity to secure it. Eventually, it would have escaped into space. Hydrogen depletion was, therefore, a real threat that if this had continued unabated, it could have led to the disappearance of the oceans and an end to life on Earth.

The process of photosynthesis releases oxygen into the atmosphere; here it combined with the free hydrogen gas to form water. Earth-Gaia had evolved a source of oxygen for the atmosphere. This was a crucial step for future emerging life. By changing the atmosphere, the bacteria had solved a potential life-threatening situation and the Earth had moved one step closer in shaping an atmosphere suitable for a wider range of life forms.

The bacteria family had produced a source of both oxygen and carbon dioxide for the atmosphere and cleaned up any excess methane and hydrogen sulphide, and in addition, made nitrogen accessible as a life building-block to species yet to arrive and ensure hydrogen depletion was avoided.

This had the dual benefit of capturing the hydrogen, stopping its release into space and increasing the water levels on Earth.

However, this created a further problem. The removal of carbon dioxide from the air during photosynthesis reduced the greenhouse gas levels in the atmosphere, which led to global cooling. This could have led to the Earth having a permanent ice-age, damaging or preventing life on Earth. This threat was neutralised by the expansion and wider establishment of the fermenting bacteria, which emit carbon dioxide and methane (another greenhouse gas) during the fermentation process.

Thus, greenhouse gasses were re-established in the atmosphere which, in conjunction with the release of gasses due to volcanic activity, established a warming influence on Earth. The absorption of carbon dioxide by one group of bacteria, and the emission of carbon dioxide and methane by another group of bacteria, eventually led to the level of these gases coming into a dynamic equilibrium, and the Earth's temperature was stabilised at a level conducive to sustaining life, even though changes in the balance between the warming and cooling influences gave rise to periods of ice-age followed by warmer periods.

Thus, Earth-Gaia had implemented the start of the process which would lead to the next vital stage of preparation of the environment to support the emergence of many more species, and more complex life-forms.

It established a stable atmosphere containing the right amount of oxygen and carbon dioxide, which provided a life sustaining content that could also enable a moderate temperature to predominate, but it was not yet the atmosphere we have today.

Thus, the equilibrium between the greenhouse gasses and oxygen within the atmosphere was not a happy accident but was a teleological sequential response which enabled the establishment of a dynamic atmosphere suitable for a wide range of life forms.

However, as the bacteria spread and grew in numbers and since some of the bacteria absorbed hydrogen, there came a depletion on the amount of hydrogen available. All life forms need the basic building blocks of carbon, hydrogen, nitrogen and oxygen, so a depletion of hydrogen was a serious threat to the evolution of life.

There is a great abundance of hydrogen in water. Water being a combination of hydrogen and oxygen, but absorbing hydrogen from this source could not be achieved by the photosynthesising bacteria. It requires a higher level of energy to split the water molecule into hydrogen and oxygen than the photosynthesising-bacteria could achieve.

Following the arrival of a further Ideation, this problem was solved by the evolution of the first blue-green bacteria (previously known as blue-green algae), SFU and its associated manifestation in the physical domain.

Blue-green bacteria use the ultra-violet part of the solar spectrum, the high energy part, to split the water molecules into their constituent parts of hydrogen and oxygen. They used the hydrogen to make sugars and carbohydrates and released oxygen into the atmosphere as a by-product of this reaction.

This was a crucial event in evolutionary history. Implementing the Ideation which established the blue-green bacteria with its dual capabilities of photosynthesis and the ability to absorb hydrogen from water which was hugely abundant, and the emission of oxygen into the atmosphere were almost the final events that enabled our life-supporting atmosphere to gradually come into existence; but again, there were still other phases to take place.

This release of oxygen gradually changed the composition of the atmosphere. The blue-green bacteria aerobic photo-synthesisers were so successful that they expanded over the Earth, but the huge release of oxygen gradually raised the oxygen composition of the atmosphere until it reached such a level that it formed a threat to life, in that too high a level of oxygen is toxic to life.

The photosynthesising bacteria had to be able to thrive and multiply in areas where they could absorb the right amount of sunlight, but not be destroyed by excessive ultra-violet radiation.

These photosynthesising organisms were responsible for raising the oxygen levels from less than 1% to over 20%, rapidly rising the levels throughout the atmosphere.

About 2-2.5 billion years ago, the levels of oxygen had increased to a level which threatened life on Earth. In fact, a considerable amount of life at that time was wiped out due to oxygen toxicity. However, the rise in oxygen levels in the atmosphere was slow over a long period of time, and there was time for a new Ideation to take place and solve the oxygen problem.

Following another crucial Ideation, which lead to another development and a new SFU for a new species to produce a solution to this threat. The new SFU produced a new species of blue-green bacteria; one that could absorb oxygen and use its oxidising properties to break down molecules, producing carbon dioxide, water and energy.

This occurred about 1.8 billion years ago. This had the longer-term effect of reducing the quantity of oxygen in the atmosphere and thus its toxicity, stabilising the oxygen level to a life-friendly level. This could be regarded as the first "breathing" organism, that is, it was able to absorb oxygen as an energy source and emit carbon dioxide.

This new capability to absorb oxygen from the atmosphere, that is to breathe, is the capability associated with all subsequent higher life forms. This organism that could absorb oxygen from the atmosphere, lowered the oxygen levels, thus indirectly saved the Earth's species from oxygen toxicity and possibly from an extreme mass extinction event as a result.

The two forms of organism, those absorbing carbon dioxide and releasing oxygen and the other absorbing oxygen and releasing carbon dioxide, is another symbiotic pairing that enabled the balance of oxygen and carbon dioxide levels in the atmosphere to stabilise at a level suitable for both forms in dynamic equilibrium.

If the level of oxygen drops below about fifteen percent, many life forms would asphyxiate and combustion would not be readily supported; above twenty five percent, the Earth's life support environment would be threatened by spontaneous combustion, and uncontrolled wild-fires, and the atmosphere would be toxic to most life-forms.

The Earth-Gaia duad has maintained the oxygen level at around twenty one percent which is ideal for life as we know it. Natural selection would favour life that could thrive with an oxygen level close to 21%. This critical oxygen level had been established by about 1.5 billion years ago.

With the stabilisation of the oxygen content, a solution to the dangerous levels of ultra-violet light radiating down onto the Earth's surface became available. Around 560-600 million years BP, another critical event took place; an ozone layer was created from the oxygen that was now in the atmosphere.

This provided a screen in the upper atmosphere which protected the Earth's surface from the ravages of ultra-violet radiation and made the Earth's surface, at last, inhabitable for a wide range of life-forms. Life was, therefore, able to emerge from the oceans and inhabit the land.

In fact, the Earth's atmosphere has been stable for millennia, which is surprising. Its composition is complex and dynamic, with many interactions between various species of bacteria, blue-green bacteria and chemicals with these interactions acting to keep it stable in composition.

As described in Chapter 2, Professor James Lovelock's view was that the atmosphere, as it is, could not have formed or remained as stable as it is by chance. It is such a curious mixture and incompatible mixture of gasses. Lynn Margulis[23] worked with Lovelock as her work involved how some aspects of the atmosphere were in part due to bacteria and other life forms

With the establishment of several bacterial species, increasingly diversified, albeit elementary life, had been established and had contributed massively to its environment. It defined the dynamics and content of the atmosphere and made land-dwelling life possible. These evolutions also enabled a stable atmosphere to form and to be stable over a long period of time.

Many of the capabilities evolved by the bacteria described above are used in higher animals today; the ability to fix nitrogen which is essential for the formation of many organic compounds, for example, and the ability to absorb oxygen from the atmosphere as an energy source, that is, the ability to breathe, albeit using different mechanisms.

The formation of the protective ozone layer ensured that the Earth's terrestrial surface was ready to receive the early life forms emerging from the oceans. These were primitive plants which possibly evolved from green algae which possibly lived along the margins of lakes about 430 million years BP.

In terms of the stable but dynamic atmosphere, it remains to be seen what affect man will have in raising the carbon dioxide levels in the atmosphere perhaps, causing some degree of global warming. Will Earth/Gaia counteract this by some mechanism, or will man find a way to restore the balance?

Professor Lovelock's view[16] relating to both the climate and chemical construction of Earth always seems to have been structured precisely to support life. This could never have happened by pure chance.

According to Matrix Model Theory, the sequence of atmospheric evolution described above was due to a series of Ideations acting through the PFU, and the associated evolution of the correct sequence of bacterial SFUs supporting the evolving bacteria and blue-green bacteria.

The Ocean Environment

Another vital control mechanism that operates on planet Earth, and without which life as we know it would not have started, is the fact that salinity of the oceans is controlled and kept within narrow limits, and has been fairly constant for billions of years. Since the oceans cover three quarters of the surface of the Earth, and life probably started there, a degree of salinity control would have been a pre-condition to the start of life.

The salinity of the Oceans has a significant part to play in the Earth's climate; it is remarkably uniform throughout the oceans of the world. It varies from 34 to 37 units of sea surface salinity, or SSS, between maximum and minimum, the lower figures being found close to the polar regions, and the higher regions found in the central Atlantic.

The factors that increase salinity are evaporation, the formation of ice and rock weathering run off. The factors decreasing salinity are fresh-water run-off from rivers, precipitation of rain and snow into the oceans and melting ice. The self-regulatory processes have clearly been very successful, since the salinity of the oceans has not changed very much since the oceans came into being.[16]

The upper three meters of the oceans contains more heat than the entire atmosphere, and the salinity affects its ability to store heat. The great ocean currents move this heat around the oceans. One such current is the Gulf stream which starts its journey on the west side of the Atlantic, in the tropics. As the warm high-salinity sea water moves north its temperature decreases, the water density increases, and it sinks below the lower salinity water, carrying with it the higher salinity content.

In the case of the Gulf Stream, the sinking higher salinity water occurs far to the north of Scotland; it then reverses its direction of travel from a north-going warm surface current to become a cooler, south-going deep current, taking the cooled water back to its point of origin, warming during the journey.

It then rises to the surface, to start the circulation again. It is a conveyor belt that warms the north and west coasts of Britain. Such conveyor belts occur in other places around the globe with different currents.

The significance of the effects due to ocean surface temperature changes is best demonstrated by the fact that they are believed to cause the so called El Nino and El Nina effects, which have dramatic effects of the climate over huge areas. They can cause curious weather events such as torrential rainfall in Peru and simultaneously droughts in the USA.

The oceans, through their currents and ability to absorb carbon dioxide and other gasses, help control and regulate the Earth's climate, although it can cause changes to the climate, it ensures that it stays within tolerable limits for life, even allowing for such dramatic events as hurricanes, tornados electric storms and flood-causing torrential rains.

Nucleated Cells

There are two types of living cells. One was the simple single cell organisms called prokaryote, which are the original simple cells, have no nucleus and form free-floating genetic material such as bacteria and archaea. The second, later evolution, is the more complex eukaryotes, which evolved somewhere about 2.0BBP, which contain a nucleus, DNA and genetic material within that nucleus. These cells are the building blocks of all life forms other than bacteria and archaea.

The evolution of the more complex eukaryotes cells is thought to have occurred by the symbiotic invasion of one simple cell into another, with both surviving and able to replicate as a more complex combination. It is thought that such an event is so incredibly unusual that it has only occurred once in the history of the Earth.

Without this event, there would be no complex life on Earth; life would mostly have consisted of bacteria. archaea and other simple life-forms. The SFU for the new complex cell was first ideated and "made to happen" using the tools of mutation and evolution to ensure the arrival of the eukaryotes. This crucial, albeit extremely unlikely event, was teleologically driven.

All multi-cellular organisms are eukaryotic including the cells of all animals, plants and fungi. Multicellular life arrived on the evolutionary scene at somewhere between 2.1 to 1.0 BBP. When the eukaryotic or nucleated cells, were Ideated and evolved, they were far more complex than the earlier prokaryotic cells. They evolved to have hundreds of times more DNA in them than that associated with bacteria. They possibly arose by larger cells engulfing smaller ones, with both surviving.

Nucleated cells also evolved more efficient means of movement, increasing their survival chances.

The Limitations of DNA

There are microbiologists who, when DNA was discovered in the 1960's by Crick and Watson, concluded that DNA explained all hereditary characteristics and that locked within the DNA and the genome, was sufficient information to furnish the life-form with all of its form, function, behaviour and instincts. However, this has been shown not to be the case[17].

As described in chapter 4, the content of DNA alone was unable to explain the migration of the eels across the Atlantic or the migratory habits of birds or the ability of a homing pigeon to find its way home or the highly synchronised flight aerobatics of a murmuration of starling.

The behaviour of colonies of ants and bees also could not be explained by their DNA alone, and neither could the behaviour of the Flatid bug or any other living organism. These are just a few specific examples; there are many others. In the case of humankind, there is the well-documented issue of the missing heredity problem.

Leslie Orgel[26], a British chemist and author of papers on the origin of life and work on DNA, was one of the proponents of the "RNA world theory". He collaborated with Crick, one of the discoverers of DNA, on a panspermia alternative theory, stating that micro-organisms, like bacteria, may have been sown by a higher intelligence. Beyond a rudimentary timeline, he concluded that the origin of life remains unknown.

In other words, it is known that life almost certainly started and became established on Earth, rather than arriving from elsewhere in the cosmos; we know approximately when, but science does not know how. DNA molecules do not carry plans relating to body-architectural instructions, they just code for the sequences of amino acids to assemble and ensure correct protein assembly.

Another curious attribute for DNA was discovered by Tomas Lindahl FRS[48], working at the Crick Laboratory, London, is that DNA has several molecular systems that continuously monitor and repair the DNA molecules, which is important in maintaining the genetic integrity of the molecule. Lindahl won a Nobel prize for his work.

However, the intricate complexity of DNA enables it to contain a vast amount of information. So the question is, what gave the DNA this data, even allowing for considerable numbers of stages of evolution; a source from within an Intelligent Universe is the only sustainable answer.

Dr D Foster,[19] a cybernetician, had the view that there is a huge amount of data required to define the form, function and behaviour of a human, and have it lodged within its genome. The source of this data must originate from a far higher intelligence than is possessed by humans.

(Ref Dr D Foster, International conference on cybernetics, Imperial college London, 1969).

His concept is that we live in a digitised universe, and this concept is, perhaps, similar to the concept of an Intelligent Universe described in this book.

The existence and contribution of the SFU/SGU/SIU families answer Foster's question; they are the sources of intelligence that defined elements of the data (information) source for the DNA; they are inherently part of the Intelligent Universe. Each generation of an organism obtains part of its coding from its parental DNA, and part from its associated SFU/SGU/SIU family.

There is also a rather fundamental question, as described earlier. Professor Sheldrake[17] asks, how, and by what mechanism is the process of the synthesis of proteins controlled and established to ensure that the required specific proteins are made in the right quantities at the right time. This is explained by the function of the SFU working in conjunction with the genome specific to each species.

If the physical structure of a human is considered, the cells of the various parts of the body contain the same genetic material; that is, the same DNA, and yet they develop to form in different ways; the arm, the leg, the head and so on contain the same "genetic program" but something makes them different, to develop as they do. Something has to have the architectural overview to determine how the body is to be correctly assembled.

This has puzzled micro-biologists for a long time, having accepted the fact that the genome could not explain everything[17] to do with heredity and body architecture; something else was involved. That "something else" is the SIU associated with an individual human, and other higher animals which, among many other activities during the development of a living entity, triggers the sequence of homeobox genes, which shall be described below.

Behaviour and instincts are not functional properties of DNA. Behaviour, in its broadest sense, is determined by a mix of SIU coding and environmental and experiential issues that an individual has been subjected to. In terms of "behaviour", the example of a bird building a nest could be sited; the bird "knows" how to build the nest without having been taught; its fledgling experiences of a nest would not have included a crash course on how to build one.

Also, some nests are quite complex, and most species have a nest design specific to its species. In fact, the memory of how to build a nest is lodged within the bird-SFU at species level. The fact that, in general, each species has a different nest design is explained by the fact that each bird species has its own SFU, which contains all the bird's instincts, including the instinct defining how to build the nest specific to that species.

Stem Cells

Stem cells are undifferentiated biological cells which can differentiate into different specialised cells and can divide to produce more stem cells. In adults, stem cells act as repair systems, repairing damaged cells and organs.

In human embryos, stem cells begin to be produced just after the fusion of an egg and sperm, the zygote stage. Stem cells differentiate into specialised cells and not only are they able to self-renew organs in some cases, and repair damage in adults, but they also assist in the production of organs (organogenesis) in the embryo. These form for example, the circulatory system, the heart, liver, nervous system and immune system. However, they are not thought to contain any aspect of the embryo architecture.

Initially, at the very start of the embryo development, some entity has to define exactly where the organs, including the heart, will start to develop and the position of the circulatory system, the nervous system and the positioning of the eyes, legs and other key body-architecture elements.

If the normal development cycle of an embryo is considered, at the point of fertilisation of the egg to form a zygote (the fertilised egg produced by the fusion of the ovum and sperm, which then starts to cell-divide), it contains DNA and its associated coding, which is based on half from the male and half from the female parents.

The SIU for the individual is also established at this instant and is also formed from contributions from both of the parent's SIUs. Within a few days, development begins, and the development axis is around the spinal cord. After week four or five, brain activity can be detected and the heart begins to beat, circulating the blood. After around five weeks, limb buds appear, and organogenesis continues.

By week six to eight, the embryo exhibits signs of movement; the eyes form by the end of the eighth week, with facial features starting to appear, the embryonic stage has morphed into the foetal stage.

When one considers the massive amount of change that has to be accommodated over a very short time period, this development is nothing short of staggering. Everything seems to "know" exactly what it has to do, when and how it has to develop, and where and how it all "fits together" to form a massively complex self-organising and self-sustaining system. Biologists currently do not know in detail how this occurs.

This emphasises the role of the SFU family. In the case of higher animals, the SIU is the dominant influencer which, together with the DNA, form the coding-sources, which contains the architecture, time and development plan, and the function of each of the components.

However, the SIU in higher animals requires physical agents in the physical domain during the embryo/foetal development to implement the required architectural plan. Among these physical agents, are the homeobox genes.

The Homeobox Gene

The homeobox gene-family are a group of specific genetic sequences that are thought to be associated with regulating the anatomical development of many life forms. This includes animals, plants, fungi and humans. They are thought to be the orchestrator of the structure, for example, of the human embryo (morphogenesis).

They appear early in the embryo development and are present at the zygote stage and initiate zygote division and embryogenesis. They are thought to influence the placing of the organs along an axis running from head to tail in animals, giving many animals their symmetry.

Not only are these genes thought to ensure or have an involvement in ensuring that the right organs form in the right place, but they also have a role in regulating cell growth, ensuring that growth is at the correct rate.

Some specialise in the structure of specific functional "blocks", for example, the eye, another for the head, another for teeth. For the homeobox gene to fully explain the eventual form and function of, for example, the adult human, it would have to contain all the coding required to achieve this, and all the coding for each stage of the human development.

It is believed that the full set of homeobox genes (over 200 in humans) appears very early in the development of an embryo. They would have to do so to be available and active at those critical early stages of development.

Although the homeobox genes within an organism play an important part in the plan of what parts develop where within an organism, they cannot explain the overall form of the organism. These genes turn out to be almost identical in flies, reptiles and humans, so it remains certain that they do not, in themselves, completely determine the form or body-architecture. However, there is currently no molecular explanation for morphogenesis (the origin and development of the form and structure of living organisms) among biologists, and it is not entirely explained by homeobox genes[17].

The SIU is unique for each embryo (as it is for the resulting individual) and interacts with it from the point of conception to guide the development of the human at each stage.

However, what "triggers" these homeobox-genes, how they are able to mutate into areas of specialisation, and how they carry the coding for the whole sequence of body plan is unknown to biologists. Professor Sheldrake[17] concludes that biologists, geneticists and neurophysiologists have not managed to explain morphogenesis, the development of embryos.

Equally obscure are the mechanisms behind the inheritance of instincts. Morphogenesis is explained from Matrix Model Theory by the human SIU, which contains the coding which explains how zygotes develop into embryos in the way in which they do, whilst the human SFU provides their instincts, as explained in chapter 3.

The SIU functions in a teleological way; it has purpose, with an end game in view from the start. The "end game" also changes with time. For example, the initial plan is to achieve a development from zygote to embryo, then to foetus; the plan then has to change to establish a baby that is capable of surviving the birth experience.

The plan then changes again to establish the infant, and later as it develops, the plan changes again and becomes that to establish the mature adult. Each phase differs in form, function and behaviour and degree of dependence. These changes could not be wholly contained within the molecular structure of DNA. The individual's SIU, in conjunction with DNA and for the early stages of development, the homeobox gene sequence implement each stage.

The Genome Project

There was a research project started in the 1980s to determine the structure of human DNA and identifying and mapping of all the genes of the human genome from both a physical and functional standpoint. The project was deemed to have been completed by 2003.

Although the genome for many species has been fully defined, it has proven impossible to work out from the genome how any species would develop and what it would look like. It was thought that a profound understanding of DNA and its sequencing could hold benefits for medicine.

In Sheldrake's view, the completion of the genome project disappointed in that it did not result in an understanding of how genes determine body architecture and traits like eye colour or height. Further, it did not provide answers to how inheritance of characteristics and traits between generations functions.

Research into genes for more complex traits, like height, eye colour and certain hereditary diseases has found that only between 5% and 50% of the traits investigated could be attributed to the DNA. To provide a specific example, there is an 80-90 percent accuracy in determining a child's height by observing the height of the parents (tall parents tend to have tall children, as previously described), but genetics account for only 5% of the height inheritance. There is something else determining height, beyond "just genes".

Since the inheritance of traits, like height, eye colour or gait cannot be explained by DNA alone, what other mechanism is at work to provide this additional hereditable information? This is known as the missing heredity problem, as previously described.

Interestingly, although it has been established that genes are involved in the formation of proteins, they cannot determine the structure, behaviour, or the instincts associated with an animal.

Looking at the missing heredity problem in a little more detail, researchers have found that individual genes from parents cannot account for much of the hereditably of diseases, behaviour, and form in their offspring.

Researchers have considered other possibilities to account for the "missing heredity" problem. The question asked was what *else* was contributing to the inherited traits in addition to the DNA? There were several proposals, but as one researcher stated, "they all lead beyond DNA as the single source of inheritance".

Matrix Model Theory proposes that this is explained by the contribution of the human SIU and genome combination determining form, function and behaviour and can, therefore, account for the missing heredity traits, and in fact, one would expect a major contribution from this source. Researchers who have worked at the cutting edge of heredity investigations have noted:

It is a sobering thought that after nearly a century of research into genetics that has used the concept of hereditability, we do not yet fully understand why hereditabilities have the values that they do.

(Visschre 2008)

Further, Professor Landecker (2013) concluded that new research in genetics, RNA and epigenetics are now casting doubt on science's understanding of how heredity works.

As if to emphasise this view, Professor Lenid Kiuglyac[46], an evolutionary biologist, took the view that no one understands why children resemble their parents; it is not just due to human genetics alone.

A further useful insight by S Jones, geneticist, (2009) took the view that the genes that would explain human genetic inheritance are just not present; other mechanisms must be involved. The characteristics and content of the SIU for humans and higher animals provide the answers to many of these seemingly intractable problems. This would imply the need for new field in biology and, quite possibly, a new extension of physics and psychology to assimilate Matrix Model Theory, which shall be further described in detail in Chapter 7.

At the instant of the fertilisation of a human egg, the zygote stage, the new SIU is formed from a mix of the content of the SIUs of each parent. Thus, it provides coding on form function and behaviour from each parent. From the first cell division, the embryo development is governed, to a large extent, by the combination of the SIU and the associated Genome.

As the embryo develops, the coding from the SIU provides the missing heredity information. It explains why offspring have many physical characteristics of their parents and may also exhibit traits associated with one parent or another according to the way the coding has mixed within their associated SIU at the point of conception.

Sheldrake concludes that molecular biology has established that morphogenesis, the coming into existence of life forms, has no molecular explanation, but seems to depend on fields. In this instance, Sheldrakes view was in the context of morphogenic fields, that is, according to his theory[5], the form and structure of living organisms are seemingly dependent on formative fields.

The SFU associated with each living entity enables them to become the "complete" entity in each case and influences their form and structure and behaviour throughout their development. In the case of many higher animals, including humans, their development seems to go through many stages, each considerably different from the previous stages.

This dynamic development requires a dynamic and progressive architecture encoded within the SIU in conjunction with the associated genome for each individual and communicated through to the developing of morphogenesis for each human in the physical domain via psi-fields, in a specific and well-defined sequence.

These explanations lead us to the conclusion that, since the domains of the unconscious have intelligence and memory enabling them to perform as they do; it is further evidence that we do live in an Intelligent Universe. Intelligence is distributed far wider than just within the brains of mankind and higher animals.

Biologists will continue their work with the genome, DNA and chromosomes. They will continue to find partial explanations how things work in the physical domain, but it is unlikely that they will be able to explain *how* they came to be that way, nor why or what the causal agency is, based on a molecular explanation only.

The inclusion of Matrix Model Theory and the associated SFU family in explaining form, function and behaviour provides the missing dimension to many aspects of the structures and behaviour of all living things.

Chapter 6
Evolution and Diversification of Life

The previous chapter reviewed the establishment of an environment capable of supporting life and enable the bacterial revolution to take place. It also covered the vital contribution of the SFU family combined with the RNA/DNA entities to the form, function and behaviour of a species.

This chapter develops this theme with a brief and simplified description of how the species diversified and proliferated, once elementary life had been established. It also covers how Earth/Gaia reacted to the various mass-extinction catastrophic events that the planet has been subjected to.

The Evolution of Species

Species tend to evolve and mutate, thereby creating new species by teleologically driven processes, rather than by random evolution and mutation events, which would give rise to a chaotic multitude of life-forms, many of which would quickly die out.

Every new evolution event or establishment of a new species has to fit in with and become part of a particular environment. There is a wide variety of species that survive in a very wide range of environments, from the burning heat of the middle of a desert, to the ice bound arctic regions.

The reason new species are first Ideated into the psi-domain in the form of a new Species Formative Unconscious is that this is an essential prerequisite to enable any new species to evolve into the physical domain; it must have an SFU associated with it in order to survive.

Evolution occurs where there is a change in the characteristics of a species over several generations and relies on natural selection. Some of these changes may give an organism an advantage over other organisms that do not have the genetic change, and they can pass this change onto their offspring by passing on the genetic change. Natural selection ensures these successful variants are more likely to replicate and more of the successful variant survive and increase in number.

The establishment of a new SFU is usually the agent causing this change in characteristics by altering a gene which natural selection can act on. Other gene-changing mechanisms include chemical contamination of the genome, pollution and ultra-violet damage. The SFU change is specific, teleological, and follows the establishment of a new SFU to support a new species or new structure or trait with an existing species.

For new species, other than higher animals, the new SFU must contain the new coding required to define the new species form and function. This would usually consist of the coding from the immediate ancestor with the addition of the new coding defined by the associated Ideation.

This prevents what would otherwise be evolutionary and mutational chaos in the physical domain due to large numbers of random evolutionary and mutational events, which would be evidenced by a vast number of different fossils, many representing organisms which had a limited term before becoming extinct. It is not thought that there is any such proliferation of fossils.

The ability for the Ideations to rapidly form new SFUs, which support new species, has led to periods where many new species appear in a surprisingly short time. One such period occurred around 541-485.4 million years before present (541-485.4 MBP) which was the Cambrian era, when many new species suddenly appeared, according to the fossil record. During the Cambrian period, the Ideations were clearly working overtime!

Many of the dates quoted here are based on fossil evidence and will be subject to change if new fossils are found, which may change the palaeontologist's view of the sequences of evolution. A specific date for the first emergence of life has not yet been determined.

There is a theory that the earliest life forms could possibly have started in the oceans around hydro-thermal vents or alkaline vents. There is evidence that early life was established between 3.4-3.7BBP based on certain microfossils found in rocks in Canada and further evidence of life found in biogenic rocks from Greenland dating from 3.7-3.8 BBP.

Evidence of microbial mats have also been found in Western Australia, dating from 3.48BBP. An important evolution was that of cyanobacteria, at around 2.7-2.1BBP which was a photosynthesising life form which produced oxygen which was released into the atmosphere.

Having established a broad series of successful sustainable living entities, as described in the previous chapter, in the form of various bacteria and archaea, further ideations were soon to see dramatic developments.

Stirrings of rapid change were present in the latter part of the pre-Cambrian period (pre-541MBP), there is some evidence of diversification; a sort of basic genetic tool kit had been Ideated and Effectuated by new SFUs using the tools of evolution, mutation and natural selection.

During the pre-Cambrian period, most life was limited to single-cell bacteria and archaea, with a few more complex multi-cellular organisms. All dates mentioned in this section should be regarded as approximate and differ according to source. The most generally accepted dates have been used here.

The formation of the ozone layer above the rest of the atmosphere provided a shield protecting the Earth's surface from ultra-violet rays from the Sun had been established by 560-600MBP, as previously described. The ozone layer absorbs between 95 and 99% of medium frequency ultra-violet, the radiation energy which is damaging to life. This enabled the land to be more easily available for inhabitation by life emerging from the sea.

Following the establishment of archaic life forms and their wide variety of body architecture during the pre-Cambrian period, the environment was well prepared for the arrival of many new species at a rapid rate in the Cambrian era.

During the Cambrian period, 541-485.4MBP there was a very rapid series of evolutions of new life-forms which were the distant ancestors of most of today's species. These new life-forms appeared at a remarkably rapid rate: in fact, they appeared so rapidly that this era is referred to as the "Cambrian explosion". Among the new arrivals were the remote ancestors of trilobites, which were hard-shelled animals living in oceans around this period. They were very successful, existing for over 250 million years.

This period also saw the arrival of the chordates, animals with a dorsal nerve cord, brachiopods, ancestors of clams and early species of primitive arthropods, ancestors of spiders, insects and crustaceans. There is also thought to have been a centipede-type animal which left the sea for land as possibly as early as 530MBP.

Also, by 500MBP, molluscs were established, and the possible ancestors of the modern arthropods, which, in turn, are the ancestors of invertebrates, evolved. The arthropods had hard exoskeletons and became permanent land-dwellers by about 420MBP. Centipedes and sea-worms, the latter being thought by some to be the earliest primordial ancestor of man, also appeared around 500MBP. Early ancestors of fish appeared, albeit a jawless species, between 490-410MBP. Earlier ancestors of fish were worm-like creatures.

Another interesting innovation evolving during the Cambrian era was the complex eye, now associated with higher animals. Prior to the Cambrian era, no evidence of complex eye structures has yet been found. Thus, the distant ancestors of most of today's species appeared during this relatively short time.

In fact, Darwin noticed that such a proliferation of life in such a short time cast doubt on his evolutionary theory: time was too short for such diversity to appear by gradual evolution and natural selection alone. When asked if he could explain such a sudden arrival of so many new species, Darwin stated that he could give no satisfactory answer.

Darwin did not consider the immense driving force of the Ideations harnessing the engines of the Effectuators; in particular, the rapid evolution of the SFU family which led to a corresponding rapid implementation of changes and new life-forms in a teleological manner. In fact, the concept would have clashed with his views. Darwin admitted that the rapidity of the arrival of new species during this period could not be explained by evolution alone.

Darwin and his successors would, in general, not have accepted the premise of teleological processes, which arises from the concept of an Intelligent Universe, or intelligence being inherent in nature. The combination of the Ideations working in conjunction with the PFU explains why so many new SFUs evolved so rapidly, leading to many new species appearing during this relatively short time-period.

Elementary life continued to progress until the occurrence of a catastrophic event. The Earth rapidly cooled, which lead to the onset of a great Ice Age. The polar caps marched towards the equator, starting from about 485MBP ending and retreating about 443MBP, the first known mass extinction of species occurred. This is known as the Ordovian-Silurian Mass extinction.

This event is thought to have been caused by a particular type of volcanic action, which released huge quantities of sulphur dioxide into the atmosphere. This gas absorbs solar radiation very efficiently, with a consequential cooling of the Earth's surface. Most life at the time was under the sea, and the Ice age caused serious damage. With an Ice age, there is a substantial drop in sea level, as more water is trapped as ice. Around 85% of all life was made extinct at this time.

Because of the huge extent of the ice sheets and freezing conditions this event is sometimes referred to as "snowball Earth".

However, extinction of life was far from total, and some life forms survived this catastrophe, those that survived were the ancestors of most of today's species. As this Ice Age waned, and the caps retreated, the fossil records show the rapid arrival of new life forms.

By 480-450MBP, the ancestors of insects evolved from species first established in the Cambrian period. Starfish and crabs appeared during this time, together with crustaceans some of which have been described as "advanced arthropods", which are invertebrate animals, having a segmented body, an external skeleton and jointed limbs, like insects, lobsters, butterflies and spiders.

After the 443MBP mass extinction, the ice melted, the ice caps retreated, which raised the sea level. Earth/Gaia had returned the environment again to one that was more conducive to life. Many of the new species were the ancestors of species alive today, although these ancestors are now largely extinct.

Between around 430-400MBP, further living organisms left the sea and started to evolve and colonise land in the form of land plants, more microbial mats and several species of fungi. One of the earliest is thought to be the lichens which could have provided a stepping-stone for marine life to further colonise land.

Further evolutions saw the arrival of the first amphibians by 419MBP; they were the dominant land animal at this time. Some of these later evolved into reptiles.

The first flying insects were also established by 400MBP, having evolved from their non-flying ancestors. Many different species, with very different and divergent body architectures, had evolved in a very short time. More new species arrived, which included ancestors of sharks and by 400MBP. Corals started to form extensive reefs providing new and vibrant habitats for a wide variety of marine life.

By 385-380MBP the first tetrapods appeared, which are four-legged creatures which were the distant ancestors of the four-legged animals we have today.

However, in about 359MBP, there was another mass extinction event, possibly due to the ice sheets again advancing from the poles, or possibly by asteroid impact. This time the extinction accounted for the extinction of around 75% of life on Earth. Once again, Gaia had to recover from a major disaster and the species that survived after the mass extinction continued to evolve, and indeed, new species were established.

Ancestors of beetles evolved after the Earth had recovered which marked the start of the Carboniferous period. Trees were established by 360-350MBP which eventually led to widespread forestation. Ferns had also appeared during this time.

When some species of plants and animals left the oceans and became land dwellers, they left the environment of weightlessness and animals needed a more rigid physical structure to counteract the effects of gravity, so skeletons evolved for some species. One key event was the fact that by 350MBP, some animals had evolved lungs enabling them to breathe, taking advantage of oxygen in the atmosphere as an energy source.

After 350MBP, there were vast forests which provided shelter and cover as well as food sources for terrestrial animals. There were also more insects, more species of crustaceans and myriapods (centipedes and millipede ancestors) had also appeared along with further evolutions of amphibians.

A key evolution had occurred around 312MBP, amniotes were established; these are a clade of terrestrial tetrapod (four legged) vertebrates, (that is animals with backbones and spinal columns) which included ancestors of reptiles; eventually, some evolved into mammals. Early versions of amniotes resembled small lizards. These were egg-layers who could lay their eggs out of water, which enabled them to spread to drier environments.

Within a few million years the sauropsids, which evolved from amniotes, were established; they were ancestors of the lizards, snakes, turtles, crocodiles, dinosaurs and birds. The earliest known fossils of sauropsids date from 320-315MBP.

A little later, around 312MBP, synapsids evolved which were the ancestors of mammals, which are sometimes referred to as proto-mammals. The period around 300MBP saw the emergence of further evolutions of spiders, turtles and beetles. Turtles were the largest amphibious animals on land between 200-251MBP.

Another notable evolution occurred around 250MBP with the establishment of Archesaurs which were later evolutions of the ancestors of a group which included dinosaurs and crocodiles and birds.

A few of these animals had no apparent direct antecedents, they "just arrived" as indicated by the fossil record. They started to form food chains with the larger vertebrates tending to eat the smaller. This proliferation of such a variety of species is strong evidence that evolution and natural selection alone could not have achieved this in such a short time.

By the start of the Cambrian period, the continental land masses had changed. Before 225MBP, there was a single great supercontinent called Pangea. This started to break up around 225MBP initially, to form Gondwana and Larasia. The Gondwana continent included Africa, South America, Australia and India. Laurasia included North America and most of the rest of the northern hemisphere. About 200MBP, Laurasia further broke up dividing eastern North America and Northwest Africa, forming the Atlantic Ocean.

This gradual breaking up of the previous single super-continent gave rise to smaller land masses and consequently, a greatly increased area of continental shelves, coastal zones and shallow seas, ideal habitats for species to form and develop and more opportunities for animals to leave the oceans and evolve to produce more terrestrial species.

The temperature average at this time was warmer and the distribution was still, and has continued to be, such that it was colder at the poles and warmer at the equator. The oceans became more oxygenated as free oxygen in the atmosphere increased and thus became more life-friendly, although the carbon dioxide levels at that time were estimated to be fifteen times higher than they are today.

Basic body structures and physical architecture of living entities diversified during this time and evolved to form the basis for all life forms in existence today. The skeleton and the eye evolved further, appearing in many of the new species. Also appearing was the blood-circulatory system, that enabled energy and oxygen to be distributed around the bodies of new species to supply the various specialist organs that were evolving.

The next era was the Permian, around 299MBP to 252MBP. This era saw further evolutions of the ancestors of the mammal together with further evolutions of reptiles and turtles.

At around 251 to 248 million years ago, the Earth-Gaia Duad was inflicted by another massive catastrophe known as the Permian extinction; the greatest mass extinction yet. This time due to the great Siberian Volcanic eruptions, which blasted millions of tons of rock, dust and debris, high into the atmosphere, and discharged huge quantities of sulphur dioxide.

This caused the Sun to be masked, and would have appeared blood red, the stars would have disappeared from view and the seas were contaminated with dilute sulphuric acid, which is toxic to many life-forms. With acid seas, and a huge reduction in sunlight caused by the emission into the atmosphere of millions of tons of debris and gasses from the massive volcanoes, plant food-chains would have been seriously damaged.

Life would have experienced conditions close to those imagined as hell, and it caused a third mass extinction. This mass extinction is known as "the Great Dying", since around 96% of all marine life and 70% of terrestrial vertebrates were made extinct.

All life on Earth today is directly descended from the survivors of this catastrophe. Marine creatures were worst affected, but even insects suffered the only mass extinction ever to have affected them. The extinction of most terrestrial life, including plants, resulted in the collapse of many food chains.

Over the following millennia, the Earth-Gaia duad once again had to rebalance the Earth as an environment that would again sustain life as the rains washed and cleaned the atmosphere and the oceans rebalanced their acidity.

As the atmosphere was cleaned and reinstated, more sunlight reached the Earth's surface, reinvigorating the remaining plant life re-establishing the food chains. Even having weathered this massive extinction event, enough species did survive to enable further evolution to take place.

New Ideations were implemented, and we entered the Triassic and the later Jurassic periods at between 250-144MBP. This heralded the next phase of life, with the arrival of the further evolutions of the mammals, and the first dinosaurs and the first large flying animals in the form of the Archaeopteryx around 150MBP, thought to be a possible ancestor of today's birds. Forests had become widespread at this time. The Jurassic period saw the dinosaurs as dominant terrestrial vertebrate.

Between 200-145MBP, flowering plants were established. Another critical development was the evolution of mammals able to give birth to live young as opposed to egg laying. This occurred around 160MBP. Bees were able to evolve after the establishment of flowering plants and modern looking birds evolved around 100MBP.

The dinosaurs flourished between 100-79MBP, and importantly, the first and earliest proto-primates had become established. The primate evolutionary path eventually gave rise to monkeys, gibbons, apes, baboons and the great apes.

Some of these are thought to be part of the distant ancestral line of humans. However, before the present cycle, there was yet another disaster to befall the Earth-Gaia planet and life at that time.

About 65million years ago, it is thought that a giant meteor, around 7 miles wide, impacted Earth and blasted a crater 190 miles across. It has been estimated that the blast impact would have been the same as one million Hiroshima atomic bombs going off at once. This also triggered further massive volcanic eruptions in the Deccan Traps. This mass extinction marked the end of the Cretaceous period and the start of the next phase of life on Earth.

Again, vast amounts of debris were blasted into the atmosphere by the combination of the two events; the devastation caused by the meteor impact and the catastrophic volcanic activity that it triggered. The debris in the atmosphere once again obscured the Sun, leading to freezing temperatures, with sulphur dioxide and carbon dioxide levels in the atmosphere soaring, adding to the dense pollution.

The seas and oceans once again became pools of dilute sulphuric acid, with molten rock raining down on Earth from the impact local to the point of impact. This caused another mass extinction where many animal and plant life species, including the dinosaurs and some flowering plants, disappeared.

It is surprising that any life survived this catastrophe. However, the event gave rise to further and more advanced life on Earth. Clearly, life, once established, has remarkable tenacity. Earth-Gaia had to work again for many millennia to cleanse the atmosphere, the terrestrial environment and the oceans to enable conditions to return to the correct balance to enable life to continue and thrive again.

As a general comment on the consequences of mass extinction events, in some cases, the extinction of one species or family of species, provided more opportunities for others to expand and fill the vacuum left by the disappearance. For example, early mammal-like animals existed during the reign of the dinosaurs but could not compete well enough to really flourish.

The extinction of the dinosaurs is thought to have allowed a rapid expansion of these early mammals, enabling them to become the dominant terrestrial vertebrae species. Darwin wrote that competition for food and space were of considerable importance in promoting evolution.

There are three main causes of mass extinctions. The first are massive volcanic eruptions which produces an atmosphere contaminated by dust, debris and gasses which suppress photosynthesis and can lead to, at least partial, collapse in food chains. The second relates to Ice-age events which, as well as causing intense cold, damaging plant life and hence food chains, also caused a reduction in sea levels as water is trapped in ice structures exposing continental shelf regions where much of life lived.

The third cause is impact events, by meteor or comet, for example, which, if large enough, can cause considerable dust and debris contamination of the atmosphere, acid rain and huge tsunamis. It is almost inevitable that, sooner or later, another impact event will cause another mass extinction on Earth; we just have no idea when.

Many life forms, however, managed to survive this devastating catastrophe of 65MBP, among them some of the molluscs, amphibians and some of the fish species along with some mammal species. We then had a phase in time, called the Paleogene, which gave the world another great proliferation of higher life forms, between around 66MBP and 23MBP, a stream of Ideations of new life forms were being implemented by new SFUs and the Effectuators.

Some were much more sophisticated life forms than previously established. Some of these evolved and many new species came into existence at this time, among them, the first horses by 55MBP, which were fox-sized animals. Grasslands had been widely established by 55MBP.

The whale appeared around 50MBP, and further evolutions of primates, a vitally important event in terms of the evolution of man. By this time, mammals were well established. Importantly, by between 63 and 25MBP, the first monkeys and apes appeared.

Each major setback, causing mass extinctions resulted in eventual further advances in more advanced and diverse species. Life forms became more complex and sophisticated. In many cases, the more complex life forms were dependent on the earlier simpler forms for their survival, often because they formed part of their food chains.

Continental drift causing a gradual movement of the continental land masses continued during this time, and the land had now formed into separate continental blocks, nearly where they are today. Some mountain ranges were formed by the movement of the continents ramming into one another, in this case the continent of India was moving north and colliding with Asia, the resulting upward movement of land mass forming the Himalayan Mountain range.

Another key feature enabling the environment to support the grazing herds occurred was the arrival of vast savannah grasslands. It is notable that these grasslands appeared much later than trees. This enabled the evolution of the grazing herds: for example, wildebeest appeared around 2.5MBP and bison about 2MBP, which in turn, enabled the evolution of animals that would hunt them; the big cats and wolves being among them.

The evolution of a more sophisticated brain enabled, among other things, animals to be able to better identify prey and to think out the tactics to succeed in the hunt or respond to threats and opportunities in the immediate environment. Intelligence was increasingly evolved into these later evolutions of species from the Intelligent Universe, and they, in turn, became parts of the Intelligent Universe.

Teeth had evolved in earlier times to enable animals to kill their prey, tear and crush the food and their digestive organs containing bacteria and chemicals that enabled them to digest the food which provided energy, which could then be distributed within the animal to maintain all the various organs and systems by some form of cardio-vascular system.

Once the food/energy source has been digested, the blood supply provided life sustaining nourishment to all the specialist cell groups within the animal's body. None of the specialised cell groups could survive alone; the interdependencies are critical and are entire; the animal life-forms are examples of ultimate system of layers of internal symbiotic relationships.

This includes the families of different bacteria which inhabit the bodies of animals and without which, the animals could not survive. This series of mutually beneficial symbiotic relationships is apparent across the animal kingdom, from the jellyfish to the horse, from the fish to man. All are part of self-sustaining systems both within themselves, with other animals and with the greater environment.

The Rise of Humankind: Homo Sapiens

Humankind is descended from primates which diverged from other mammals around 75-85MBP. Evolution then implemented a further sequence of Ideations and their resulting SFU families gave a corresponding sequence of hominid ancestors; in particular, the lineage which diverged from the chimpanzee around 7-13MBP. The chimpanzee brain size is approximately 400ml.

The first of the great apes, appeared around 6-8MBP with a similar body architecture as modern man, but much smaller brain. It is currently thought that man did not evolve from apes or gorillas but shared a common ancestor with these primates.

A possible early ancestor of man, Ardipithecus, is evidenced in the fossil record by between 3.5 and 5.8MBP, which may have been biped, that is, he may have walked upright on two legs: it was a forest dweller. A later evolution appeared by 4.2-1.9MBP in the form of Australopithecus aferensis, thought to be a more likely direct ancestor of modern man. He had a brain size of 380-430ml. There is some evidence of the use of stone tools at this time.

It is thought that Australopithecus was a pre-human species of the Hominoid genus. The earliest currently known representative of the Homo genus is Homo habilis who evolved around 2.8MBP, (probably evolving from Australopithecus) where there is evidence of more sophisticated use of stone tools.

The actual lineage of man's ancestors is open to question and occasional discoveries of new fossils causes new ideas to be considered. Homo habilis had only a modest increase in brain size compared with his predecessor and was larger than that of a chimpanzee.

Fossil evidence suggests that Africa was the cradle of human evolution and many fossils of the above species have been discovered there. At several points in the evolutionary trail, there were migrations out of Africa to the north, to Europe, Asia and elsewhere.

The environment now included all the necessary support life-forms to enable Homo genus to evolve: the trees to provide shelter, the grasses to support the grazing herds which was a possible food source, the fish, birds and the fruits and seed plants to provide the complex food chains to provide alternative and diverse forms of nourishment.

By 1.8MBP, Homo erectus had arrived, which is thought to be a possible common ancestor to both Neanderthals and modern humans, with a brain size averaging 930ml, considerably larger than that of Homo habilis. This greater brain size possibly demonstrated greater intelligence. The arrival of Homo ergaster between 1.9-1.4MBP, who evolved in Africa, represented further evolutionary progress. At that time, there is evidence of the controlled use of fire, cooking and the manufacture and use of ever more complex stone tools.

The next evolution was around 1.2MBP in the form of Homo antecessor, who may also have been the direct ancestor of both modern man and the Neanderthals.

A key feature in man's evolution is the very rapid increase in brain size in man's ancestors over the next million years; the reason for this rapid rise is not known to science. From about 2 million years ago, through to 800,000 years ago, the human ancestor brain-size increased, but only slightly. After 800,000 years BP, the brain size increased rapidly, in fact, it doubled over a period of around 600,000 years.

This implies that each generation had 125,000 more neurons in their brains than their parents! This was an extraordinary development a giant leap in Ideations. By 200,000 BP, the brain size was nearly that of modern man. This increase in brain size enabled the higher conscious to be further evolved from the earlier, rather basic version.

This development strongly indicates that there is a teleological aspect to evolution and evolutionary direction for Homo sapiens. This evolution gave Homo sapiens greater intelligence than any species up to that time: the ultimate distribution of capability from the Intelligent Universe, making Homo sapiens a major contributor to the Intelligent Universe.

From about 800,000 through to 100,000 years before present, there is thought to have been a divergence in Homo Sapiens, based on a differentiation of mitochondria (a structure found in large numbers in most cells, associated with energy production) between those in South Africa, in Central and West Africa and Eastern Africa.

What is known as "The Great Leap Forward" occurred just after this divergence, accompanied by a rapid rise in sophisticated tool making. It has been postulated that brain size alone does not define or predict intelligence; it appears to be more a question as how the brain is "wired"; the sperm whale, for example, has the largest brain size of any animal that ever existed, but it does not appear to have an intelligence superior to that of humans.

John Hawks[49], Professor of Anthropology, University of Wisconsin, states that the human brain has tripled over the last three million years, with most of that increase occurring in the most recent period. This dramatic change created a species with reasoning powers and intelligence which were superior to its predecessors, probably because of not just the brain size, but also the interconnectedness within the brain.

This gave the larger-brained hominid better ability to invent tools, hunt more successfully, also an improved ability to co-operate with others in the tribe with the development of complex language beyond the earliest of man's ancestors, which was probably when communication sounds were probably little more than those exhibited by chimpanzees.

They were able to build better shelters and clothe themselves more efficiently making them more resilient to cold weather. This enabled them to migrate into cooler northern latitudes and they developed cultures and traditions which helped bind the tribe and establish laws and taboos for the overall tribal benefit.

It is possible that modern man is descended from Homo heidelburgensis 700,000BP-300,000BP and/or Homo rhodesiensis, 800,000BP-120,000BP, each eventually had a brain size of about 90% that of modern man.

Early Homo sapiens that were anatomically close to modern man evolved between 400,000 years and 200,000 years before present, whilst their behaviour and language capabilities are more difficult to date, it was probably established by (very approximately) 50,000 years ago, where we have the arrival of fully modern man.

The first early anatomically and behaviourally modern man, Homo sapiens, lived in Europe in 43-45,000 years ago. His brain size, interestingly, was around 1600ml, a little larger than today's "modern humans". Cro-Magnon, a later arrival around 23-27,000BP, lived in Europe, and is now referred to as "European early modern human".

Neanderthals also had a slightly larger brain size than modern humans at 1200-1900ml but became extinct by about 35,000 years ago. Modern man has an average brain size of about 1200ml.

Direct ancestors of Homo sapiens are believed to have left Africa in a series of migration events between 70-300,000BP and their migration and establishment out of Africa completely replaced all earlier Homo species; they populated Europe, South East Asia, Oceania and beyond.

If it were the case that random steps in evolution alone gave rise to increasingly sophisticated Homo species, as ancestors to modern man, it would be expected that the fossil record's archaeological layers to be littered with many Hominoid fossils, representing different species that were evolved but failed and became extinct, perhaps rapidly or perhaps slowly, after a few thousand years of just clinging on, as natural selection dictated.

There is no such apparent mass-proliferation of Hominoid fossils. Those that have been found seem to represent development, with rapidly increasing intelligence and capability, indicating that evolution is not a series of random events.

The followers of Darwinism would state that each creature "evolved" from a specific ancestor in a specific manner and this, along with natural selection, is certainly a key mechanism. However, if there had been no "Ideation" or design, to influence the structure of a new evolution, and therefore, no teleological influence, and no corresponding SFU for each of the Hominid ancestors, it is difficult to believe that evolutionary and natural selection processes alone would lead unerringly to the lineage that led to modern man as described above.

There would appear to be relatively few Hominid-like species in the fossil records which would indicate that the number of species in the line were relatively few, and that, therefore, design and implementation has always had a teleological influence. Random diversification of the Homo species does not seem to have occurred.

During the evolution of man, it can be noted that there was a period of around a million years of slow and stable evolution with Australopithecus afarensis but then, there was a series of sudden transitions, as previously described, known as "punctuated equilibria" which moved the evolutions rapidly towards modern man with his greatly enhanced brain size.

The theory of punctuated equilibria goes rather against conventional Darwinism. This theory is based on the idea that, in evolutionary biology, once a species appears in the fossil record, the population will become stable, showing little evolutionary change for a considerable time. This state of little or no morphological change is known as "stasis".

When significant evolutionary change occurs, punctuated equilibria theory proposes that one species has split into two distinct species, rather than one species gradually transforming into another. Standard Darwinism proposes changes by "gradualism." However, there is little evidence of gradualism in the fossil record.

Matrix Model Theory proposes that changes are "step functions" based on new versions of the SFU family being Ideated which enabled new species to evolve. The evolution of man (shown in Fig. 9) demonstrates the clear and distinct step changes between the evolution of Australopithecus through to Homo sapiens.

Interestingly, Australopithecus was around for upwards of 2 billion years, far longer than Homo sapiens—so far. Each step of evolution established a new species, and the arrival of Homo sapiens is based on the establishment of a sequential series of ancestral species.

There is evidence that by (very approximately) 160,000 BP man's ancestors had some degree of spiritual awareness. Evidence for this is the presence of grave goods and burials, in some traditions, the red-ochre painting of the deceased before interment, certain "shamanic" images in cave paintings, among other examples, which indicates a belief in some form of "life after death."

This demonstrates some instinct that there was an "otherworld" or spirit world. This implies the capability for abstract thought and some kind of "common store" of spiritual experiences. This is strong evidence that, by this time, the higher conscious in Homo sapiens had further evolved to the sophisticated level apparent in modern man.

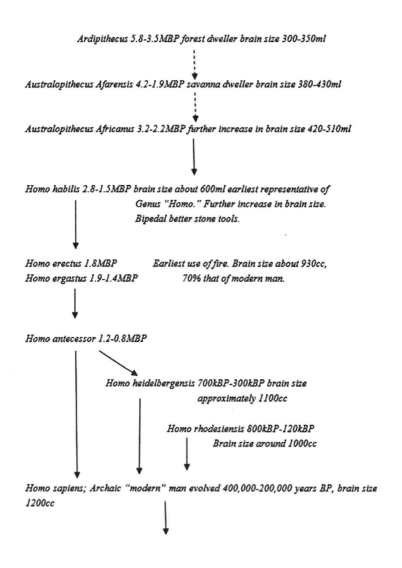

Fig.9 One possible line of human evolution (*not proven and open to question. Dates approximate*).

An approximation of the possible evolutionary line of Homo sapiens. They originally evolved in Africa. The evolutionary line between Homo ergaster and Homo sapiens probably evolved through Homo rhodesiensis, antecessor or heidelbergensis. Between 800,000 BP and 200,000 BP, the brain size doubled, which demonstrates exceptionally rapid evolution.

167

The evolution of the higher conscious was fundamental to the evolution of modern man. It was a feature which, above all, differentiated man from all other animals and gave man the unique capability to be aware of himself and, according to the various traditions, believe in aspects of another world, a world of spirit forces, perhaps of gods and the spirit world of the environment, according to his various traditions and cultures.

As described earlier, among the important aspects of the higher conscious is the capability for abstract thought, conscience and other enhanced conscious-capabilities. The main features of the higher conscious have been described in chapter 3.

Homo sapiens was thus, the ultimate inheritor of the Earth-Gaia environment. Modern man had arrived and had become the dominant species. Interestingly, one could speculate that where two Hominin species co-existed, it is possible that the larger brain version (more intelligent?) killed off the smaller brain competitors on the grounds that they were in some way "different" and therefore, may be a threat.

Even modern man has consistently killed off both animals (wolves, bears, tigers, spiders, snakes and insects) which he perceived as a threat, and other tribes and even nations of humans for various reasons.

The constant local and global wars we witness today are testament to this tendency! However, Neanderthal man has a slightly larger brain size, and was of a sturdy physique compared to Homo sapiens, indicating that he may have been able to look after himself in a conflict situation on a one-to-one basis, so his disappearance may have been due to interbreeding, disease or inability to adapt.

Modern genetics indicates that Neanderthal is not closely related to modern man[58], based on mitochondrial evidence, but do have a degree of Neanderthal DNA in them, although other sources claim there was a close relationship.

When "modern" man moved out of Africa, his migration took some tribes west to Europe, some east to Asia and, eventually beyond, whilst some remained in Africa.

The ultimate arrival of modern man was thus enabled by the formation and stabilisation of the Earth's environment, crucially the atmosphere, and a whole series of Ideations leading to a vast, complex and interdependent diversity of life forms, including the forests, trees, grasses and the denizens of the oceans and rivers, the diverse species of land dwellers and creatures that could fly. This created a complete environment which would allow the higher animals, including man, to survive.

Homo sapiens have progressed from the earliest ancestors of man, in the form of a biped with a brain size of one third of modern man, who used basic stone tools, to modern man's ability to produce the works of Bach, the theories of Einstein and putting a man on the Moon in, roughly, 2.2 million years! This achievement of the nature establishing Intelligent Universe is amazing.

Man is, by far, the most complex of all life forms so far Ideated and Effectuated, with his cultures, traditions, his science, technologies, his mythology, capability for abstract thought, religious and esoteric belief traditions.

The stone-age started around 500,000 BP (lower Palaeolithic) when man used stone knives, axes and flint implements, although he probably manufactured many articles out of wood, leather and other materials that were freely available at that time, but these would have long decayed away and are not apparent in the fossil record. The advance of man was also characterised by his inventions and his cultures.

Humankind had been successful hunter-gatherers until perhaps 12,000 BP, when tribes increasingly became farmers. This period marked the start of the agricultural revolution. Humankind stopped total dependence on hunting and gathering, but found it easier to grow the essential plants that he had gathered, so he knew where it was. He penned animals he hunted, so they were easily accessible and he could breed them to increase numbers.

History has shown that farming, which necessarily involves fencing off large tracts of land, cannot co-exist easily with hunter-gatherers, who need free access to all land to hunt and survive. This inevitably leads to the extinction of the hunter-gatherers or their transformation to become farmers themselves.

Then, somewhere around 6,500 BP (late Neolithic), someone, (perhaps a genius?) somewhere, discovered how to make metals, among them tin and copper from various rock-types, which they had learned to mine. This led to the discovery of how to make bronze.

This involved identifying the raw ore-containing rock, finding the sources of it, mining it and working out how to build a furnace of some kind to smelt it and extract the metals. In the case of bronze, he also had to deduce that mixing tin and copper produced a better and harder metal for tools. These are not obvious discoveries.

This they achieved and it led to superior tools both for agriculture and for hunting and warfare. Writing was invented, perhaps, around 6,000BP in Mesopotamia. This was a revolution which enabled thoughts, ideas, stories and knowledge to be permanently recorded and communicated to others.

About 5,500 BP the wheel was invented, ships were built, building bricks were used and the plough came into being, pulled by oxen. This represented a series of very great technological advances over a relatively short time. It was also notable how rapidly technologies in one culture spread to others, possibly aided by trade or travel connections, but in part, due to the cross communications between the SIU/SGU/SFU family at the tribal and species level.

As one tribe solved a problem or invented a new technology, others would be more likely to arrive at the same ideas or solutions, due to the interactions between their species-level SFU.

Since the Earth-Gaia Duad always finds solutions to the forces threatening life on Earth, man should be aware that, should he become a threat to Earth/Gaia and its environment, either through his activities which deplete key resources or through causing pollution or worst of all, through his sheer numbers due to human overpopulation which threaten the planet and other species, he may be 'evolved' out of existence.

Mankind risks becoming extinct, becoming another of the life forms that were Ideated, bought into being, then eliminated to make way for another. There is no guarantee that man, in his current form, is the end-product of the Ideations and of evolution. There are several mechanisms that could precipitate man's extinction, perhaps, by mass starvation due to the planet being unable to feed the ever-increasing masses, or perhaps, pandemic disease or nuclear folly.

There is also the possibility of disaster resulting from climate change, which, if not managed, could well lead to large parts of the Earth being reduced to arid or desert zones, unsuitable for agriculture with a rapidly rising human population, leading to mass migration of people from lands which cannot feed their populations to those with land that can feed them. There will also be far more chance of wars between nations as they fight over water and land access to feed their populations.

A significant crash in the insect population, particularly the pollinators, due to extensive use of powerful pesticides could also trigger a catastrophic reduction in crop yields, possibly leading to mass starvation. Humankind is intelligent enough to avoid these disasters, but it would probably require some kind of international co-operation on a grand scale and a substantial change in man's global lifestyle and attitude to nature.

Chapter 7
The Matrix Model

Overview

So far, the various domains of the physical and psi-domains have been considered as separate entities. This chapter will now show how they inter-relate and inter-connect forming the Matrix Model which applies to all living and non-living naturally occurring structures.

The same Matrix Model applies, with variations in the content of the individual domains, to all life-forms from the most basic living entity, represented in this book by the protoid, right through to the later evolutions which included bacteria, multicellular life and higher animals including Homo sapiens.

In addition, Matrix Model Theory provides a fundamental understanding as to how living entities evolve, function, interact, replicate and survive. The Matrix Model for each species includes its physical aspect, its associated domains of the conscious and unconscious and the domain of the environment relevant to the species.

The simplest and earliest evolution of the Matrix comprised only two nodes, the Universal Unconscious (the UU) and the Primary Formative Unconscious, (the PFU). They are both elements of the Intelligent Universe. As described in chapter 1, the UU was the source of all Ideations (designs). The PFU instigated, and was the catalyst for, the Big Bang, the formulation of the laws of science and the formation of the Cosmos.

Cosmos building included the formation of many phenomena and structures, which included the exploding supernova, the stars, galaxies, the formation of the solar system and planet Earth, with its amazing life-friendly environment, which were all established by the PFU using natural processes.

The Earth-Gaia environment was formed and evolved to support a wide range of life-forms. It includes a multiplicity of self-sustaining and self-regulating systems, which provide a vigorous and dynamic stability to the environment.

Once the initial environment was established, the PFU influenced natural processes to ensure the environment evolved to ensure it was always life friendly. A specific example, which was crucial to establishing suitable environment, was the establishment of the atmosphere, already described in detail evolving through several stages, and solving many serious problems as they arose.

A Theory is a system of ideas, or a model, which is intended to explain certain phenomena. Matrix Model Theory has been introduced in this book to explain many phenomena which, currently, mainstream science has no generally agreed solutions.

Many examples have been described throughout this book. Matrix Model Theory explains the triggering of the Big Bang, and establishment of an expanding universe. It explains the much later establishment of planet Earth and its complex environment.

Having established these, the next evolution was to evolve the first Species Formative Unconscious (SFU) to support the protoid. The Matrix Model for the protoid, introduced in chapters 5 and 6, is shown in Fig. 10. This is comprised of five basic nodes or domains.

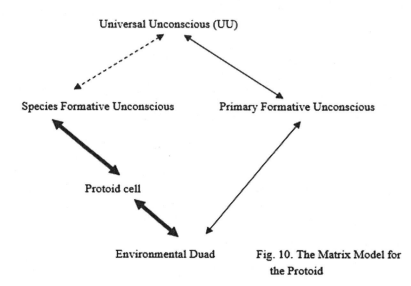

Fig. 10. The Matrix Model for the Protoid

The Matrix Model for the protoid also applies to later evolutions of all simple life-forms, including bacteria and archaea. This is a considerably simpler model than the one that later evolved for higher animals. The dominant input to the protoid cell is shown in the figure by the thick line between the cell and its SFU and its immediate environment.

Lesser, but important links between domains relevant to the cell are shown by solid lines, and the link between the Universal Unconscious and the protoid SFU is shown by a dotted line, which indicates a low level of information flow. This model contains all the domains and information sources and flows that enabled the protoid cell to come into being, to exist as a self-organising, self-sustaining structure and be able to replicate.

The SFU provided the initial coding defining form, function and behaviour, for the cell. It also provided the "trigger" to ensure the replication process happened. The basic awareness of the immediate environment surrounding the protoid (cognition) is provided, in part, by its SFU and does not constitute any degree of "consciousness" but evolved into consciousness with the evolution of higher animals.

The Species Formative Unconscious (SFU) domain ensured the correct assembly of the original amino acid chains and proteins which formed the structure of protoid cell and ensured the establishment of that species as the first viable life-form on Earth.

The SFU for the protoid differs from those of the many later evolutions of different single cell, bacterial and archaea species only in the *content* of the associated SFU domains and the physical realisation in each case, which is represented in the Matrix Model by the "physical domain".

Its ability to function was also assisted, as described earlier, by its SFU providing a degree of "awareness" of its environment and degrees of essential behaviour by means of the "borrowed mind" function. The SFU supplied this function, since the cell at this stage of evolution has no brain/mind and borrowing extremely basic cognitive or very basic mind-characteristics, was essential for survival.

As previously described, the SFU for all species usually provides "instincts" based on the collective experiences of many millions of members of that species' ancestors. However, in the case of the first protoid, there were no ancestors to provide these experiential memories; the protoid was the first living entity. The SFU collective unconscious for this cell was therefore "empty".

As thousands of generations of protoids lived and died, their experiences were lodged within the SFU and started to form a level of elementary instincts within their collective unconscious sub-set of its SFU.

A degree of cognition is essential for any living entity to survive. The protoid SFU provided this, ensuring that it collected the correct materials from the environment to provide its energy requirements and ensure that it collected and processed the correct materials from its environment to allow it to create a copy of itself for replication.

The SFU then triggered the whole process of replication, ending when cell-division took place (it is likely that the protoid replicated by cell-splitting), so that one protoid becomes two; essentially, it had then solved the problem of replication. There would have been, in all probability, billions of generations of protoids before later evolutions of more advanced life-forms came into existence, and the protoid either evolved into a more advanced species or eventually became extinct.

The Matrix Model for all bacteria species is identical in terms of the nodal structural to that just described for the protoid, but the SFU coding is different, and the cell structure (physical aspect) domains are more complex. Also, the awareness of the environment was more sophisticated due to evolution and mutation adding complexity and cognition into the organism's structure from their associated SFUs.

As Matrix Models evolved, they supported later evolutions of ever more complex species. Many more Matrix Models and their associated SFUs evolved which led to more species being established.

Continuing this evolutionary theme, an example of a much later evolution of the Matrix Model is that for the bee which is shown in Fig.11. This Matrix Model is similar for all insects, including ants and termites.

This later evolution shows a total of nine nodes. In addition to the domains described above for the protoid and bacteria, there is the SGU node which, as described previously, evolved so that each hive or bee community, had its own SGU, each one supporting one hive or bee-community providing the ability for the bees within each hive to function as a super-organism or as a mutually co-operative community. The bees generally act with purpose and each bee knows its function due to its close communication with its associated SGU.

The bee-SFU is common to all bees of the same species and contains instincts common to all bee communities and some memory patterns of the key experiences of millions of generations of previous bee-communities, which are lodged in the SFU domain as instincts.

Matrix Model for the bee (the same structure for termites, ants and other insects but with different SFU, SGU content, and different lower conscious and physical domains)

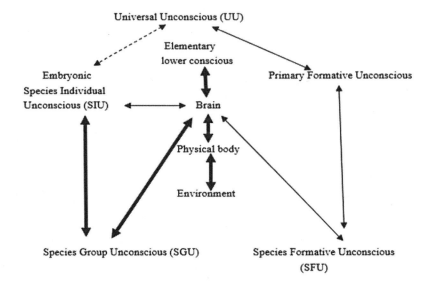

Fig.11. Typical Matrix Model for a bee. The overwhelming influence is from the SGU acting at group (hive) level. This is supported by a basic lower conscious and a strong interaction with the environment. A similar Matrix Model would apply to termites or ants and other insects. The bee-SGU is marginally different for each beehive and is unique to each hive. It operates on every bee in the hive using psi-fields. The elementary SIU gives the bee a limited degree of ability to function as an individual.

Bees have the largest effective brain in the insect world, having around one million neurons; humans in contrast have over one billion. Thus, by interfacing with its SFU/SGU/SIU, the bees are provided with a degree of instinctive "knowledge" of which plants and flowers to approach for nectar, how to communicate with other members of its community and how to play its part in enabling the hive to act as a coherent community, as described in chapter 4.

This is due to the SFU/SGU/SIU nodes providing an element of "borrowed mind". Although bees have a brain, it is distributed across its body and has several basic functions. This is because, as evolution of all species continued, increasing amounts of mind/brain-related functionality was transferred from the

SFU/SGU/SIU nodes to the developing brain and genome of the species in question, providing later species with greater degrees of independence.

It is interesting to note that the olfactory part of the insect brain is apparently the same as that of humans. Recent research has shown that some insects have a degree of consciousness and even the possibility of a degree of self-awareness.

The SFU/SGU/SIU combination continues to provide the insect with formative coding which, in conjunction with the bee-DNA, ensures that bees of a specific species are all constructed in a virtually identical way, and have very similar behaviour and function, with the queen exhibiting her own form, function and behaviour. Bees also have a relatively sophisticated ability to communicate with one another.

Also appearing in this Matrix Model is the bee lower conscious. This provides the bee with a much greater ability to have a conscious awareness of its environment and respond to threats and opportunities as they appear. It provides the basic fight or flight capability and the determination to protect its hive, protect its queen and co-operate in the formation of a new swarm as a newly hatched queen departs from one hive to form a new one.

As previously described, when a new queen leaves a hive to form a new hive, the bees that leave with her, essential to the establishment of the new hive, must "know" which of them must do so and the sequence of activities they must complete to establish the new hive. Part of this comes from the new hive-SGU and part from the bee's SFU, which is the source of all instincts for the species.

The bee has a certain degree of independence as seen by its embryonic SIU, although it has a dominant SGU. The SIU also provides the bee with a degree of long-term memory within its basic personal unconscious. The combination of the SFU, SIU and SGU provide the bee with a degree of "borrowed mind" when required to enhance its own cognitive capability. This provides each bee within a hive to have an enhanced ability to interact with its environment and interact with other members of its hive.

The bee SFU in particular also provides a functional memory in the form of instincts of, for example, which plants to access for nectar, since each foraging bee must function efficiently from its first forage, without spending long periods of time "learning" which flowers to access, based on the combined experiences of the bee's ancestors for that species of bee.

The Matrix Model is easily extended to higher more complex animal groups. The SFU for each species, as previously mentioned, contains some memory function and a compilation of the stronger memories and experiences of billions of ancestral members of the species. Instincts enable some innate inborn ability to behave in a certain way: the SFU for each bee species contains the set of instincts, memories and influences relevant to its associated species.

Fig 12 shows the overall structure of the Matrix Model for humankind, with the interconnections of the ten nodes which represent the complete entity which we call human.

The Matrix Model for Humankind

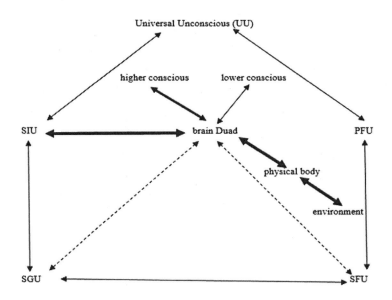

PFU=Primary Formative Unconscious SFU= Species Formative Unconscious
SGU=Species Group Unconscious   SIU=Species Individual Unconscious

Figure 12. *The Ten-domain Matrix domains for a human, showing the interconnections between the various nodes and how they relate to one another. The collective unconscious proposed first by C Jung resides within the SFU which contains the archetypes, as described in chapter 3. Instincts are also sourced from this domain formed by vast numbers of memories from countless generations of humankind ancestors. The personal unconscious resides within the SIU. The higher conscious domain which evolved for humans is also included. All higher animals have the same ten domain Matrix Model, as shown above, but with different content in each domain. There are also lesser links between the PFU and environment and also between the SIU and the physical body from the point of conception.*

178

This is a much later evolution than the Matrix Models so far considered. This is the most complex of all the models and supports the most complex of all animals.

Although the Matrix Model domains are arranged in the same structure for all higher or more sophisticated and complex animals, including all mammals, apes, monkeys and birds and several other species, the content of the domains is hugely different for each species. For some species, the higher conscious domain is either missing or has considerably reduced functionality compared with that corresponding domain for mankind.

Also, the content of the SFU/SGU/SIU domains are radically different between the various species because they ensure each species is structurally and behaviourally different. Similarly, the content of the genome for each species is different and is species-specific. The genome is part of the physical body domain.

The function of the higher conscious domain has been described in detail in chapter 3, and it is a key difference between man and earlier-evolutions of animals, as shown in Fig 11, where the node is missing altogether. In man, the higher conscious is very well developed. Some higher animals have been shown to have some of the characteristics provided by the higher conscious, including aspects such as loyalty, affection, friendship and other emotions.

In all higher animals, the SIU node evolved to give higher animals, including man, a great deal of independence compared with much earlier evolutions of life. The borrowed mind has a far smaller contribution than in early life-forms, although the SIU still interacts continuously with the brain-duad in the case of higher animals although much more of the role of the borrowed mind attribute has, by evolution, been permanently installed in the higher animal's brain and more of the form-coding evolved to be resident in its genome, although the SIU still makes crucial contributions, one example being how it provides an explanation to the "missing heredity problem" previously described.

Evolution provided each new species with increasingly more complex brain and mind capability, and therefore, have much more autonomy than earlier, less complex species, giving them an enhanced ability to think more for themselves, and, therefore, be more independent.

Where the link between domains is strong, the interconnection is continuous and is shown by a continuous line linking the nodes. Where there is a very dominant interaction, for example, between the SIU and the brain-duad as shown in Fig.12 there is a wider, more solid line denoting much stronger information flows.

Images, thoughts, memories and symbols flow between the SIU to the brain-duad. The brain filters and processes this information and it affects conscious thoughts, motivation, decisions, prejudices and actions. One of the key information flows is that of long-term memories, which flow from the SIU personal unconscious into the brain on demand, to be made conscious.

For all higher animals, including man, the brain-duad is the key communications hub. It has continuous inputs from the physical body senses which relate directly to the environment, as well as the strong inputs from the higher conscious, the lower conscious and the SIU. There are also lesser or intermittent inputs from the other domains of the unconscious shown in Fig.12 as dotted lines on the Matrix.

In all Figures, the links between the domains indicate various degrees of communication which is enabled by means of psi-fields; the Matrix is based on information flows.

The sensory inputs to the brain also provide inputs from the senses which allow an awareness of the environment, and which relate to the environment. For ancient man, this was a vital set of inputs, since a keen awareness of the conditions and activities of all relevant aspects of his local environment was important to his survival. Post industrial revolution, man has become more insulated from "nature" in its widest sense.

In western societies, we no longer (generally speaking) have to hunt for food, nor do we starve if there is a harvest failure, nor do we live in a degree of fear from predators; they have largely been contained or eliminated. This has caused, over a long period of time, a diminution in our closeness, respect and knowledge of our environment and nature for most people, with potentially seriously negative consequences.

The Matrix Model also demonstrates the inter-relationship between the psi-domain and the physical domain entities, since the domains of the unconscious, together with the higher conscious and the psi-aspect of the brain, are all domains within the psi-domain. It shows diagrammatically that the living world depends totally on a continuous and harmonious relationship with the psi-domains and the physical domains.

As previously described, the Intelligent Universe can be described as originally existing solely within the Universal Unconscious. For higher animals, intelligent capabilities and attributes evolved into their associated SIUs. Thus, intelligence, in all its various forms, from the merest degree of cognition and basic environmental awareness found in, for example, bacteria, through to the vastly more sophisticated intelligence of higher animals and humans was established.

Intelligence, or "mind stuff", thus became widely distributed in nature following millions of years of evolution and the basic need for each generation to have the mind-tools required to survive and thrive. The distribution of intelligence throughout all forms of life and within nature eventually gave us an increasingly Intelligent Universe.

This level of intelligence within nature ensured a teleological progression of evolution of life-forms and the environment in which they could survive; intelligence begets purpose. Every living entity across every species could effectively be regarded as a "cell" in the universal mind.

The Environment

The environment is essentially a duad functioning in both the physical domain and the psi-domain; each domain has a different environment. The physical environment for any species includes the parts of the cosmos, at least the Sun and Moon in particular, that any species is aware of, but is dominated by the local micro-environment surrounding each individual organism.

All life-forms were dependent on their local environment to supply food, water, warmth from the Sun and shelter of some kind. In many cases, they also needed an environment that could provide a degree of protection from predators. The environment is a broad and diverse domain of the Matrix Model. All higher animals, including humans, interact continuously with their environment via their senses and it has a direct effect on their behaviour and decision making in many circumstances.

To a large extent, modern humankind has replaced many of these hard-won goals with societies where money buys their shelter, food and heat, he has his water delivered "on tap" and their energy is similarly supplied, and they generally have their shelter built for them.

This has widened the gap between modern man and his natural environment, and greatly increased man's vulnerability, since the traditional survival skills have been largely lost and a dependency on generally available electrical and gas energy and on the efficiency of global farming. Global trade has grown to the extent that failure of any of these functions could prove catastrophic.

The night sky with a celestial canopy of stars and planets and the dominant Moon were as familiar to our ancestors as an important part of their environment as they are to people today. During the day, the giant form of the Sun was and is dominant.

There is also evidence among some early traditions, including shamans, that they believed that the Earth was populated by a realm of spirits, that had to be appeased or could perhaps, be approached to assist a tribe or individual. To the Shaman and his tribe, this assumed "other world" was, to them, an important part of their perceived environment.

The Physical Body

The physical body domain of the Matrix Model for humankind is a complex collection of cells, organs, muscle and bone. This represents the individual's physical presence in the physical domain. This physical entity exists only for as long as man is physically "alive", and the entire structure returns to the earth or air after death, and the entity: decays and ceases to exist as a physical, living entity.

The physical aspect provides humankind with senses to allow awareness of, and interaction with, the physical environment; the ability to see either food or danger, the ability to fight or flee and the ability to procreate, communicate with others and form communities. These capabilities enabled him better to survive and flourish over a wide range of situations, threats, climates and environments.

Homo sapiens is not just an animal living within the environment but is inherently part of it. They have evolved capabilities that enable their survival and for them to flourish, and by the actions of people over many centuries, have changed the environment, in some cases irreversibly.

The move from hunter-gatherer to farming, with the fencing of land, the mass felling of trees to form fields, removed vast tracts of land from wandering herds and grazing animals and removed woodland habitats for thousands of species.

Humankind uses and absorbs resources from the physical Earth, in terms of food, water and air and many other materials and emits waste products and exhaled air which he changes, causing it to be slightly richer in carbon dioxide, and lower in oxygen than the air he inhaled.

The human body is amazingly complex, incorporating millions of bacteria of differing types which have specific functions and without which the body could not survive, many forming symbiotic relationships with other structures within the body.

Earlier chapters have described the capability of bacteria to multiply very quickly; there are therefore mechanisms to automatically regulate and stabilise the number of each bacteria type within the human body or else their numbers would overwhelm their host.

These mechanisms ensure that the numbers created by cell division are matched by the bacterial mortality rate, without any conscious effort from the host. There are several other complex and essential regulatory systems within the physical body and such systems form part of the human overall self-regulating, self-sustaining systems.

Every species has a unique physical domain which is the entirety of their physical form/body, whether it be a bacterium, an insect or humankind.

The Human Brain Duad

The brain has a physical aspect which can be measured, weighed and analysed, and a psi-aspect which shadows the physical brain but exists wholly in the psi-domain. Both aspects act as the communications hub with the other domains of the Matrix Model, and there are continuous flows of information between them. As described earlier, the combination of the physical brain and psi-brain form the brain-duad, that is part of the overall individual human mind.

The physical and psi-aspects of the brain for every individual maintain continuous links with the domains of the unconscious, particularly their associated SIU. The brain-duad has the capacity for rational (or, some might say, occasionally irrational) reasoning and thoughts, and to make decisions, based in part, from the physical inputs from the five senses: sight, hearing, touch, smell and taste.

The body responds to commands from the brain, some of which are due to thought processes, some are automatic, some instinctive. The physical brain also incorporates a physical *short-term* memory. In terms of structure, the brain is a complex collection of specialised cells, as detailed in chapter 3, arranged in a form of interconnected nodes, enabling electrical impulses to travel around inside the brain and be processed.

They enable the brain to form symbols, images, thoughts, reason and make decisions with the additional benefit of continuous inputs from its associated SIU for each individual, its internal structure, the environment and the other nodes of the Matrix, as shown in Fig.12.

The brain-duad is also the communications link between the unconscious domains and the higher and lower conscious domains, the physical body and the senses linked to the environment. Thoughts, ideas, memories and intuitive influences flow from the SIU and, to a lesser extent, the other elements of the SFU family. These thoughts, ideas and memories can be made conscious by being channelled into the brain-duad domain, and thence into the conscious domains.

Post-death, the physical brain dissipates and decays away whilst the psi-aspect continues as part of the post-death individual. This enables the psi-brain to continue to communicate with the Matrix Model domains of the unconscious and the higher conscious, which also survive death. This further enables the post-death humankind to continue with a conscious awareness of their psi-domain and with their psi-environment.

The brain function is not just a "data processing" entity, but forms complex 3D images, thoughts, sometimes abstract and ideas. Some of these thoughts and images are influenced by the content of the SIU which contains the personal unconscious, which is the main *long-term memory* store for man and higher animals, as will be described in detail in the next section. Such thoughts and images are also influenced by stimuli from the immediate environment and are also shaped, among other things, by memories of previous experience, prejudice, inclination, culture and instincts as well as logic.

Scientists can tap into the physical brain, measuring electrical activity and analysing the correlation between specific locations in the brain and the associations with some physical functions; for example, the locations responsible for sight and hearing capability have been mapped as specific physical locations within the physical brain.

Other key functions of the physical body are controlled by the brain. Feedback loops between the body and the brain enable key parameters of the physical body to be controlled, for example, body temperature and the cardio-vascular system and heartrate among many others, to ensure that the overall human-body "system" functions as a series of stable, self-regulating systems, without conscious involvement.

The way in which the unconscious domains access the brain-duad of an individual to make symbols, events and images conscious, is by creating the electrical activity in specific areas of the brain. This is achieved by psi-fields which are generated by the domains of the unconscious, the two conscious domains and the brain-duad itself.

The physical brain operates and functions primarily by the interactions of vast numbers of electrical signals, via a network of different specialised structures, including neurons and axons. The interconnecting nerve fibres form a three-dimensional grid[53] carrying electrical signals which represent the language that the brain understands. They enable the images, symbols and events to then become conscious and have some form of meaning to an individual.

The images experienced during dreaming may be of almost any type; realistic or sometimes confused, bizarre or even fantastical, replays of actual events, or distortions and scenes of events which in fact may never have happened. Dreams are certainly capable of creative imagery.

The themes originate in certain domains of the unconscious, although there are many theories as to why we dream and whether there is meaning in the content; dreams have been the subject of much research. We become consciously aware of the content of our dreams whilst we sleep, although many may be forgotten, or perhaps, consigned to the memory within the personal unconscious domain when we awake.

A holistic consideration as to how the brain-duad functions and what it processes in parallel (thinking, dreaming, imagining, analysing, together with emotional and metaphysical thought), indicates that it must have active overall control mechanisms, co-ordinating these sometimes-parallel activities.

Francis Crick[56], famous molecular biologist, found himself forced to the conclusion that these parallel brain functions must depend on "some kind of overall control system.". For humans, such an overall control system is provided by the SIU operating and interacting with the brain-duad of an individual.

Memory

The memory capability, which enables the storing and retrieval of information based on past experiences, information passed on by others, or by personal observation. It is a vital facility in enabling man to survive. He must have the ability to recall locations, identify colleagues and recall events and above all, learn.

In this case, the ability to learn, meant the ability to remember solutions to problems that have previously been solved or information taught by others, especially those relating to the location and identification of food sources, threats to safety, knowledge of the local environment and procreation.

Attempts have been made over the years to isolate the physical location of the memory faculty within the physical brain. It was thought that there was some form of electro-chemical trace left within the brain as the "memory trace". However, so far, all attempts to isolate such traces have failed[17].

Also, all attempts to localise the memory have failed; the researchers have found that even when they believed that they had found the memory location within the brain, they were amazed to find that the memory survived destruction of their supposed memory location.

If humans are supposed to have a specific memory trace for every experience they have had, there would be vast numbers of traces stored in the brain; but no such trace has ever been identified.

It is currently thought by some scientists that the hippocampus, a part of the physical brain, may play a part in memory, since when it is damaged, it can restrict the ability to store new memories. However, experiments have shown[5] that memories are not actually *stored* in the hippocampus but "somewhere else", a location unknown to science.

It would seem that, whilst the hippocampus was in some way necessary to *access* the memories, it was not in itself, the actual memory store. Eric Kandel[57], who was awarded a Nobel Prize for work on memory, made the point that although the hippocampus was required for the initial storage of a memory, it was not required once the memory had been stored.

Some extreme experiments have been, unfortunately, carried out on animals by Karl Lashley[30] where the entire motor cortex of the animal was removed, and yet memory was still retained. Lashley made attempts to find memory traces within the brain. In a wide variety of experiments, he taught animals a wide range of tasks, some simple and some complex.

He then cut various nerve tracts or removed portions of their brains and measured the effects on their memories of the learned tasks. He found that with rats, even when nearly the entire motor cortex was removed, they remembered tasks they had been trained to do.

With chimpanzees, who had been trained to open various latch boxes, he removed almost the entire motor cortex, and they were still able to open the boxes; they had retained their memories. Different areas of the animal's brains, including the cerebellum were destroyed, with no long-term reduction in their memory capability.

The long-standing theory, that specific "memory cells," or specialised RNA-type cells, host memory data has now largely been abandoned.[17] As Francis Crick[56] described, almost all the molecules in the body are replaced in timescales that vary between a matter of minutes or hours, others may stay active for a matter of years, whilst neurons which are cells within the brain, in general, last a lifetime and are not replaced when they die.

However, 80% of RNA cells die in less than 2 minutes, the rest die within 5 to 10 minutes, and some last for up to 5 hours. If memory traces had been stored within these cells, they would vanish as the cells died. This would make it difficult for any form of long-term memory traces to be maintained.

A mechanism whereby some molecules might have the capability to pass on their memory traces to replacement molecules before they died would be the only viable solution, however, no such mechanism has ever been found.

As Sheldrake writes[17], more than a century of well-funded research has failed to pin down memory traces in the brain. He concludes the reason for this is that they do not exist!

Further research looking for memory mechanisms in chemical changes, changes in neurons or other cells within the brain, has resulted in the conclusion that by some means, memory "resides" elsewhere than in the physical brain.[12]

As previously described, the proposal made by Professor Freud and Professor Jung[20] is that each individual has a unique personal unconscious. According to Matrix Model Theory, this is inherently a sub-set of his SIU. The psi-brain which exists together with the physical brain, as a duad, contains only short-term memory capability.

All higher animals, including rats and chimpanzees, have their associated SIUs, which contains their personal unconscious domains which, as described earlier, is their source of long-term memory storage. This provides a comprehensive memory store for the important or key memories of the individual's experiences. In the case of the animal experiments described above, the animal's memories of this training would be permanently stored in their personal unconscious domain.

These memories may well have been quite strongly etched into the animal's personal unconscious since the training was accompanied by constant repetition.

Such strong memory traces within their personal unconscious would have enabled them to recall their training, even after the removal of parts of their physical brains.

The memories were there, permanently ready for recall, as demonstrated by these experiments. The brain-duad interfaces with both these domains of the unconscious, moving content from the personal unconscious long-term memory into the physical short-term memory when required, where the content can be made conscious.

This explains why no long-term "memory traces" have ever been found within the physical human brain: they simply are not there. It also explains why, having trained rats and chimpanzees, destruction of major parts of their brains did not stop them remembering their training.

The SIU, with its personal unconscious, contains the memories which can be accessed by the brain-duad to restore memories to the conscious faculties, even when these memories are from the distant past-experiences of the individual.

These memories are induced into the conscious by psi-fields interacting between the brain-duad and the SIU. These stimulate the brain, inducing electrical impulses which can be measured, and which form the complex images which constitute the memory. These signals are the "language" of the brain.

Short-term memory remains a faculty within the brain-duad. Experiences for an individual are, therefore, transferred as memories to the SIU and its associated personal unconscious within a short time. They then become permanent memories which can, in most cases, be accessed at any time.

As an individual ages, their brain's ability to interface and interact with the domains of the unconscious can become impaired and consequently, their ability to access the personal unconscious and its memory bank becomes less efficient, which has the effect of the individual experiencing apparent memory loss: although the memories are still there in the personal unconscious part of their SIU, they cannot easily access them.

If there is serious or extreme damage to the brain, although the memories still exist undamaged in the personal unconscious, both the physical and psi-brain may not be able to function to retrieve these easily, even though the brain has an amazing ability to "re-wire" itself following damage. In many cases, this reconfiguration may result in the memories once again becoming available from the personal unconscious.

With some cases of brain impairment, for example, in some cases of dementia, the short-term memory is poor, but the patient often has little difficulty in remembering things from the more distant past. However, the condition can become so severe, that even access to all memories can become difficult.

This breakdown in the brain-SIU communication link will lead to severe impairment of many faculties and would lead to symptoms which include a complete mental malfunction.

Having reviewed many of the above experiments and their conclusions, Sheldrake writes:

Memory is both everywhere and nowhere in particular.

Sheldrake also states that our memories may not be wholly within our brains. This is one of the key contentions of Matrix Model Theory.

If memories held in the personal unconscious have not been accessed for a long period of time, they may be more difficult to access; but they are still there. Since all levels of the unconscious are psi-domain based, they are not held within the physical domain and are thus "non-material".

Acquired Characteristics

Mankind is adept at learning to solve problems. Ancient ancestors, perhaps, had to solve problems concerned only with getting enough to eat and making structures to provide him with shelter, and protect himself from predators. Learning was originally passed on from one generation to the next by example, word of mouth and, much later by writing.

Evolution is enabled by changes to the genes of a species. Lamarck, a 19th century zoologist, along with Charles Darwin assumed that learned behaviour could be *inherited*. This implied that learned behaviour somehow modified genes.

This is known as Lamarkian inheritance. In modern times, geneticists insist that learned behaviour cannot be passed on by inheritance since the genes cannot be modified because of characteristics that life-forms acquire during their lives, or through things they have learned during their lives.

Lamarkian supporters, who site examples of learned behaviour being "passed on" to their offspring, assumed that, somehow, genetic modification must take place but could not suggest how this could occur.

There is an epigenetic mechanism which can affect which traits are inherited, whereby although genes themselves are not modified, they can be affected by chemical modification, which is not a genetic modification and not part of the DNA sequence.

In this case, a chemical attachment to DNA can determine which genes are switched on or off, and this determines which proteins a cell makes. But genes in themselves cannot explain form, function or behaviour as previously described.

In current science, there is no known mechanism whereby behaviour that has been learned by one member of a species can cause specific modifications to the genes of that individual such that their offspring, or indeed other members of the species, would be able to inherit or be aware of that learned behaviour. An alternative mechanism will now be described.

McDougall's Experiment with Rats

To demonstrate this concept of learned behaviour being made available to the next generation, some experiments were undertaken by William McDougall[5] at Harvard in 1920. He trained rats to escape from a water maze by swimming to a ramp, climbing it, and exiting by one of two exits.

The brightly illuminated exit gave them a small electric shock as they passed through; the dimly illuminated one was harmless and they could escape consistently without discomfort.

The first generation of rats made an average of 165 errors before they were consistently leaving by the painless route. Subsequent generations learned more quickly and by the thirtieth generation, they made an average of only 20 errors.

Although he interpreted this as evidence for the Lamarkian inheritance mechanism whereby the rat's genes had been modified by the learning, many biologists found this difficult to accept. No one else had an explanation for the result.

However, the experiment was repeated by Francis Crew in Edinburgh (1936). The very first generation of rats he used (obviously different entirely from those used by McDougall) learned very quickly, averaging only 25 errors from the start; his rats seemed to have learned some of the lessons originally learned by McDougall's rats. The rats were unrelated, so could not have passed on any memories by any genetic modification mechanism.

This can be explained by Matrix Model Theory, since the SFU can provide a species wide memory as instincts where the memory traces are very strong, which is one of the prime functions of the SFU. The methodology of this experiment would have resulted in extremely strong memory traces within the conscious and unconscious domains of the rats.

The information flow, relating to the rat's experiences was from each individual rat's SIU, then though to the group's SGU, and finally, due to the magnitude of the unpleasant experiences and repetition, through to the species SFU, where they were lodged within the collective unconscious as instincts. Here, the instincts so formed can then become available to all members of that rat-species.

The large number of repetitions of the experiment by the first rats led to a reinforcement of which was the "painless exit", which made it *more likely* that the subsequent rats would choose that correct exit. Clearly, the rats' memories generated by the experiment would be very strong, due to a combination of pain and repetition.

Further tests were done in Melbourne by Wilfred Agar, who also found similar results; the rats used in his experiment improved at an increasingly rapid rate right from the initiation of the experiment. He also repeated the test with rats not directly descended from the previously used rats, and they also showed a similar improvement. They appeared to have absorbed the learning of other rats, even when unrelated.

Lamarkian theory supposed that the rat's genes were supposedly modified by experience, so that memories could be passed on to offspring by genetic modification. The results of these experiments demonstrate that the Lamarkian theory is wrong, since the results were the same, even for the rats not related to the rats used in earlier experiments.

Genetic information could not have been passed on to the unrelated rats used in later experiments. The rats that had "solved" the escape problem were able to share their knowledge with other members of the species via their shared SFU, even sharing these memories with rats that were completely unrelated, but of the same species.

Since these memories which provided the solution to the problem was available only as an instinct, and not as a clear memory, the results of the later generations of rats were still not 100% but appeared to follow on from the best results of previous generations; they were more likely to choose the painless exit.

The Lower Conscious

As described in chapter 3, the brain includes a faculty which is the ability to make images, thoughts and ideas conscious. In general, the facility of the conscious is that which gives us an awareness of our environment and ourselves. It is a centre of mental activity which, to a certain extent, determines our courses of action.

Each of these levels of the conscious are centres of cognition, which is the capability of the mental act of acquiring knowledge which includes perception, intuition and reasoning but have many different roles.

The lower conscious domain is that primal faculty which includes the base survival drives which enabled the earliest ancestors of humans to survive. It includes a level of reasoning which includes the fight or flight decision-making attribute: the drive to feed the body, hunt and procreate.

These attributes are a characteristic of many animals; it represents the "animal" aspects of humankind. These attributes have enabled them to survive and adapt and take action to ensure they and his offspring survive. The positive aspects of the lower conscious can include the nurturing and protection of offspring and partner, the drive to cooperate with other members of the tribe to achieve common objectives, logical thought and certain forms of problem solving.

Thus, the animal aspect of man was vital to his survival in earliest times and is still very much part of man today: civilised behaviour is just a thin veneer which can crack and be displaced by "animal man" when certain situations arise.

The earliest evolution of human's very distant ancestors had only a lower conscious and a basic, primitive higher conscious This level of consciousness enabled them to adapt to environmental changes, hunt, make tools and communicate with others, and importantly, find a mate. It also enabled them to form into tribes for mutual benefit; a lone hominoid was, and still is, very vulnerable.

The Higher Conscious

The other conscious element of the Matrix Model for man is the higher conscious. It is a much later evolution than the lower conscious domain for Homo sapiens and was directly related to the very rapid increase in brain size over a short period of time from around 800,000 years ago. It is one of the ways in which man differs from most animals.

The attributes of the higher conscious include, among other attributes, a level of appreciation of creativity, spirituality, our understanding of the concept of justice and integrity among many other attributes and is a key aspect of an individual's personality. The higher conscious also provides an appreciation of art, love, hate, abstract thought and conscience.

Conscience is defined as a sense of right or wrong, that to some extent governs a person's actions, or sense of guilt or anxiety. Clearly, the effect of conscience on any individual, and what weight he or she places on it, depends on culture, tribal or family tradition or peer pressure and personality. The higher conscious is also characterised, in some individuals, by a spiritual belief system to some greater or lesser extent.

Mysticism and religious beliefs and superstitions stem from this level of consciousness. As man evolved, so his higher conscious evolved and continues to do so. Many in modern society reject spiritual beliefs or religions of any kind since they prefer a completely mechanistic core belief system.

Since, like religion, the mechanistic world view can neither be proven to be correct nor disproven, it is a "faith" on the same footing as the religions that some disparage. All these belief systems stem from the higher conscious and are also strongly influenced, and even defined, by group culture and tradition.

These can be referred to as "soft" attributes because they are not directly associated with man's survival, they vary between different societies and even change with time within each society. The other difference between lower and higher consciousness is that whereas the lower conscious is, to a large extent, common to all mankind and originates from the times when the first Homo sapiens and his ancestors walked the Earth and is, therefore, independent of race, culture of tradition, the higher conscious is strongly dependent on all three, which is why. these attributes are not universal and differ between cultures and with time.

We can take a few examples to illustrate this. In historical times in the western world, slavery was regarded as just and beneficial (to the victim) providing him with work and Christianity thus "saving his soul". However, cultural change and a massive shift in values in later times in western culture, made slavery the embodiment of injustice and a despicable imposition on the victims.

Another justice example, whereas some cultures perceive judicial execution as acceptable; other cultures find it barbaric.

Different cultures have evolved different values, traditions and concepts of justice and these in turn have evolved over time, even within one tribe or grouping. Thus, the values established within the higher conscious of any tribe or culture are changeable over time and are never absolute.

Different values in appreciation of music, art, literature and poetry can also be identified; they are strongly dependent on the culture creating and experiencing it and demonstrably varies even between individuals of the same culture; there is an individualistic aspect to it.

The higher conscious function, although present in all mankind, is not universal in its reasoning. It is an extremely important element of man being able to define values, direct the perception of a society, and in part, inspires man to seek knowledge in general, and within the fields of science, religion and mysticism.

As has been described in the previous chapter, from his earliest evolution, humankind has been a thinking reasoning creature, creating explanations for the phenomena and events they experienced in the environment, nature and the skies and cosmos around them and invoking myths, legends and folklore to pass this understanding to the next generation.

There is some direct evidence for the establishment of the earliest higher conscious faculty from as far back as 160,000 years ago. This timeline is not known exactly; it may have coincided what has been called, the "great leap forward" in more advanced cognitive thinking which has been put between 70,000 and 200,000 years ago, and possibly related to the time when Homo sapiens' brain size massively increased over a short time as previously described.

One clue is to find out when humankind had developed a spiritual dimension which, in part, is evidenced from finding examples of cave paintings, some with a distinctly shamanic frame of reference to produce art images and carved religious objects, as previously mentioned.

Evidence of a belief in a world beyond the physical is found in that they buried their dead, sometimes with basic grave goods implying some form of ritual. This is strong evidence that these early people had a conscious belief in an "otherworld" Middle-Earth or spiritual dimension, according to their culture.

Grave goods were thought to be of use to the deceased on their journey to the afterlife and perhaps to make the afterlife more comfortable. There is evidence that, among Homo sapiens groups, there has been found evidence of bodies buried covered in red ochre (the red colouring associated with life) together with offerings of food, tools, fresh flowers deposited in the grave and ritual burials. These are examples of some concept of an "afterlife" among these people.

One of the earliest figurines discovered is the half-man (woman), half lion found in the Stadel Cave in Germany, dated to be about 32,000 years old, the Palaeolithic era. This is another indicator of the higher conscious evolution; the ability of man to form abstract thoughts, leading to art based on imagined beings which do not actually exist.

Stone goddess figurines have been found, thought to date back to Mesolithic times; one such example known as the Venus of Dolni Vestonice, is the earliest known depiction of a human body from roughly 4,900 BP.

Shamanism is one of the earliest known and widespread of belief systems[38]. The Shaman was often a tribal elder who was believed to be able to travel to the realm of the spirits and negotiate with the spirits on behalf of the tribe or perhaps, to cure an illness in one or more individuals. This belief system still exists in some parts of the world; there are many different traditions and many different roles.

In some traditions, the shaman would enter a trance-like state, often by rhythmic drumming or dance. Having gained their perceived access to the world of the spirits, they would be expected to fight or placate malevolent spirits or gain favours from friendly ones, to protect the tribe from enemies or bring about a beneficial outcome of behalf of the tribe. An example could be healing the sick or perhaps, somehow enabling a successful hunt.

According to some traditions, becoming a shaman was associated with some form of "initiation" ritual, whereby the shaman is "reconstructed" mentally or physically. They were effectively early priests, doctors, or sorcerers and would have been powerful folk within the tribe. These belief systems were certainly not essential for man to survive, and not an evolutionary necessity, but stems from the evolution of the higher conscious.

Having such a strong awareness of "other-worlds" is a rather sophisticated evolution of thought, unique to humankind; an abstract attribute and would have been especially important to the tribes, as they were sometimes only one step ahead of starvation or death by disease and would possibly have seen spirits in almost everything around them.

They believed they needed to enlist the help of these spirits in any way they could, according to their tribal traditions. Such belief systems were part of the tribal culture and probably helped bond the tribe together and were an important faculty of the higher conscious.

These early ancestors of man could communicate well, lived in communities, and had their own mythology, which enabled them to pass on an understanding of the world around them, give knowledge necessary for survival to their offspring and, as their higher conscious evolved, describe their understanding of values and their understanding of a "spirit world". To many of these cultures, spirits were present in everything within their environment: wells, mountains, streams, forests and animals.

Where war, crime and destruction are instigated by man, it is often the lower conscious suppressing the higher which is the cause. This can, in some individuals give rise to irreconcilable inner conflicts. With other individuals, the higher conscious can be under-developed or perverted which can lead to the domination of the lower conscious.

The higher conscious can also have negative attributes: it is also the domain of envy, greed, hatred, harmful religions and distortions of religion and negative aspects of the occult. Very strongly held religious values and views which instigate the destruction of others who think differently has been common in history and can still be observed today.

Conflicts between the higher conscious, which contains the "conscience" attribute, and the lower conscious, if not reconciled, can possibly lead to mental stress or illness; however, these are the fields of the psychologist and psychiatrist.

The higher conscious functions in both the psi-domain and the physical domain and is the only conscious domain that survives death. The lower conscious becomes redundant and dissipates post-death.

The higher conscious does have crucial role post-death, in that it provides post-death mankind with a domain of consciousness, and therefore, a conscious awareness of the psi-domain environment. It is also an element of the personality. It continues post-death, together with the other associated domains of the unconscious.

The higher conscious is a faculty which is highly evolved in man but is also present to a lesser extent in some other higher animals. Some have evolved a limited and varying degree of higher conscious capability. They can happily live their lives without any need or capability to consider notions of justice, truth or mysticism. Emotion in some form has sometimes been ascribed to some higher animals.

Some observers consider that basic emotions of anger, happiness, sadness, jealousy, loyalty and sympathy have been associated with rats, dogs, horses, elephants and cats, among others. This is contested by some: others doubt that animals exhibit, for example, loyalty which would be evidence of at least a basic level of higher conscious. However, based on anecdotal evidence, it would seem likely that some animals do have rudimentary elements of the higher conscious faculty.

The Species Individual Unconscious (SIU) in the Matrix Model

The SIU, described in detail in chapters 3 and 4, is the next domain of the Matrix Model. It is the node that communicates directly and continuously with the brain-duad for man and higher animals. The SIU, as previously described, is unique for every individual higher animal and for every individual human.

For all higher animals, the SIU provides a continuous source of information, thoughts and ideas and influences interacting with the brain-duad, and provides crucial heredity and developmental coding as previously described.

The Species Group Unconscious (SGU) in the Matrix Model

The SGU functions have been described in detail in chapter 3. It performs vital roles for many species, including insects and animals.

The Species Formative Unconscious (SFU) in the Matrix Model

A further domain of the Matrix Model is the SFU. The attributes of this were described in Chapter 3 and particularly Chapter 4. This level is common to the entire membership of a particular species, and each species has its own unique SFU.

The Primary Formative Unconscious (PFU) in the Matrix Model

The Primary Formative Unconscious, the PFU, has been described previously and was the original catalyst for the formation of the cosmos and instigated the laws of science and all the other Effectuators which subsequently evolved. It was also the generator of the first protoid-SFU which itself was the ancestor of all subsequent SFUs, for all the later species of life, from the original protoid through to man.

The Universal Unconscious (UU) in the Matrix Model

The Universal Unconscious represents the most remote domain of the Matrix for every life form. It is the level at which all forms of living and non-living forms are interconnected.

The Universal Unconscious is the original source of primordial intelligence which evolved into the Intelligent Universe.

The Mind and the Matrix Model for Mankind

The Matrix Model Theory is of fundamental importance in understanding the *mind* of humankind and the elements of its structure. The Matrix Model also helps to explain some aspects of human behaviour, including those more intangible aspects relating to religious, mystical and many esoteric traditions which are almost universal, in one form or another, across most cultures right back to and including our most distant ancestors.

Matrix Model Theory also explains aspects of para-normal phenomena, which will be described in detail in chapter 8. The elements of the Matrix Model which correspond to the "mind" are shown in Fig. 13. The mind of man is an extremely complex entity and it is that part of an individual responsible for thoughts, behaviour, intelligence and intellect.

The mind includes the faculty to bring into consciousness original, abstract or creative thought. It is the entirety of the brain-duad, together with the domains of the conscious and unconscious, as shown in the figure.

The mind is usually defined as the set of cognitive faculties that enables consciousness. It is also widely accepted that the mind enables the individual to have "subjective awareness and intentionality" towards their environment; to have consciousness including thinking and feeling. It also defines personality, emotions and instincts.

The Mind Domains of the Matrix Model for Mankind

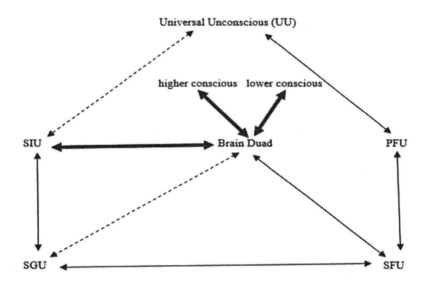

PFU is the Primary Formative Unconscious SFU is the Species Formative Unconscious

SGU is the Species Group Unconscious SIU is the Species Individual Unconscious

Fig. 13. The mind domains of the Matrix Model. Here, the physical body and environmental domains have been removed leaving the domains of the unconscious and the brain-duad together with the conscious domains. This eight-domain model applies for mankind and, with modifications to the content of the domains, for all higher animals.

There have been many profound philosophical debates about the nature of the mind as an entity. The mechanistic view is that the mind is a mechanistic faculty which is formed from chemicals and complex cells and is part of the brain located only within the skull of an individual.

Matrix Model Theory as described in this book, rejects this view. Whilst the lower conscious and physical aspect of the brain exist in the physical domain, the domains of the unconscious, the psi-aspect of the brain and the higher conscious domains reside in the psi-domain but are active in the physical domain and interact with all domains.

The "location" of most of the domains of the mind, are therefore, not within the skull of an individual nor within the brain. All the domains of human's Matrix Model representing the mind, except for the physical brain and the lower conscious, survive death.

As higher animals evolved, additional mind-nodes also evolved and all higher-animal Matrix Models are structurally identical to that of mankind, but with different content in the nodes, and varying, but lesser levels of higher conscious complexity.

The activities, decisions and behaviour of an individual are largely controlled by the mind. The brain-duad enables logic, physical short-term memory, reason and rationality to determine decisions and actions.

In the case of humans and higher animals, the brain-duad is the central communication hub of the Matrix Model, and all information flows from each domain contributes to thought processes. The "mind" of the individual is still centred on the brain-duad for an individual and has continuous intercommunication links with the SIU and to a lesser extent the SGU/SFU: it is a fully integrated system.

The information flows to and from the SIU and the domains of the conscious are strong and continuous; those from the other domains of the unconscious are usually weaker and more intermittent, as indicated in Fig 13.

These various domains can present a massive flow of information into the brain-duad which carries the risk of mental overload. To prevent this, the brain-duad includes filters. These filters are applied in a very sophisticated way and have evolved to be able to prioritise according to the "value" of the input information. Thus, all information flow into the brain-duad is immediately assessed and either prioritised or held in memory for later consideration or discarded.

Matrix Model Theory demonstrates the links that exist between the physical domain and the psi-domain. It also defines the elements of humankind which survive physical death, and continue as an active reasoning entity, existing entirely in the psi-domain after the physical aspect of a human has dissipated.

The Relationship Between Zones of The Mind

There is a direct correlation between the human mind, those of higher animals and the mind of the Intelligent Universe, as shown in Fig. 14.

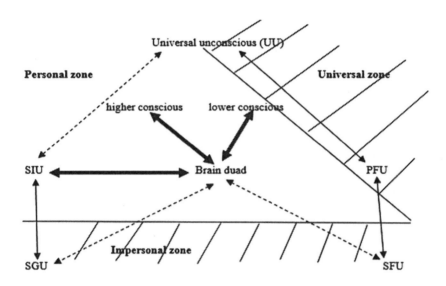

Fig 14. *The mind domain for higher animals and humankind is divided into three zones. The universal zone is pertaining to the Intelligent Universe and interconnects all minds and the PFU by the universal unconscious. The impersonal zone pertains to all members of a species, and the personal zone relates entirely to the individual members of a species. The SIU includes the long-term memory function within the associated personal unconscious. The SFU includes the collective unconscious which provides instincts to all members of the species.*

The Monad

The word "monad" in the context of this book simply means an entity having a form of existence exclusively within the psi-domain, except for man-made objects which exist entirely as monads in the physical domain and have no psi-domain representation, since they are not natural constructs.

A Duad has an existence both in the psi-domain, and a corresponding existence in the physical-domain. No life form or natural creation, like a rock, tree, or ocean, can exist as a monad only in the physical world. Whilst man has an existence in the physical world, the duad with his psi-aspect continues; when he dies in the physical world, his psi-aspects continue in the psi-domain as a monad; the physical aspect dissipates.

Thought Monads

A Thought Monad is a mind-construct comprising a powerful thought or idea, created within the conscious domains which is then transferred to the domains of the unconscious. Thoughts generated by the conscious mind are usually benign; they are generated and soon fade and dissipate or are routed to long-term memory.

Unless they are of special interest, they are quickly replaced by new thoughts. There are, however, a small number of powerful thoughts or images that under certain conditions, persist as dominant entities within the mind-domains of humans.

Such Thought Monads can become long lasting, fading slowly over a considerable time, and eventually dissipating unless they are rejuvenated and reinforced by further energy from further visualisations or experiences of the same nature, which effectively reinforce that particular thought image.

Thought monads can take the form of images, symbols, a sequence of events resulting from a dramatic or traumatic event or an intensely desired outcome of an event; a desperate "wish". They can be the powerful imprint of an event which has already happened or of a visualisation of a desired event which has not yet occurred. They are the result of powerful or often-repeated thoughts, events or traumas or strong emotions.

In many cultures and traditions around the world, there have always been practitioners of so-called "magic" ritual or religious rites, by various names, to generate and reinforce a desired outcome of an event. Such concentrations of thoughts can sometimes become Thought Monads. This may be motivated by the need to achieve a positive outcome such as healing someone, or perhaps, achieve a good harvest.

Some of these Thought Monads are reinforced by some form of ritual, or a group reinforcement of the intended outcome. The essential pre-requisite is that the Thought Monad construct is driven and reinforced by emotion or very intense concentration, or in some traditions, some form of ritual. In some cases, this reinforcement is based on a deliberate process.

Religion and so-called magic traditions have always been in some way connected. It could be said that the former is designed for the masses and the latter intended for some versions of an adept or trained individual. Both go back in history for many thousands of years, and both are inescapably part of man's history across many cultures.

The generation of powerful healing Thought Monad images have, anecdotally, led to cures; these are sometimes labelled "miracle cures" or the result of faith healing, where the powerful images are transmitted to the mind of the patient by the practitioner or faith healer. There has been no scientific proof for the effectiveness of either "magic" in the usually accepted meaning of the word, nor indeed in faith-healing: evidence appears to be purely anecdotal.

The tenants of religions, being based on faith, tradition or cultural belief, have gatherings or congregations to perform group prayers which is another way of reinforcing, in some cases, the need for a particular outcome; the co-ordinated thoughts of many, being stronger than the thoughts of any individual. The focus of these thoughts is, for most religious traditions, some form of deity, which provides a "target" for the Thought Monads.

A powerful visualisation of a traumatic event which passes beyond the conscious domains of an individual and its associated SIU, can occasionally pass into the memory stack of the SGU, which is the domain of the unconscious common to a group, or perhaps extend even to the SFU domain. Such images or experience-based memories can then occasionally be disseminated more widely to other individuals via their own SIUs, which have continuous access to the common SFU or SGU as demonstrated by McDougall's rat experiments described earlier in this chapter.

The unpleasant experiences of the rats during the experiments due to repetition and electric shocks, caused the formation of Thought Monads, which were distributed to the rat's SFU by means of psi-fields and became available to all rats of the species as instincts.

Where Thought Monads transfer between the SIUs of two individuals, a degree of thought transfer can occur, and this is the basis for telepathy, which will be discussed in detail in chapter 8, together with the research references that have proven its existence.

In this case, the Thought Monad can be generated at an individual level, whereby one individual concentrates intensely on an image or thought, thus generating a Thought Monad, which they then "send" to a colleague, and in some cases and under certain conditions via their SIUs; the image can then become conscious to that colleague. This is a weak and unreliable link but has been shown to function based on stringent laboratory tests.

Where a group or crowd strongly visualise a common thought or idea, they can collectively generate a Group Thought Monad, reinforced by collective thought.

Neither the sender of a thought monad, nor the recipient, need to understand the mechanism or even be aware of the process, no more than a car driver needs to understand how a car's internal combustion engine works. In some cases, a weak Thought Monad can be unintentionally created and transmitted to an unintended recipient, perhaps, during a conversation which causes the recipient to become aware of a new subject, for example, before it has been mentioned by either party.

As discussed before, this accounts for the "little coincidence" of the recipient becoming aware of the new subject, perhaps, a person or event, before it had been mentioned. It can also account for the frequent experience of someone "knowing" who is calling on the phone, before answering it[17].

The ancient belief system of the "middle Earth" described by Professor Brian Bateman[39] in his book, "The Real Middle Earth". Bateman describes a belief system from the Anglo-Saxon and Norse traditions and mythologies. It was a world of interconnectedness between all things, a web of life where everything gave and took from the environment and everything was inherently part of the environment, and everything depended on everything else.

This concept, however, was largely abandoned by, firstly Christian influence and later, by mechanistic science. This interconnectedness is, however, a fundamental principle of Matrix Model Theory.

The rebirth of a modern version of the web of life has, to some extent, been championed by the various strands of the green movement. Scientists such as Lovelock and Fritjof Capra, among others refer to these interdependencies which give us an improved understanding of elements of environmental science.

The domains of the Matrix Model demonstrate the interconnectedness between the universal zone, the impersonal zone and the personal zone, which form the web, according to Matrix Model Theory.

The Matrix Model and Life After Death.

As previously described, Matrix Model Theory predicts that most of the domains of the Matrix associated with an individual survive death. The domains of an individual which survive death include the surviving *personality.* This is derived from his or her higher conscious and SIU, with its associated personal unconscious and their associated psi-brain.

Thus, this continuance of life after death is wholly in the psi-domain; the individual post-death continues to exist as a sentient, reasoning, conscious being, but devoid of the physical body and the lower conscious, which have no role outside the physical world.

Humankind, therefore, continues after death as a monad in the psi-domain. They continue as individuals located within the psi-domain having conscious awareness of the psi-domain environment around them, with the ability to continue an existence, interacting with their psi-domain environment, moving, observing, but now decoupled from the physical environment.

The post-death human monad can be aware of other animals around him in the psi-environment; there is a full flora and fauna existence; they will still see birds flying, as the psi-aspect of their duads and butterflies and other insects will still similarly be visible.

To a post-death human, therefore, the psi-environment looks similar in many aspects of the physical world, complete with the psi-aspects of planets, stars, mountains, forests, rivers, oceans, lakes, waterfalls and forests which collectively form a complete environment.

Changing "time eras" in the psi-domain is no more possible in the psi-domain than it is in the physical domain. The human post-death monad cannot "pop back" to see how the Saxons lived. With just a limited flexibility, they are locked into their own time, even in the psi-domain.

The psi-domain only contains the psi-aspects of naturally occurring entities; man-made objects have only a physical aspect and do not form duads and have no existence in the psi-domain.

The monad entities within the psi-domain are eternal: there is no "second death". All entities continue to "appear" in the psi-domain in their original form; for example, when the Earth is eventually consumed by the Sun, it will continue in the psi-domain in its "pre-death" form.

Professor H H Price,[18] Fellow of Magdalene College, Oxford, and later Fellow of Trinity College, Oxford and Wykenham Professor of Logic, was best known for his work on "Philosophy of Perception" and had theories relating to the "afterlife" as he called it. He postulated that in the state of life after death, the self would exist in a kind of "dream-world", a world of mental images.

This is not unlike a description of the psi-domain, where the images are contained within the domains of the unconscious and higher conscious and are a combination of our own memories and an awareness of a psi-world which is a psi-representation of the existing physical cosmos.

Price further postulated that his "dream-world" would not follow the laws of science in the same way that our dreams do not. He also believed that entities would be able to communicate by "dream telepathy".

He eventually referred to the various experiments on such topics as telepathy, concluding that the evidence was sufficient to disprove the mechanistic theory that all mental phenomena originated from purely physical and chemical activity and processes within the body. He believed that current mechanistic theories concerning the mind could not explain mental phenomena.

Although different in many ways to the concept of the psi-domain, the idea of a mentally vibrant post-life existence is present in both ideas. He postulated that ideas and thoughts will be communicated between post-death human entities in the psi-domain.

Traditions Relating to the Empowerment of Material Objects and Places of Power

The generations of powerful Thought Monads created by individuals or groups with a common objective, assists us to explain why man, from earliest time, has included in his religious traditions and cultures, various shapes, symbols or material objects as representing centres of power.

In some cases, the symbol may, for example, have been in the form of a woman carved out of wood or stone representing fertility, or a representation of a source of nurturing, typically as a representation of the Earth goddess. In other cases, the form of a man would be manufactured, perhaps symbolic of strength or perhaps a phallic symbol denoting fecundity or in some cases, a war god.

Some of these ancient relics have taken the form of a simple shape or symbol. Archaeologists have discovered many such artefacts from ancient civilisations. They can also be encountered in modern society as a visit to many churches or temples or other religious buildings will testify.

There has always been a broad category of physical objects that, throughout history, have had some profound significance to a culture, tribe or civilisation. They could include idols, figurines, symbols, talismans or other artefacts made from a wide variety of materials.

The significance could be religious, spiritual and extended to include not only physical objects, but also to include places, spaces or buildings, depending on culture and tradition. Objects, spaces or buildings were made or crafted, sometimes at considerable cost in terms of labour.

One has only to consider Stone Henge and the massive effort the tribe that built it would have expended to move the blue stones from Wales and assemble them to be as they are, to create a sacred space. Similarly, the incredible skill and investment of resources to build cathedrals, churches, temples and pyramids is testimony to what they meant to their societies.

Sometimes, smaller objects were made of gold or silver to ensure that they did not physically degrade over time, implying that in many cases, they were of great importance to the tribe. They may, in fact, not have been regarded as "gods" but rather as representatives of some sort of spirit world, but have some specific reason for their manufacture, perhaps, as representing some spirit-entity; perhaps, to aid fertility, the production of a good harvest, to repel "evil", have a role in healing or any one of many topics of critical importance to the tribe or group.

There are many examples that archaeologists have found that relate to human's esoteric history. These objects were, and in some traditions still are, revered, and were sometimes associated with supernatural powers, in that they were considered, in themselves, to be able to bring about desired outcomes. This could, for example, be a request to bring about problem-resolution perhaps success in battle, or perhaps, they hoped they might obtain a glimpse of the future.

Sometimes, these objects were thought of as having the ability to influence events on behalf of the tribe, group or community by intervening with higher powers: the gods. Sometimes, the objects could become viewed as gods or objects of supernatural power in themselves.

In many ways, they can represent other ancient beliefs in the need to appease the "otherworld entities" be they spirits or gods, according to the countless traditions and cultures which humankind has constructed over many thousands of years.

This perceived "empowerment" is due to the generation of powerful Thought Monads associated with the object by the group leader, priests and followers of the tribe, sect or religion, associated with the object.

The tribe or group thought that the power resided within the object itself, or perhaps, thought that the object had the capability of "channelling" the required energy appropriately on behalf of the group to enable a desired outcome of a situation to happen.

Thus, in this way, a symbol could have been perceived as a source of energy, or power to the believers and followers of a tradition; an object held in awe, a centre of focal point for religious activity, rites or worship as far as the tribe or group is concerned.

In fact, the "power" clearly did not actually reside within the object, but within the minds of the tribe members; the object was acting as a focal point. This had the effect of reinforcing and regenerating the Thought Monads residing within the tribal SGU.

Thus, the group or tribe effectively indirectly "empowered" the symbol or object to the point where they believed it could influence events in the material world due to the collective power created within the group unconscious of the sect, group or congregation, and the focus provided by the symbol. The symbol itself had no inherent power.

The symbols or objects were sometimes carved in a variety of materials in a shape to symbolise the Earth goddess, or to represent planetary gods according to the many traditions, for example Venus, Mars, Jupiter, also Thor from Norse mythology who was associated with thunder, storms and protection of mankind, or other nature representatives like Herne or the Green Man and many others. The esoteric history of mankind is incredibly diverse and rich and were constructs of the human higher conscious.

Earth goddess symbols have been found in caves, as early as the upper Palaeolithic times and ancient Crete and other ancient civilisations. Many other symbols are well known; they appear in many forms such as amulets, corn dollies, symbols such as a broken cross or cross, a crescent or any one of countless others each having meanings and levels of importance according to the culture, religion and society in question.

Such objects could be made of carved wood, or even be large natural objects such as a particular tree or be formed from gold or stone, according to the culture. Such objects could similarly be empowered by the tribe. Some traditions recognised a place of power, rather than an object, examples include the Druid's oak grove, a temple, a church or a cathedral, a cave; there are many other examples.

This belief in place or object-empowerment is not limited to physical symbols; for example, even today, there are wells in England where people leave offerings to encourage the powers they associate with the well to assist them in a certain endeavour; usually associated with healing.

A specific example can be found at the Chalice Wells in Glastonbury in England where people tie strips of cloth to the branches of nearby trees overlooking the well, in this example, specifically associated with healing. The branches get crowded with cloth ties, so belief in this tradition continues today.

There are also various amulets, or as further examples, the athame and the cauldron of the wicca, or magician in some traditions, which the followers of these traditions believe are empowered to gain their assistance in a specific endeavour.

Once a tradition has evolved and changed, and belief systems have been replaced by new belief systems, or perhaps by conquest, the stone gods or the many other symbols and the places of power, can fall into disuse: the associated Thought Monads are then no longer reinforced and the assumed power and effectiveness of the object fades and vanishes, becoming once again a physical object of no consequence, except perhaps, of interest to the archaeologist or historian.

Chapter 8
The Para-Normal

A Problem Field for Researchers

The field of the para-normal is broadly defined as those associated with events or phenomena that are beyond explanation using the established laws of science. The subject includes telepathy, psycho kinetics, poltergeist phenomena, out of body experiences and pre-cognition among several others.

There has been a considerable amount of research over many years on some of these subjects which involve para-normal events or capabilities. Telepathy has been confirmed by strictly controlled experimental research and, as will be shown, the results have proven the existence of telepathy beyond reasonable doubt.

These results are always criticised and openly rejected by many scientists, who, in some cases, dismiss the existence of para-normal effects out of hand. Typically, the critics will dispute the validity of the methodology of the experiments and research, and if this fails, in some cases attempt to discredit the researchers.

The critics have, in some cases, failed to properly review the laboratory experiments, the details of which, in many cases, are available as published papers from reputable institutions. It has to be reasonable to examine the various experiments that demonstrate a para-normal effect to help eliminate flaws and errors or problems with methodology, which can be useful.

Criticisms should start from an open-minded viewpoint, as some are, and allow the evidence to lead to the specific criticisms, rather than, in some cases, the critics start from a viewpoint that the results must be flawed somehow, or fraudulent and therefore, even the flimsiest criticism will do.

A few of the many experiments that have been undertaken under rigorous laboratory conditions, by scientists within credible institutions, shall be described in this chapter.

In one case, the main critic, who was a strong sceptic concerning telepathy, becomes a research supervisor, re-designing the experiment in conjunction with the researchers to eliminate the many criticisms that he had documented. This resulted in extremely solid results. This demonstrated the positive benefits of rational criticism by a constructive sceptic.

One of the problems with the investigation of para-normal effects is that they are difficult to reproduce reliably and repeatedly under laboratory conditions. There are several reasons for many scientists not wanting to research these fields; among them, the most basic driver of research projects; why spend valuable research dollars on these subjects when, even if the effects are established or confirmed, there is no money to be made as a result, and no obvious benefits to be gained.

For example, if telepathy is proven to be a real effect statistically beyond doubt, so what? The keepers of the research purse strings would far rather invest in a new saleable product, or perhaps a new drug that would make money and benefit humanity.

This, in practice, has meant that the research into the para-normal that has been done, was usually carried out in universities which have an appropriate faculty, since these are the institutions that are most likely to engage in pure research without the need for a specific financial return.

It is surprising then that there is so much research data available on a few of the para-normal subjects, and much of it heavily analysed and scrutinised. Some of the research that has been done and results have been provided as detailed below. An explanation for some of the para-normal events shall also be provided, based on Matrix Model Theory.

Firstly, one aspect that has historically given the various fields a bad name, is that early or historic experiments were wide open to fraud and charlatans, some of whom made a living out of claiming capabilities, which later proved to be hoaxes or fraudulent.

A further problem is that so many of the events are anecdotal; that is passed on by word of mouth with no real evidence to substantiate the claims. Science demands much more that a series of anecdotes. Only cases where proper rigorous experiments have been concluded, performed by credible scientists working within credible institutions will be described in this chapter.

Another reason for some scientists to refuse to accept of evidence of the para-normal is that, should it be proven that such effects exist, it undermines some of the currently held fundamental tenants of science and implies that a new approach to some aspects of science is needed, or at least, a new extension of existing science. This could include requiring a new understanding of fields, the mind, and how mind and matter interacts or indeed, how minds interact.

Nikola Tesla[32], an inventor and physicist took the view that should science start studying non-physical phenomena, it would make more progress in ten years than it has made in several centuries.

It is a recurring theme in this book that some new approaches to some aspects of science is required: one, that accepts that living entities require, and have, a non-physical (psi) dimension as well as a physical dimension. Tesla, perhaps, alludes to this.

Noetic Science

This is a fairly new branch of science and is based on investigation and research. It is a branch of metaphysics which includes abstract concepts such as "being" and "knowing". It is attempting to reconcile the world views of those that see reality in strictly objective terms with those that perceive that a subjective view also has a part to play if a holistic solution is required.

It can be regarded as a branch of parapsychology that is defined as the study of mental phenomena which are excluded from or inexplicable by scientific psychology. Noetic science is also concerned with investigating the power and source of human intelligence, which includes how thoughts cause physical effects.

One institute that is following this path is the Institute of Noetic Sciences (IONS). This organisation was started by ex-astronaut and moon-walker Dr Edgar Mitchell[44]. He concluded that there is a great deal more complexity and mystery to reality than science would have us believe. Mitchell saw the limitations of a mechanistic worldview.

There are different methods for observing the world around us. Science is based on observations followed by measurement and experimentation and analysis. This has proven to be outstandingly successful as an *objective*, disciplined interpretation of many physical phenomena relating to the physical world and has been the basis of countless incredible achievements.

But there is another method that can explain our world, and that is *subjective* which includes intuition, feelings, emotions and instincts. This method relates to explanations which are occasionally beyond rational explanation but are still conceived as being, nevertheless, real and part of holistic reality.

Thus, subjective experiences may be beyond physical matter and consciousness or, in other words, beyond the brain/body processes. An alternative explanation to the mechanistic view is that there are many complex relationships between the physical and non-physical worlds. Noetic science applies good science to study subjective experiences and the ways that consciousness may influence the physical world.

Matrix Model Theory, as introduced in chapter 7, describes how the conscious domains, together with the *unconscious* domains, have considerable and vital influences over the form, function and behaviour of all life forms from bacteria to humans: indeed, the unconscious domains were instrumental in the establishment and shape of the entire cosmos, as previously described.

What this means, in practice, is that whereas conventional science is based on external observation and measurement of phenomena, mostly limited to the physical domain, Noetic science attempts to explain such events by considering such subjects as intuition or explains experiences which are inconveniently beyond the material, or so called, "rational" explanation. Such alternative explanations may be equally valid.

The field includes concepts of "consciousness" and certainly overlaps, in many ways, some of the content of parts of this book.

Mitchell is quoted as responding to critics as follows.

"IONS it is breaking down barriers and finding things; that's what science is all about; new discovery. There is nothing that IONS has done or demonstrated that doesn't have good science behind it; sceptics be damned".

Einstein believed that the experience of the mystical is a beautiful emotion and is the source of all art and science; it may well be that he was speaking from personal experience.

Experiencing so called "para-normal" phenomena may well turn out, in many cases, to be "normal" once the fields of science are expanded to include alternative views.

It is possible that further research will lead to new theories and a far better understanding of the conscious and unconscious domains. This could also include research into psi-fields; the mechanisms that explain how the domains communicate with one another.

Another scientist to contribute to this wide-ranging debate is the English physicist and astronomer Sir James Jeans FRS[14] when he stated:

The stream of knowledge is heading towards a non-mechanical reality; the universe begins to look more like a great thought than a great machine.
Source. James Jeans in his book "The Mysterious Universe"

There are other organisations besides IONS also attempting to get a more holistic theory reconciling these fields of objectivity and subjectivity. They include the Metanexus Institute, specifically researching links between science and philosophy, and "science and non-duality" which is exploring the nature of consciousness. This organisation believes that consciousness cannot be explained in terms of the existing laws of science and believe that, therefore, a new branch of science must be developed.

These thoughts are closely in line with some of the themes of this book, but from different starting points and in some cases, different contexts. When science expands research into the conscious to include the domains of the unconscious, we will get closer to understanding the human mind as a vast holistic entity being at the same time, individual, but also, on occasion, interconnected with other individual minds, and ultimately, indirectly, with minds of the entire species and beyond. This understanding is demonstrated by Matrix Model Theory.

A few of these fields shall now be explored, and strong experimental evidence for the existence of what is still referred to as "para-normal" phenomena shall be described.

Telepathy

This is probably one of the most researched of the fields of the para normal. This is a phenomenon whereby one person appears to be able to transfer thoughts to another with no physical medium being involved. It is, in effect, thought transfer to some greater or lesser extent. Some animals also appear to have the capability to some degree.

As the following descriptions of experiments show, the effect of telepathy appears to be an imperfect means of image or thought transfer; the "signals" appear to be weak and easily drowned out by other inputs to the senses. The results are never a 100% success, but when statistical analysis is done, they show the effect exists, greatly beyond that which can reasonably expected by chance alone.

Its success appears to depend on such variable parameters as whether the "sender" (the person attempting to send a thought or image) and "receiver" (the person attempting to capture the thought or image) know one another and have some degree of empathy. It also seems to depend on the state of mind of the participants, whether relaxed, tense or in a hypnagogic state (a state of being half-awake, or halfway between sleep and full wakefulness).

Success also seems to depend on the environment. It also appears, from the test results that, perhaps unsurprisingly, some individuals have more capability than others. Experimenters, as described in detail below, generally go to great lengths to ensure their experiments are sound and not subject to fraud or accidental transfer of the subject matter by physical means. The experiments are invariably overseen by sceptics (those who's initial view is that telepathy does *not* exist) to ensure thorough scrutiny of experimental methodology.

Sheldrake's Experiment with Dogs

Professor Sheldrake[17] is a fellow of the Institute of Noetic Sciences, a visiting Professor at The Graduate Institute in Connecticut. He has also published more than 80 papers in Scientific journals, belongs to many scientific societies including the Society for Experimental Biology and the Society for Scientific Exploration; he is also a Fellow of the Zoological Society and the Cambridge Philosophical Society, and has travelled giving lectures in many parts of the world.

Sheldrake[33] became interested in observations that some dogs seemed to "know" when their owners were coming home, even when the journey was out of the usual routine. Sheldrake carried out experiments, described in his book "The Science Delusion", with a terrier. The pet dog started waiting for its owner, at a specific place in the house, just before she set off homeward, when she had "formed" the idea of going home.

The dog did this whatever the time of day the owner set off for home, even at non-routine times, on 85 out of 100 times. This 85% "hit" rate is massively above statistical chance. Sheldrake then continued the experiment by continuously filming the place where the dog waited on a time-coded videotape. In this case, the owner was sent by Sheldrake at least 5 miles away from home and did not return until Sheldrake phoned her out of the dog's hearing, which was at random times.

She travelled by taxi, in a different one each time to avoid any familiar sounds influencing the results. Sheldrake's results showed that when the owner was not coming home, the dog was in the waiting place only 4% of the time, but when the owner was on her way home following the call, he was there 55% of the time. This is extremely statistically significant and demonstrates that the dog appeared to be "aware" of the owners return, far more often than statistics would indicate.

According to Matrix Model Theory, this implies that there is a link between the owner's mind and the dog's mind via their respective SIUs. When the owner consciously made the "go home" decision, specific and clear images would have appeared in the owner's conscious, perhaps definite images of "home" or the house.

These images could then be transferred across to the dog's SIU by means of psi-fields and then be turned into conscious images in the dog's mind. The mental image of "home" in the owner's mind would stimulate similar images in the dog's conscious. The pet dog could then react and go to the "waiting" area. This is evidence of some degree of telepathic capability between the owner and her dog.

A Telephone Experiment Indicating Human Telepathy

Sheldrake[17] has over the years built up a database of over 4,000 case histories of human telepathic experiences. A further experiment that he carried out was to examine the reports that some people often seemed to know who was calling them when the phone rang, before picking up.

Sheldrake recruited subjects who stated that they often knew who was calling them. He took the phone numbers of four people who they knew well and who phoned them regularly. The subjects were in a room by themselves with a phone without a caller-number ID system. The identity of a caller was then selected randomly by Sheldrake and his assistant by the throw of a dice. The selected person was then phoned and told to call the subject.

When the phone rang, the subject had to say the name of the caller, which was recorded. The times of the calls were random, and no mobile phones or computers were permitted inside the subject's room. By pure chance, the subject would be right one time in four, 25%, but she achieved 45% which is highly statistically significant.

This experiment has been successfully replicated in the universities of Frieburg, Germany and Amsterdam, Holland. Reproducing results of an experiment in different locations in different laboratories with different teams and getting similar results, are powerful tools in establishing the credibility and reliability of results.

This can be explained by Matrix Model Theory where conscious images, in this case from the caller, can be transferred to the person receiving the call by psi-fields between the SIUs of both parties, and thence transfer across to the receiving person's conscious. The caller would have formed a mental image of the friend they were calling, which transferred to the subject's SIU, and thence into the subject's conscious.

Rudolph Peters and E G Recordon Observation

A further example of telepathy[17] is provided by Sir Rudolph Peters, formerly professor of biology at Oxford University, as described by Sheldrake. This example was published in the "Journal for Psychic Research." Peters had a friend who was an ophthalmologist, E G Recordon, who had a young patient who had sight impairment and other disabilities, including mental disorders.

Yet, the patient seemed to be able to read the letters on the eye test board remarkably well, considering his condition. He could, however, only read the letters when his mother was present in the surgery; she was, of course, able to read the letters perfectly well. Further research carried out by Peters and Recordon included inserting a screen between the boy and his mother to eliminate any visual clues passing between mother and the boy.

They then advanced the research by moving the mother to another location and provided her with a set of cards which had letters printed on them. After shuffling the cards, a researcher held up the cards one at a time to the mother. The boy, at the other end of the telephone line, had to guess what was on each card, and the mother responded with a "right" or "no".

In the trials with pack with letters, there is a 1 in 26 chance of being right by pure guesswork, which corresponds to 3.8%. The boy actually achieved a score of 38% over the whole trial; ten times that which would be expected by random guesses. Sheldrake writes that when he was wrong and had a second "guess" he was right 27% of the time.

With the numbers the results were similarly astounding. Overall, the results were such that they were millions of times higher than would have been achieved by random chance alone.

The researchers had shown that telepathy, in this case, had been demonstrated beyond reasonable doubt, and the reason why the effect was so strong was thought to be because the very close bond that had arisen between mother and son due to his disabilities and his dependency on her.

In this case, it indicates that emotional links between the "sender," in this case the mother, and the "receiver", the boy, are far stronger than usually found between two people. The closeness of the SIUs of each of them would indicate close emotional ties between the two, and consequently, close ties between their SIUs.

This strong communication possibly developed to an unusual degree between the two to compensate for the boy's disability. Accounts for the astonishingly high "hit" rate that cannot be explained by conventional science and can only be explained by the existence of a telepathic link. In this case, the mother so much wanted the boy to do well in his sight tests, that she unwittingly formed Thought Monads of the letters on the sight test board and "transmitted" the correct answers to her son via their SIUs by means of psi-fields.

Further Telepathy Experiments

In a completely different context, there was further research using cards where the person acting as the "sender" in one building would transmit the image of the card he had selected to a "receiver" person in another building, ensuring that collusion and communication between the two was impossible.

Many of these tests were carried out at Duke University Northern California. Locating the "sender" and "receiver" in different buildings addressed the possible criticism of the tests in that it eliminates "leakage," where there are hints or clues even subliminally provided to the "receiver".

The results, described below, show a consistently high hit rate, statistically much higher than would be expected by random chance alone. Many of these tests were carried out between individuals who were either strangers, or who did not know one another very well, so the "bond" between them was either loose or non-existent.

In these cases, one might expect less of a telepathic success than between people who knew one another well. Some specific examples of successful tests along these lines shall now be provided, together with the associated statistics.

A Brief Note on Meta-Analysis

Before describing the experiments, it is necessary to briefly describe meta-analysis, which is another field of statistics, Statistics is a branch of mathematics that enables the analysis of data to establish trends, or whether an assumption is likely to be true or false. One specific branch of this subject allows analysis of large amounts of data, from many different studies, with a view to establishing the likelihood of a particular hypothesis.

The subject of meta-analysis enables the results of many experiments to be combined to provide a more robust conclusion. This is of particular importance when dealing with the subject of the para-normal, where large quantities of data, sometimes from many different experiments, are essential in determining whether a proposition is true or false.

To return to the simple example of flipping a coin a large number of times, introduced in chapter 2; if the coin was fair and had no bias, and if the coin-flipper was also fair, we would expect the same number of heads and tails to occur. The probability of a head being flipped would be 1 in 2 or 0.5. Our hypothesis would be that the coin is fair, so we would expect the result (that is, the ratio of the number of heads to the overall number of coin tosses) to be around 0.5 if the hypothesis is true.

For example, if the coin is tossed 5 times, the probability of getting 5 consecutive heads would be

$P = (1/2)^5$ which is 0.03125

When using meta-analysis, it is also part of the process for the researcher to set a "significance level" usually with a p=0.05 which is $p = 5 \times 10^{-2}$. If the result is below this number, the hypothesis would be rejected since the data would not support the hypothesis; if the results are above this figure, the hypothesis would be accepted, since the data would support the hypothesis.

It is important that, to determine whether a hypothesis is true of false, many results must be recorded. This involves accruing a large amount of data and applying meta-analysis. It is also important that all results are recorded; those which support the hypothesis and those that do not.

In the coin flipping test above, if we only tossed the coin 5 times, and got 5 consecutive heads, the results gave a p=0.03125 which is 3.125×10^{-2}, which is below the significance level of $p=5 \times 10^{-2}$, so the hypothesis that the coin is fair has not been upheld. The result here, however, would not be conclusive since there had not been a sufficient number of results, and therefore, the data would be insufficient to draw a conclusion.

Suppose though that we flipped the coin 10 times and got 10 consecutive heads, the probability of this is $P = (1/2)^{10}$ which is approximately 9.76×10^{-4} which is significantly below the significance level, and we would start to suspect that, either the coin or the flipping technique was not "fair", since the hypothesis that the coin is fair has failed. To really prove to a high level of certainty that the coin is not fair, several hundred coin-tosses would have to be performed and the data recorded.

In short, the results from the meta-analysis develops a single conclusion that has great statistical power. In general, the larger the value of p above p=0.05 (that is $p=5 \times 10^{-2}$), the more likely the hypothesis is *true*. Conversely, the smaller the value of p below $p=5 \times 10^{-2}$, the more likely the hypothesis is *false*.

Meta-analysis techniques clearly lend themselves to analysing the results from telepathy and other para-normal experiments where large amounts of data are collected from many experiments and where the para-normal effects are small.

The hypothesis that "a para-normal effect has not been upheld" will be proposed here; so, if the value of p is above 5×10^{-2}, the hypothesis has been upheld and telepathy has not been demonstrated. However, if the value of p is less than 5×10^{-2}, then the hypothesis has not been upheld and telepathy has been shown to exist. This chapter will examine some of these experiments and analyse the results.

Some Zener Card Experiments

Zener cards were invented by psychologist Karl Zener, and they consist of a pack of cards with each card having one of five different symbols on them. The symbols are a circle, a square, a simple cross, three vertical wavy lines, and the fifth symbol is a five-pointed star. They are sufficiently different to be difficult to confuse in describing and have no emotive bias.

Early experiments using the cards were arranged such that there were two individuals, one a "sender" who would select a card at random from a pack of

Zener-cards and, by concentrating on the image, would attempt to "transmit" the image to the second individual, the "receiver," who would have to "guess" the symbol.

Clearly, the receiver would have a 1 in 5 chance of guessing right, provided the selected card was replaced back into the pack after each test, and provided the pack was shuffled between each test (ensuring random selection from the same number of cards at each attempt).

These early experiments came into much criticism for the methodology used, and the way the results were analysed. Rhine[34] repeated the experiments with each criticism (and there was a total of 35 counter hypothesis and criticisms in all), taken into account.

Rhine and his fellow experimenter published their work in a document called "ESP after 60 years" Rhine and Pratt, (ESP refers to extrasensory perception) in which he describes these counterhypotheses and criticisms which included, statements that the statistics were analysed improperly, biased selection of results reported, hypothesis relating to the management of errors in experimental records, hypothesis including sensory leakage, suggestions of incompetence, among others.

Rhine and Pratt answered each counter hypothesis or criticism and ensured, having repeated the experiments, that the results were sound, and all criticisms were responded to in subsequent experiments.

Among the steps taken, the American Institute of Statistical Mathematics were asked to audit the mathematics that were applied. They issued a statement confirming that Rhine's statistical procedures were "not in the least bit faulty". In most experiments, all results were reported and merged into the data overall.

Over a period of 60 years, ESP (telepathy) studies were published using 77,796 subjects who did between them 4,918,186 single-trial "guesses". Most of these tests were carried out by psychologists and other scientists. In 106 studies, which was the great majority of the studies: the authors arrived at results significantly exceeding chance expectations.

Double-blind techniques were used which reduced to insignificant numbers any inaccurate recording of results. Both the subject and experimenter results were recorded without knowledge of the scores against which they were to be matched. This is to prevent the "receiver" having been told that he has "guessed" right being less likely to choose the same symbol immediately afterwards; thus "guess" or choice is completely unbiased.

Further errors were reduced by having two or more experimenters overseeing the matching of scores. Also, all the test results were saved and checked for errors several times. Data tampering was eliminated by having several copies of the data independently saved.

The possibility of inadvertent sensory clues was eliminated entirely. Often, the experimenter and subject were in different rooms. Those who criticised the experiments on the grounds of incompetence were able to check the experimental methodology.

Fraud was also eliminated, since it would have required the collusion of several teams of 2 or more experimenters to falsify the results. Also, at least 6 successful studies (which demonstrated telepathy exists) were gathered from experimenters who were sceptics: that is that their opinion, before the experiments started, was that telepathy did not exist, which is the predominant view among mainstream scientists.

One of these experiments placed the "sender" person and "receiver" person in different buildings over 100 yards apart. After 1,850 "guess" trials with the cards, the expected results would be to correctly guess one attempt in 5 by pure chance alone, that is a total of 370 correct results. In fact, they achieved 558. The probability of these results being due to pure chance were calculated to be one chance in 100 million! These are impressive results and constitute further evidence that indicates that telepathy, by whatever mechanism, does exist.

It is interesting that the standards applied in examining and analysing the methodology applied to these tests greatly exceed the methodology normally applied to most scientific experiments, showing the extremes that the critics had gone to try to cast doubt over or reject, the results that they found threatening or worrying since they could not be explained by mainstream science.

These tests, with such a high probability in favour of demonstrating telepathy, show that the interconnecting fields between the domains of the mind of one person and another allow the existence of the phenomenon of telepathy. The proposition here is that the mechanism for the interconnection is the psi-fields interconnecting their SIUs.

It may be either an evolving capability and not yet fully developed or a faculty which our ancient ancestors had to some greater degree than we do now but has faded over many generations as it has fallen into disuse. Telepathy can be explained by Matrix Model Theory which predicts the ability of minds to communicate with one another, to some degree, via their psi-fields, and the SIUs of the individuals, although the effect is weak and intermittent, and therefore, not particularly useful. Its most interesting aspect is that it demonstrates an aspect of the human mind and supports one aspect of Matrix Model Theory.

Other tests using a pack of cards with five different symbols on them carried out at Dukes University gave less conclusive results[17]. After hundreds of thousands of tests, they ended up with a 21% hit rate, when the pure chance figure would be 20%, not nearly as impressive as the results described above, but still statistically significant due to the huge number of tests.

Ganzfeld Research

Another rigorous test to research telepathy or ESP (Extra Sensory Perception) effects is known as the Ganzfeld environment. In these experiments, the "receiver" person was seated in a comfortable chair, in a room, with half table-tennis balls covering their eyes.

Red light was beamed on the table tennis balls, and white noise was played in the background. This provided an environment of sensory deprivation, blocking out intrusive sounds and sights to completely isolate the "receiver" person.

In a separate room, the "sender" person was stationed and had to choose at random from a set of slides to look at and try to "send" a "thought", of the selected image to the receiver person. At the end of the tests, the receiver person was asked to describe the images sent from a set of four slides.

The replies were recorded and independently judged as to whether they were "hits" of "misses". After many tests, meta-analysis was used to indicate whether telepathy had been demonstrated. This research will be described in general terms but should be regarded as a stepping-stone to the more rigorous methodology of auto-Ganzfeld, described later.

One of the most important researchers who used this technique to research whether there was evidence for telepathy was Charles Honorton, an American parapsychologist and research fellow initially at the Maimonides Medical Centre and later a researcher at Edinburgh University. There were 42 Ganzfeld studies performed in 10 different laboratories.

Across these studies, it had been calculated that the hit rate would be 25% if the selections were the result of pure chance. They achieved 35% which is considerably above the figure predicted by pure chance alone. Having analysed these early test results from the large number of tests performed, (using meta-analysis) he found that the overall probability of the results being due to pure chance turned out to be 1 in 1 billion!

Additional analysis demonstrated that this overall result could not have resulted from either selective reporting of positive results or non-reporting of negative results.

However, as is inevitable, the results were criticised on several grounds, mostly by a sceptic Ray Hayman, a cognitive psychologist. Honorton welcomed the critique and worked together with Hayman to perfect the experimental methodology, and in 1986, they issued a joint communiqué in which they agreed on the problems with certain aspects of the experimental methodology relating to the experiments carried out above, and how these could be overcome.

This included using a computer and a random number generator to select the "targets" (the images which the sender would attempt to send to the receiver) and include automated data-storing of the results: that is, recording the "hits" where the receiver guesses correctly, and the "misses" where he or she gets it wrong.

There were also further improvements to eliminate sensory leakage to make it impossible for the receiver to become aware, even subliminally, of clues or cues making a "hit" more likely. The "hit" or "miss" criteria was also criticised, and a more concrete decision-making method was evolved. This much upgraded methodology was called "auto-Ganzfeld".

Auto-Ganzfeld

The improved technique in auto-Ganzfeld used both static targets, using a pool of 80 still pictures as well as dynamic targets in the form of a pool of short video clips. In addition, the whole experiment was critically examined by several dozen parapsychologists and behavioural researchers from other fields, and most importantly, by sceptics.

The computer not only selected the target at random but also selected the 4 frame judging panels which were presented to the receiver. The receiver then scored each of the 4 options on a 40-point score scale. The computer automatically stored the score results in each case, and the experimenters were blind to the results; they did not themselves know which target image was correct.

A total of 100 men and 140 women participated as receivers over 354 sessions across 11 separate experiments. The receiver had to select from a sub-set of four comprising the real target and three "dummies". Chance alone would give a 25% hit rate over a large number of tests.

These results, presented below, showed results between 50% and 75%, which were *very* significant, demonstrating that the results, based on the percentage of hits, was massively above what would be achieved by chance alone. The results were published in the Journal of Parapsychology in 1990.

It has been established by other research that individuals are more receptive and have more success if they are in a calm relaxed state of mind. Best of all appears to be a half asleep or hypnogogic state. It is also possible that in a hypnogogic state, the receiver's SIU is more sensitive to psi-fields emanating from the sender.

It is possible that this relaxed state of mind improves the "signal to noise" ratio for the receiver, which is based on the theory that received signals during telepathic events are weak and easily drowned out by normal sensory inputs. The Auto Ganzfeld environment produces this environment, since external visual and audio stimuli are greatly attenuated or eliminated, as described above.

When Honorton used receivers with an arts background, he found that the hit rates were higher; in one set of tests, he used 20 music drama and dance students, from the Juilliard school, where a hit rate of 50% was achieved against an expected probability of 25% by pure chance. The musicians alone achieved 75% hit rate over many hundreds of tests. These are some of the best results ever achieved by Auto Ganzfeld.

By 1989, having further improved the experimental methodology, a further 355 tests conducted by 8 different experimenters had been concluded using Auto-Ganzfeld. These yielded significant results to the earlier Auto-Ganzfeld tests, giving a hit rate of 34.4%. In statistical terms, this gives the equivalent of a $p=5 \times 10^{-5}$.

Remember that the hypothesis here is that "telepathy does not exist" so a p value *above* $p=5 \times 10^{-2}$ would demonstrate that telepathy did not exist; but with a p value so extremely low, in this case $p=5 \times 10^{-5}$, the hypothesis (that telepathy does not exist) is false; therefore, telepathy was strongly shown to exist from this data and experiment.

Yet another meta-analysis was carried out by Daryl Berm, John Palmer and Richard Broughton, where they selected those studies and experiments which adhered most closely to the Ganzfeld process methodology, and an additional ten new experiments, which had been published since 1999, were also included.

The results were again shown to be very much above what could be expected from random chance alone, confirming earlier results.

In terms of yet more analysis carried out in 2010 by Storm, Ressoldi and De Riso, analysing 29 auto-Ganzfeld studies carried out between 1997 and 2008. Of the 1,498 studies, 483 produced results with a hit rate of 32.2% which is very significant (with a $p= 1x10^{-3}$) greatly exceeding results due to chance alone.

Further wide-ranging analysis were carried out by Storm and Ertel, where they analysed results from the earliest pre-communique days (the original test methodology) combined with the latest Auto-Ganzfeld results from many different sources, overlooked studies, and Melton and Wiseman's database of 1999.

The result overall gave confirmation that the effects were way beyond what could be achieved by chance alone, and further strongly indicated that telepathy does exist. They also calculated how many studies that showed chance-alone (no effect) would have to be done and *not* reported (or filed) in order to reduce these overall results to that one would expect from chance alone; it comes to a total of 857 studies; not a realistic proposition in practice; so, the "filed non-reported" effect was thus eliminated. In any case, the automated computer storage of *all* the auto-Ganzfeld results eliminated this possibility anyway.

Overall, the results are not explicable by chance alone, and the hypothesis that the effect is due to some form of telepathy has been demonstrated beyond doubt. Because of the success of the wide range of experiments, other institutions around the world have continued the experimental work with auto-Ganzfeld, including Amsterdam University, the University of Edinburgh, and Gothenburg University in Sweden and Cornell University in the USA. The arch-critic and initially arch sceptic, Ray Haymen, then concluded:

"The Auto-Ganzfeld experiments have produced intriguing results; if other independent laboratories can produce similar results with the same relationships and same attention to rigorous methodology, then parapsychology may indeed have finally captured its elusive quarry".

The "elusive quarry" is proof-positive that telepathy exists.

Honorton's willingness to accept all and any criticism and work with his critics, improving the test methodology and the analysis, certainly worked in the long run, frustrating as it must have been at the time.

More recently, Edinburgh University experiments have achieved a hit rate of 33% (against pure-chance results which would have given a result of 25%) using full Auto-Ganzfeld methodology, which closely replicates earlier work by Honorton. This answered Ray Haymen's conclusion that the tests needed to be replicated yet further, since they have been and gave similar results.

Yet further work by M Schilz and D I Radin, 2002 found a total of 929 hits out of a total of 2875 sessions reported by researchers from 15 different research centres giving a hit rate of 32.3%, compared with a result of 25% which would be expected by pure chance alone. This work closely confirmed earlier results.

Yet criticisms still abound on the internet, mostly of the older pre-1986, some of which may have been valid for the early experiments, but as improvements to the methodology were made, the results remained fairly consistent, so these criticisms have been answered.

I have yet to see a valid criticism of the later Auto-Ganzfeld results, although more than one critic has stated that it cannot be telepathy since, "there is no known mechanism to support it." This comment demonstrates the inbuilt resistance that some critics have in accepting even the most meticulous and rigorous experimental results. These results indicate a phenomenon not currently explicable by science. Matrix Model Theory provides the basis to explain these phenomena.

Auto-Ganzfeld Relating to Dream-State in the Receiver

A series of studies by Ullman, Krippner and Vaughn 1989, were conducted at the Maimonides medical centre. In this methodology, both sender and receiver subjects stayed in the lab, and the experimenters waited until the receiver fell asleep. This was an experiment to explore the idea that the "dream state" was more conducive to successful results relating to telepathy.

Once REM (Rapid Eye Movement) was detected in the receiver, it implied that the receiver was starting to dream. The sender was then alerted, and they would concentrate on a target with the goal of influencing the sender's dream. After a period of sending, the receiver was woken up and asked to describe his/her dream.

A transcription of the receiver's dream content was then given to independent individuals who served as outside raters. They compared the descriptions to several pictures, one of which would be the target. The judges themselves did not know which of the pictures was the correct target, (blind judging).

The results were significantly above what chance alone would predict. The descriptions of the images given by the receiver was, in many cases, sufficiently similar to the target image rather than the dummies (images that had not been sent), that they were regarded as "hits".

This demonstrates that the communication of the image is more dependent on the unconscious mind than the conscious mind, and it would be interesting to expand the work to include different personality types, and work on what personal profiles provided the best results, following the earlier work by Honorton and his musicians.

Spontaneous Telepathy

Telepathy within the family group or peers, is not uncommon from an anecdotal point of view, and this is difficult to measure or quantify. This is when someone seems to spontaneously experience telepathy, where images may come into the conscious mind of something which someone else immediately refers to, which may seem to be a random coincidence.

It is also the faculty which enables groups to operate towards a common aim with no apparent communication. An example of this telepathic communication is allegedly encountered among the Australian Aboriginals or the south African Bushmen (unfortunately all anecdotal, and therefore unacceptable as credible evidence). The Aboriginals regard it as not unusual for one of their number to suddenly go "walkabout" heading home over some considerable distance to meet with a relative who had suddenly been taken ill.

In terms of the Bushmen, explorer Van der Post refers to the hunting group returning home with their catch to be greeted by tribal members who already knew what they had caught and had completed the food-preparation accordingly. Clearly, it is almost impossible to find any rigorous laboratory-quality tests to measure such random effects to enable them to be regarded as acceptable evidence for telepathy.

If the sender and receiver are related or know one another well, as was the case in the Peters and Recordon observation described earlier, their SIUs might be better attuned, and we might expect the results to be better than if they were strangers.

This is where the concentration on the image impresses, to a slight degree, the image as a Thought Monad carried by psi-fields by the sender's SIU. The fact that hit rates which would be expected to be 25%, but, in practice, achieved results of around 33% rather than a 100% show that the telepathy effect, although demonstrated beyond doubt, is weak, and many distractions of other inputs into the layers of both the conscious and unconscious preclude anything like a reliable means of communication.

The effects do, however, provide further evidence for the existence of the domains of the SIU and consequently psi-fields, and that it can influence mind-content in some situations.

Professor Alistaire Hardy FRS[43] concluded that:

Telepathy does exist and has been proven.

If telepathy was a capability among our ancient ancestors, it is probably a capability which has been partially lost because humankind simply doesn't need it. Evolution is such that any capability which remains unused diminishes over time. However, there is no way of knowing whether our ancestors had the capability, or to what extent.

Professor Alistaire Hardy's view is that, in order for minds to communicate with one another, there must be a common stratum, which he refers to as a "group mind". This is very similar to the Matrix Model Theory proposition relating to the existence of the SIU/SGU/SFU family domains, in that for the duration of the communication between the sender and receiver, their SIUs are in communication, temporarily forming a group mind.

The reason why these conclusions are important is not because the weak telepathic phenomena are, in themselves, likely to be particularly useful, but rather that they strongly indicate an aspect of "mind" capability which warrants further research to determine the mechanisms involved in telepathy and the information fields (psi-fields) which this implies.

Interestingly, Nikola Tesla was responsible for many inventions and was considered by some to be a genius was asked where original ideas come from; are they entirely internal to the individual or is there some other explanation. Tesla's[32] view when trying to explain the source of his original ideas was that he considered his brain to be a receiver which collected knowledge and inspiration from the universe. He did not know what the source was but wrote that he *knew* it existed.

Perhaps, eventually some mathematician may produce a mathematics which proves the existence of the psi-domain and predicts para-normal effects. They would then cease to be "para-normal" activities but would be regarded as just become another branch of science.

Psychokinesis (PK)

There are at least two different definitions of the phenomena of psychokinesis; the first implies that a physical object can be made to move by the mental will of a subject. Another is based on the idea that the outcome of a random event can be influenced by the mind power of a subject. These effects will be covered in this part of the chapter.

Work by Helmut Schmidt and Others

(Reference Journal of scientific explanation, 1987, Volume 1, No.2, and other work prior to this date)

This interesting experiment describes experiments that used a random number generator, which is an electronic device which generates millions of numbers in a random manner and examine whether a subject could influence the outcome of experiments which use such equipment.

In Schmidt's experiment, he used a random generator which had two outputs: one represented "heads" and the other "tails". The random generator was programmed to count upwards at 100,000 times a second, and the count was stopped by the random output from a Geiger counter. The output was recorded as a "head" if the count stopped on an even number, (visually represented by a red lamp) or a "tail" if the count stopped on an odd number (visually represented by a green lamp). The outputs were recorded.

If the random generator provided truly random outputs, the system would be expected to be give an equal number of heads and tails over a period of time, and that would be represented by an equal number of red lamp and green lamp displays.

Subjects were asked to concentrate on, for example, making the red lamp to flash more often than the green lamp by mind power only. Schmidt pre-selected his subjects on the basis that they showed more "promise" than others which is valid since some may have the capability and others may not, and it is whether the effect existed or not which he wanted to determine.

His first experiment showed that subjects were able to deviate the expected 50% red and 50% green outcomes by a significant amount, demonstrating that, after analysis, the effect was certainly present with a 1000 to 1 chance against the effect being due to random chance alone (Schmidt, 1971 New Scientist and Science Journal).

In the second test, Schmidt used two subjects who had the best overall performance in demonstrating PK. These tests showed the effect was present with a 1 in 10^7 (ten million to one against) chance of the effect being due to random chance alone.

The third set of figures combined many experiments from 27 other researchers and, using meta-analysis the overall figure was calculated to be 1 in 10^9 (one billion to one) chance of the effects being due to random chance alone.

A critique of some of the earlier experiments was authored by J E Alcock who analysed Schmidt's work. He states that Schmidt has "accumulated some pretty impressive evidence that something other than chance is influencing subject's scores".

His main criticism is that Schmidt failed to "nail down" what was going on. This is a curious criticism, since Schmidt appears to have merely documented results that showed the effect existed, he did not set out with the intention of providing an explanation. It would indeed be interesting to consider alternative explanations for the effects described in these experiments, but it is almost certain, based on these results, that some intervention by the "mind" of the subject is involved.

Alcock's second criticism concerns the randomness of the random event generator. Clearly, this is important since if it is not truly random, there would be a bias in favour of one particular outcome, for example, slightly more heads than tails. However, Schmidt and his team ran the random generator overnight on occasions to establish that the output was truly random by checking all the outputs generated from many runs to establish that they really were "random" and therefore gave, approximately, an equal number of red and green lights, as would be expected.

Alcock also raised a further criticism that, overnight, the mains voltage supplying the generator would be more stable and more likely to be free from mains borne interference, whereas the experiments were carried out during the day, when the supply may be more variable. This would appear to be a criticism based on the assumption that quantum changes in the random radiation relating to the Geiger counter source is mains voltage dependent; this is extremely unlikely.

The key and valid criticism was that the experiments had not been replicated at that time. However, to answer this they were later replicated. Also, it was suggested that the results should be automatically recorded. Again, this is a question of methodology. Alcock sums up by stating that "in his opinion the experiments were flawed" but did not specify in what way.

Based on the above summary, that is a bit of a stretch. To answer these criticisms, the experiments were modified, and the work was repeated as described below. Clearly, having results which cannot be explained by current science, having critics and sceptics analysing the experiment methodology and results is important, and indeed inevitable. When the comments of critics and sceptics are used to improve the experiments, the results hold far more credibility.

The data from Dean Radin, Bell Laboratory 1981 (Mental Influence on Machine-Generated Random Events; six experiments) showed the effect was present, and the results demonstrated that a figure of 1 in 10^5 against these results being due to random chance alone. That is, one hundred thousand to one, thus the hypothesis that PK exists had been strongly demonstrated in this experiment.

Further work was completed by R D Nelson, Princetown Group (Nelson, Dunne and Jahn, 1984. School of Engineering, Princetown University.) This work showed that the PK effect was present with odds of 1 in $10,^4$ (ten thousand to one) against the effect being due to random chance alone.

Dean Radin also used the same equipment as Schmidt and performed his own checks to ensure that the equipment was truly "random" before conducting his own experiments, the results of which are described above.

The differences between the results in the various experiments is because different subjects were used, the assumption being that some individuals are more capable of demonstrating the effect than others. Also, it would seem to depend on how long each experiment lasted; subjects seem to become less effective over time, as they become less able to concentrate or even bored. The formation of strong Thought Monads requires a powerful level of concentration, which could induce tiredness and a reduction in performance.

In order to answer the criticisms described above, Schmidt published a much later paper entitled "Observations of a PK effect under highly controlled conditions" (1993).

In this work, five further different experiments were analysed and published. All were under tight supervision by independent observers. Steps were taken that enabled the observers to evaluate the results independently without having to trust the reliability of the equipment or the experimenter. Results were recorded automatically on a computer.

Independent observers did the analysis after the tests; the computer printed out the results which were sealed until the end of each experiment. Also, the *observers* decided in advance in each case whether the subject should attempt a "red" light predominance or a "green" light predominance in each test. This is to eliminate any possible bias in the results due to lack of randomness in the generator.

At the end of the experiment in each case, the observers analysed the results without having to consider the reliability of either the experimenter or his methods. In some of the experiments, the independent observers supervised one another! These tests showed that the PK effect was present with a statistical probability of around 8000 to 1 against it being due to random chance alone.

The tests were carried out by Morris and Rudolph (test 1), Rudolph is a professor of Computer and Information Science at Syracuse University, and Shiltz (test 2), then Morris and Hardin (test 3), Hardin is professor of Philosophy at Syracuse University, then Braud, (test 4) and Steppe (test 5) who is a theoretical physicist at Lawrence Berkeley Laboratory his papers cover elementary particle physics and the foundations of quantum theory.

This answered the critics. Even James Alcock, after he had analysed the raw data from the results obtained by Morris and Rudolph, wrote that the study was well executed and merited further replications.

It has often been said that when exceptional findings are made in a scientific experiment, then exceptional analysis will be applied to the experiment, the researcher and everything contributing to those results.

These results show that the PK effect certainly does exist, even though it does not yet have an explanation based on current science. These results are particularly interesting since they were carried out by highly reputable university laboratories and were the output of a particular series of specific experiments, thus eliminating the "filing cabinet effect" (where failed results are not published) and fraud, unless one believes in a massive conspiracy involving many reputable scientists.

Although the PK affect is certainly present, it is inconsistent in that it cannot be reproduced on demand, and it is also a weak phenomenon in that it takes many tests to statistically establish the fact that the phenomenon exists at all.

Schmidt writes that the results of these experiments conflicted with what quantum theory would predict, in that the Geiger counter, which controls the random number generator, appeared to be affected by the subject's mind. The Geiger counter "stop" command was instigated by a quantum jump in an atom from one state to another, which should, according to quantum theory, be random, and not capable of being affected by a mind.

It implied that when a system includes humans, either some aspect of quantum theory may be compromised, or at least have certain aspects which perhaps become questionable or that human minds can affect experiments in certain circumstances; these explanations are in conflict with the accepted laws of physics.

Alternatively, as Schmidt also notes, the subject's mental effort does not affect the quantum jump per-se but does affect the overall system outcome. The subjects may have no knowledge of the internal design and workings of the equipment (some subjects certainly did not), but they only concentrated on the colour of the lamps, "willing" them to be a particular colour, in other words, willing one of the two colours to predominate.

The mechanism causing this effect is clearly highly debatable and are not understood by science; only the results are clear. This gives rise to the interesting corollary; can scientists observing an experiment in any field of science unintentionally influence the result, by unintentionally "willing" the result towards a particular outcome?

However, the PK effect is obviously small, and many experiments had to be performed to detect the effects using statistical analysis. In practice, therefore, the effect on other experiments would be probably small. However, as Schmidt concludes:

These results leave, I think, no doubt that the PK effect exists in discord to currently accepted laws of physics.

Some additional evidence relating to how "mind" can affect outcomes shall be described later.

Work on Dice Throwing

L E and J B Rhine[31] (Rhine and Rhine, Journal of Parapsychology) were scientists who performed a considerable number of experiments to investigate whether certain individuals could influence the fall of dice. Initially, the dice were thrown manually by the subject, but, following criticisms by critic J E Alcock, (who appears to have been a frequently intervening critic in the fields of parapsychology) who suggested that the results could be influenced by the skill of the thrower, a mechanical thrower was used for subsequent experiments. Later in the series of experiments, the dice were first put into electrically driven rotating cages to ensure randomness in the tumbling of the dice before they were thrown.

Also, different faces of the dice were selected to be the "target" result, and great effort was put into ensuring that the dice were balanced to avoid any mechanical bias in the way the dice landed. The subject had to try to influence the face of the die that would land face up by power of his mind, or "will power" only, and with no physical contact between the subject and the dice permitted.

Eventually, they had data from a total of 621,216 dice throws. The combined results showed that there was indeed a phenomenon at work, with the calculated odds against the results being due to random chance alone at 10,115 to 1 against.

It was also noted that "hits", that is when the subject's efforts gave the intended result, occurred in clumps, particularly at the start of sessions. This is possibly due to the subjects probably feeling fresher and had higher concentration at the start of sessions and, as they tired during the sessions, their concentration waned, and the success rates declined.

When these starting "clumps" were analysed in isolation, the odds of the effects being due to random chance alone dropped to 1×10^8 to 1 against (that is one hundred million to one against). These results indicated strongly that some form of paranormal effect was at work and warranted the publication of the work.

Some critics have suggested that it is possibly due to some form of pre-cognition, that is an ability to "foretell" the result, rather than psychokinesis, which is also possible, but equally remarkable.

It is difficult to separate the effects of pre-cognition and psychokinesis in this experiment. The subject had to call the intended result before the throw took place in all cases. The "pre-cognition" effect could be eliminated if the required result were decided in advance by the experimenter, rather than the subject.

Radin and Ferrari conducted a meta-analysis of 140 dice studies and found similar positive results confirming the previous results. Again, the confirmation of the results by different experimenters was important and adds greatly to the credibility of the results.

As a follow-on from this work, Schmidt reproduced the earlier work by Rhine on dice experiments, as described above. He also measured whether subjects could have any measurable effect of stationary dice, by placing a die on a sensitive scale, and seeing if the subject could have any measurable effect on the dice's weight. No change in measured weight was seen.

As he states, "This suggest that the PK could not be considered as a force, comparable to electric of magnetic force". He also states that Rhine's work and subsequent improved experiments with new ideas, "has confirmed the existence of PK." However, dice-gamblers need not get excited; the effects, although significant and measurable, are very small, and they would almost certainly lose a lot more money than they made!

PK Placement Study

A different approach to demonstrating a PK effect was undertaken at Princetown University's "Engineering Anomalies Research Program". They constructed an apparatus that caused the cascade of 9,000 polystyrene balls to fall in a random manner through a matrix of 330 pegs into 19 collecting bins. The balls were counted electronically as they fell into each bin, and the results were recorded on a computer database.

The experiment was designed to see whether a subject could influence the mean fall of the balls in a particular direction; that is to influence the balls to fall more to the right than the left, or more to the left than the right. Several tests were done to establish the "mean" spread without the subject influencing results before the tests began and the subject was introduced.

Subjects were then asked to concentrate on shifting the mean of the fall either to the right or the left as they fell. Over 3,000 tests were done using 25 subjects and the data analysed. The results clearly demonstrated that there was an effect well beyond expected statistical spread or any effect due to random spread variation alone. In this case, the effect would be due to PK rather than any form of pre-cognition.

This experiment, unfortunately, does not seem to have been repeated to confirm the results, but they have been included here because of the reputation of the experimental institution, the number of tests done, and the number of subjects used, which seems to indicate fairly strong base of data.

It would be useful to see if these results were replicated elsewhere using different experimenters and following an in-depth critique of the experiment described above.

Explaining Psychokinesis Using Matrix Model Theory

To explain the PK effect in terms of Matrix Model Theory, we recall, once again, the existence of the Thought Monad. This is the coming into existence of an entity which is formed by a powerful conscious thought-image, possibly induced by extreme concentration on the part of the experiment's subjects. With this effect, the subject at the start of a PK test concentrates strongly on a particular outcome, and a temporary, but strong Thought Monad is created.

This Thought Monad can be transmitted by the psi-fields between the subject and the PK target. It is possible that this can occasionally have a very slight effect on events in the physical world given a particular set of circumstances. Similar fields are also responsible, as described above, for the telepathy effect.

These results seem to imply that some modification to the accepted laws of physics (see Schmidt's conclusions above) may possibly need to be made for *systems which involve human observers*, or at least experiments should be designed to account for them.

In the broader fields of science, there are also implications. For example, it follows from the above that it may be possible for observers of an experiment in other fields (other than PK research) to be able, unintentionally, to affect the results of an experiment in a manner that may not be repeatable in subsequent experiments.

If this is true, it implies that the methodology used for any experiment should, wherever possible, be chosen to eliminate this effect and provide an experimental environment that will eliminate the effects of "mental influence" from observers affecting the results. Researchers usually insist that experiments which demonstrate either expected or particularly, unexpected results, should always be repeated preferably in a different lab, carried out by different experimenters.

This will minimise the effects of mental influence affecting results. This may imply that, where possible, keeping experimenters away from the actual experiment and automating the whole process as far as possible may be a wise policy.

It may be that, where possible, experiments should be designed from the start to eliminate the Thought Monad effect on results; possibly by designing experiments in such a way that, at the time of, and for the duration of, the experiment, there are no observers. Everything should be done automatically, and the scientists are presented with the results after the event.

In conclusion, Nobel Prize Laureate, Professor Brian Josephson[50] proposed that explanations for both telepathy and psychokinetics might be found in quantum theory.

This is an interesting point; there is a strange effect in quantum mechanics called by physicists "quantum entanglement"[51]. If two quantum particles are split from a single source, a curious effect is observed. Each particle has a number of specific characteristics, one being what physicists refer to as "up-spin" or "down-spin", as *either* can have *either* spin until such time as one of them is measured to deduce its spin.

The other particle must then instantaneously adopt the opposite spin (by the rule of conservation). They cannot both have the same spin. If they are separated, even by a large distance, once the spin of one is deduced, it appears that the other particle reacts instantly to adopt the opposite spin; it is as though the second particle seems to "know" what spin it must adopt.

The two particles remain entangled in such a way that a change in one particle results in an instantaneous change to the other. There is currently no known mechanism for communication between the two particles, and if such a communication were to be postulated, it would have to operate to transfer the spin information between the particles much faster than the speed of light, since the effect appears to be instantaneous; this would violate relativity theory.

The "spin" between the two particles seems somehow to be entangled; the answer to this conundrum is not clear. Perhaps, the answer is related to psi-fields? Einstein called this effect, "spooky action at distance."

In this case, this explanation could revolve around the fact that it demonstrates that the activities in one system can be remotely affected by the activities in another previously related system. The two particles seem to communicate spin information with one another by a means that also defies any generally accepted explanation by modern physics...so far. No doubt research continues. Doubtlessly, there are several theories to explain these phenomena and possibly an answer will be found.

An Out of Body Experience

There is one additional subject worth covering here, which breaks the rule of only recording, in this chapter, experiments that involve what we have described as para-normal events, when they are based on experiments that have been conducted in credible research institutions with a great deal of rigor and control.

The subject about to be described relies solely on anecdotal evidence, because, by its very nature, this type of experience could not realistically be transferred into a laboratory environment, and therefore, rigorous experimental methodology could not be applied.

Doctor Eben Alexander,[35] is a neurosurgeon and an academic who taught brain science at Harvard medical school. On some occasions, he had patients who, as a result of serious illness, described out-of-body experiences, that is, where they experienced an experience where their consciousness seemed to have enabled them to observe events from outside their bodies. Eben regarded with a degree of scepticism; he would put their reports down to hallucination brought about when their brains had suffered trauma.

However, Dr Alexander suddenly became ill with a rare form of meningitis which attacked his brain; he was hospitalised. The doctors found that the entire neocortex, the part of his brain that managed thought processes, including sensory perceptions, cognition, and many other functions, had shut down completely. He was in a vegetative state, with no measurable brain activity at all. He was in a deep coma; scans showed no evidence of electrical brain activity of any kind.

His experiences subsequently are particularly interesting. His medical records of the time showed and confirmed no brain activity. He became aware of other "entities" around him; he could hear sounds and was aware of lights and he found himself moving into a lush green valley with waterfalls.

He observed a sky with clouds and tree fields and rivers. He experienced rain and even saw fish in the waters. He states that he "found himself as a speck of awareness among pulsing swarms of millions of butterflies".

The doctors at the hospital were meanwhile deciding whether to terminate his life support system, since there were no indications of any brain activity; but fortunately for him, he suddenly came out of his coma and became fully conscious. He recalls that he also "met" a person who he later came to know was his long dead sister whom he had never known.

He met her for the first time whilst he was in his coma; he recognised her from a photograph which he received four months after his experience! Understandably, Dr Alexander believed that he had experienced a glimpse of what he referred to as "heaven".

There have been many other similar out of body experiences recorded over the years. They are invariably attributed to delusion or abnormal brain activity under extreme conditions, for example, following a near-death experience or during major hospital operations. Some mystics and shamans also describe, in different ways, various descriptions of out of body experiences.

However, in these cases their brains were functioning normally during their experiences, so they cannot be regarded as similar experiences to that of Dr Alexander. This case is unique in that Dr Alexander's brain was monitored and declared "dead" during his experience, with no activity recorded on the monitors. He had, therefore, formed conscious images within his mind that were clearly outside his physical brain envelope.

What he experienced, had not occurred "inside" his head, but in the psi-domain, particularly from the viewpoint of his own SIU, and the functioning of his psi-brain, whilst his physical brain was "switched off". The experiences he encountered generated memories which were stored, not in his brain since that was not functioning, but in his personal unconscious within his SIU, which he was later able to access and restore those memories to consciousness.

His experiences during the event were undertaken by his unconscious and higher conscious domains; the elements that survive death, and the memories of it were stored in his personal unconscious. Clearly, anecdotal evidence of this kind, of which there are many examples, do not lend themselves to acceptance by the scientific community, since the effects cannot easily be explained by current science, or even in this specific case, by current neuroscience.

Perhaps, as the evidence mounts, experiments will be devised that will reproduce these effects under strict laboratory conditions and perhaps the reality of so-called out of body experiences will be explained, which may then demand a new branch of neuroscience. Perhaps, such work will also provide laboratory-grade proof that will establish the reality of the psi-domain. Matrix Model Theory provides a viable explanation.

Chapter 9
In Conclusion

An overview

The previous chapters of this book have described some of the many and various parts played by the Intelligent Universe in the establishment of the cosmos, its evolution from the time of the Big Bang and the establishment and evolution of the solar system. One question that still puzzles science is, where did the energy come from to produce the matter that expanded from the Big Bang.

One idea is that, perhaps, dark energy fluctuations flooded the universe with sub-atomic particles; another proposed by Hawking[7] is that the total energy within the universe is exactly zero: he states that matter has positive energy, but this is balanced by gravity which has negative energy, and the net sum of the two is zero; they cancel one another out. With this explanation, there would be no need for some mysterious source of energy.

It is also generally accepted that there are black holes that have been established throughout the universe; they are places with incredibly high gravitational field; in fact, gravity is so strong that no matter, nor even light can escape; that is why they are called black holes.

This raises a further question; at the instant of the Big Bang, where the total mass of the universe was contained within a tiny sphere with a singularity, it would have been a vast black hole, with stronger gravitational field than any other currently in the universe: how then, did the matter escape the massive gravitational field and expand as described in chapter 1, which reflects the current mainstream view of science?

It is proposed here that at the instant of the Big Bang, different laws of science applied; and, with the Primary Formative Unconscious, the PFU, providing the catalyst for the event, the laws that applied at that time enabled expansion, and the establishment of the "strong nuclear force" that enabled quarks to bond to form atomic nuclei. The rest then followed in the stages described in chapter 1.

The Big Bang must have been such an extraordinary and unique event that it has only occurred once in the known history of the universe; otherwise, there would be other Big Bang events creating expanding spheres of matter all over the universe; and yet, as far as we currently know, the event has only occurred once.

The Intelligent Universe, with its complex, dynamic domains of the unconscious, also ensured the establishment of the cosmos and planet Earth with an amazing series of events, some of which have been described in earlier chapters, which provided it with its critical distance from the Sun, a Moon, an atmosphere, oceans and an environment capable of supporting a vast range of life and subsequently, the complex pathways of evolution enabling the incredible diversity of the species.

There were several exceptional events in the formation of the cosmos; the establishment of the laws of science, which included the, as previously described, like the electric charge of an electron, or the mass critical numbers of a proton as a ratio to that of an electron, which, had they not been exactly as they are, stars would not have formed and supernova would not have exploded; events which established the heavy elements (heavier than hydrogen and helium) which were essential for the formation of rocky planets and, eventually, life.

Another strange event was the arrival of the eukaryote molecules; they possibly may have evolved by the invasion of very simple cells, the prokaryote cells, into one another, and both surviving, the event, as previously described, has only happened once in the entire existence of planet Earth.

Whatever the mechanism, this provided these complex cells with many times more DNA that the prokaryote cells and were essential for the establishment of complex life, which is structured from these eukaryote cells.

The arrow of evolution travelled inexorably from the earliest establishment of an environment that could support life in its earliest form, which occurred very soon after the formation of the Earth, through to the arrival of modern man.

The proposal that the first living cell on Earth formed from a series of random interactions between naturally occurring chemicals has been shown to have been impossible, as described in earlier chapters: it occurred due to a series of teleological processes. Hawking's view[7] is that science has come to realise that things happen, not in a random manner, but that there is a "certain underlying order". This view is supported in various ways by other scientists from various disciplines.

Natural selection, which is a powerful tool of evolution, has been described in earlier chapters, which tends to prefer or "select for" organisms that are better adapted to their environment or have an advantageous trait compared with other members of the species, and they will tend to produce more offspring that will inherit the beneficial trait.

It is a vital characteristic of evolution, aimed at improving and strengthening species as they evolve. The current view among some scientists[24] is that nature and life are inherently intelligent, and have varying degrees of cognition, even without the need to assume an overall design or purpose.

However, it is difficult to see how any intelligence in nature could proceed and achieve what has been achieved without any degree of purpose, and the evolution and establishment of enabling mechanisms. It is also impossible to see how the first living cell and the subsequent evolution and diversification of complex life could have occurred without both design and purpose.

We live in an Intelligent Universe, and intelligence begets purpose. The establishment and evolution of the cosmos, and indeed, the emergence of life itself without a teleological influence has been demonstrated to have been an impossibility from both a mathematical and information standpoint.

It has also been concluded[24] that it is almost impossible to explain complex structures such as the human or higher animal's eye having resulted from a series of random genetic mutations and natural selection.

Matrix Model Theory has shown how the various domains of the unconscious and conscious interact with one another and with the physical aspects of humans and animals, and to their environment. It also provides a new definition of, and structure of the human "mind" as a sub-set of the Matrix Model.

The existence of the domains of the personal unconscious and the collective unconscious has been widely accepted for many decades[20]. It is a small step to propose that other domains of the unconscious are active, not just within man, but within all other species, particularly higher animals, to some greater or lesser extent. Every living entity can be regarded as an element of the Intelligent Universe and contributes to it[14].

Information flows take place on a continuous basis between all the domains of the unconscious and the domains of the conscious. They determine, in part or wholly, the physical architecture, physical development, function and behaviour of every living entity for each stage of their life cycle. Such information flows are supported by psi-fields.

We thus return to the idea that all living entities exist in a "sea" of psi-fields and that each life-form "tunes" into those domains of the SFU family that are specific to them which they require to function, develop and interact with their environment.

For humans, this interface takes place from the instant of the establishment of the zygote (the earliest stage of the egg after fertilisation by sperm), and the SIU domain, which is a mix of the SIU content from both parents. The resulting new SIU for the human offspring remains an important influence and information source throughout the individual's life which provides, in conjunction with the organism's genome, the totality of the inherited traits and characteristics.

Fields

In the world of physics in general and the discipline of telecommunications in particular, observers are familiar with fields which support the ability of systems to transfer information between locations which are physically separate. When we consider the functioning of the domains of the Matrix Model, there is a web of information flow between each of the domains.

These information transfers are clearly achieved by fields, albeit not field systems with which science is currently familiar. A "field", in this case, is characterised by the mechanism whereby one system is able to affect another at a distance, by transferring information between two points. The field can carry coding or information which defines the way one system (for example the SIU), can affect the receiving system (for example the brain-duad of an individual).

The characteristics of fields used in radio telecommunications differs considerably from light, although both are electromagnetic fields. Light has a much higher frequency than those used in typical radio systems. Human and animal eyes are tuned to be excellent receptors of light but have no sensitivity to radio frequencies.

Similarly, we have been able to measure and characterise the effects of gravitational fields; they are not electromagnetic but are a different type of field altogether. A key characteristic of psi-fields is that they can transfer information between entities in the psi-domain to those in the physical domain and vice versa.

We all live in a mix of psi-fields emanating from all living entities and the various domains of the unconscious in the same way that we live in a mix of radio fields emanating from many radio and TV transmitters around the country, transferring vast amounts of information from the transmitter to the receivers, when the receivers are tuned to the correct frequency.

We are not "tuned" into any radio frequencies, so we don't notice them. When it comes to the vast number of psi-fields washing around the planet, each individual living entity receives those specific psi-fields relevant to them. These fields link their unconscious and conscious domains, in fact, interlinking all the domains of their "mind", which are directly relevant to them forming a complex web.

Typically, and importantly, psi-fields provide links between all animals and their associated SIU/SGU/SFU family, and, in the case of higher animals, most strongly to their own unique SIU. Simple organisms do not have an SIU domain as described in chapter 7. These links are established at the instant of conception, and instantly start the processes of influencing the animal's structural development (morphogenesis). Every human is linked to the Homo sapiens SFU, their group SGU and their unique individual SIU.

Several attempts have been made by scientists of various disciplines to define what is meant by "life", or rather "living entities," to differentiate between animate and inanimate objects. It appears that at some level, there is a common thread linking all living things in that they all depend on organised flows of information between their internal systems, and between the psi-domain and their physical systems.

These include their brain-duad and genome, their life-support systems, their replication-systems, and are represented by the associated domains of the Matrix Model representing their species. These information flows exist in all living things from the simplest bacterium through to the extremely complex higher life-forms, including mankind.

These information flow processes influence form, function and behaviour and include the elements of coding missing from their genome (solving the missing heredity problem), defining their body architecture, traits and how this architecture changes with time. These information flows include those that flow into and from the entity's immediate environment.

The essence of Matrix Model Theory is to provide a comprehensive description of these information flows: where they flow from and where they flow to, and what information (coding) is transferred. This is particularly relevant to the structure and function of the mind of mankind. The overall model demonstrates and defines how every organism functions.

Telepathy: Communication Between Minds

What is clear from the work of many scientists including Professor H H Price[18], Honorton, A Hardy, Schmidt, Sheldrake and various other researchers into telepathy cited in this book, is that the telepathy phenomena exists and has been proven. The phenomena could give another insight into the nature of the mind.

It has been proposed in this book that telepathy could also provide further insights into, more specifically, the domains of the unconscious. This indicates a need for further research into, not just paranormal phenomena, but also into the mechanisms that enable these phenomena to be realised.

Initial indications from the work on telepathy demonstrate that some individuals can "tune in", partially and intermittently and temporarily, to the SIU of another individual. This contact enables information transfer between the two individuals, which is the essence of telepathy. This capability seems also to be present in some animals, and between some animals and humans.

The highly detailed research which has proven the existence of telepathy is described in chapter 8. The elaborate methodology that was developed to collect and process huge quantities of data was sufficient to convince even the harshest sceptic, among them Haymen, who conceded that parapsychology had "finally captured its elusive quarry".

Further research work by Berm, Schilz, Radin and several others has replicated and confirmed the results achieved by Honorton. Professor A Hardy FRS concluded that telepathy does exist and has been proven. This proof is in direct contradiction to the existing laws of physics. The results of these research projects demonstrates that further work to establish an extension of these laws is now essential.

A Research Project to Investigate the Function of the SGU

To extend research into the SGU function in action, to further understand how it operates, it would be interesting to gather data on the electrical activity within the brains of several individual starlings within a particular murmuration over a period of time. Sensors are becoming smaller and less intrusive, so this may eventually be a practical proposition. If the brain activity could be measured and characterised, firstly, when the starlings were behaving normally, as a group of individuals, under the influence of their individual SIUs.

Then, secondly, these measurements could be repeated when they were flying as a tightly controlled aerobatic murmuration under the influence of their flock-SGUs, as proposed by Matrix Model Theory. This experiment may demonstrate whether there was a high degree of commonality of brain electrical activity when they were acting in their tightly controlled aerobatic events.

This would demonstrate the difference between brain activity when the birds were under the control of their individual SIUs, that is, when they were behaving as individuals, with that when they flipped to being controlled by their Species Group Unconscious; their flock SGU, that is, when they were flying as if under the control of a "single mind".

If the brain activity during aerobatics was similar or even identical in many birds, this would indicate that an outside agency had taken control, since such homogenised brain activity could not be dictated by any individual starling. This data would provide evidence for the existence of the SGU for starlings.

Missing Coding

Science is gradually discovering the nature of the information coded in DNA, following the work of Crick and Watson. This work was further progressed by completion of the genome project, as described in chapter 5. Science has also made amazing progress in gene editing to eliminate some inherited genetic disorders in some cases.

It is known that DNA and the genes influence many aspects of the structure of an individual, but a full understanding of the nature of the coding within DNA, and the exact format of the coding within the domains of the unconscious is not yet known. However, the totality of the coding in both is essential to fully determine form, function, behaviour and development of all living entities.

This book provides an explanation as to how they can influence the form, physical development and behaviour of man, animals, plants and trees and indeed all life forms. It is now known that there is more to defining the physical structure of life-forms and their serial development than genes alone. As detailed in Chapters 5, the missing heredity problem shows, the "genes are just not there" to fully explain various inherited traits and characteristics.

It has also been esablished[17] that the DNA content and the outcome of the research on the human genome structure and content do not fully explain the inherited architecture, characteristics and traits of an individual human or indeed of any species.

"Something else" is at work, providing the missing coding and information to provide the missing elements for the organism and its development. This missing factor is provided by the SIU in higher animals and the SFU or SGU in other life-forms.

The description of Matrix Model Theory has touched on many fields of science including, microbiology, cosmology, physics, psychology, the environment and wider fields of science, as the references listing at the end of this book testify.

Evolving Paradigms

Noetic science takes a quite different and constructive approach to understanding the cosmos and events within it. The purely mechanistic world view is increasingly being subject to criticism[17] as it becomes clear that it is failing to be able to answer many critical questions.

As we referred to the conclusion reached by Sir James Jeans in chapter 8 where he expressed his view that the purely mechanistic view is disintegrating.

The direction that the Institute of Noetic Science (IONS) will take in the future is interesting, in that it is one of the institutions that are attempting to change the paradigms of main-stream scientific thought and replace it with a wider, deeper and less restrictive or dogmatic approach, free from preconceived ideas and unhelpful prejudice but using good science.

This unorthodox approach is likely to arrive at new discoveries and new understandings and explanations across many fields of knowledge. However, new paradigms relating to the totality of reality, consciousness, what is meant by "life" and the mind are evolving and have been evolving for some time.

For example, professor H P Yockey,[42] who has been quoted previously in this book, did considerable work on the origin of life. He wrote:

Information Theory and Coding Theory show why life could not originate protein first, RNA first, in a pond, on a rock or on other planets.

He clearly rejects, not only the spontaneous mechanistic origin of life, but also the panspermia theory. As a chemist, he also considered how chemicals could be "organised" by information code in nature; and indeed, where the code could have come from in the first place.

He wrote:

The problem with the origin of life is to explain how information began to govern chemical reactions through the means of a code.

Even the simplest viable life form has enormous complexity which enables it to be self-organising, self-sustaining, had the ability to replicate and have a degree of cognition. This implies access to an enormous quantity of information. The source of the information governing specifically how the interaction of chemicals could form the first living cell, was the coding emanating from the first SFU.

Life could only start with the teleological application of the species formative unconscious, which, as part of the then Intelligent Universe, ensured the coding applied to the formation of amino acids, with left-hand only chirals, to form the right proteins to ensure the structure of the first living cell.

The new paradigm that we are moving towards, accepts that there are enormous interconnections between all living and non-living entities and their eco-systems[24]: that everything is interdependent and affects everything else, either through weak or strong interactions.

Chapter 5 described how bacteria and other prokaryotic organisms were the driving forces in the formation of the atmosphere and warded off ecological disasters by acting, for example, to reduce and adjust oxygen levels to avoid oxygen toxicity and, at a different stage of atmospheric evolution, acted to prevent hydrogen depletion, and acted to avert other disasters.

The atmosphere became suited to the establishment, evolution and sustaining of life[16], and remains a dynamic, stable self-sustaining system, relying on many living sub-systems for its content.

It is also necessary to find an answer to the problem of where the essential coding required for life to start, evolve and thrive, originated. According to Matrix Model Theory, the original source of the coding was an Ideation from the Intelligent Universe, which gave information flows to the newly established SFU, which evolved from the PFU.

This coding defined the structure, function and behaviour of the protoid and was passed to the protoid proto-RNA to ensure it was established as the first living organism, as described in this book.

We could describe the concepts that are arising from these evolving paradigms as "Jung and Freud meet Einstein and Hawking" in that the new model of "reality", involving some aspects of theoretical physics, quantum mechanics and cosmology combines with the world of the domains of the conscious and unconscious.

This new reality transcends the standard traditional model of a reality limited to three dimensions plus time and that life started due to a sequence of random chemical reactions, which is the essence of the mechanistic paradigm.

The existence of the psi-domain as the dominant domain of the mind, helps to explain the age-old traditions of mysticism and various aspects of religions, since the originators and practitioners may have, in some way according to their various and many traditions and belief systems, experienced some aspects of the psi-domain.

Archaeological evidence of ritual burials, temples, shamanic cave paintings, stone "gods", evidence of ritual killings and evidence of grave goods, all point to belief systems dating back to our distant ancestors, that there is an "otherworld" be it of spirits, ancestors or other disembodied entities according to some of the many ancient traditions which developed over many thousands of years.

Although these belief systems are not necessarily directly related to the psi-domain described in this book, they imply that, to a wide extent, man has from early in his evolution been instinctively aware of a post-life continuation of some kind.

This awareness could possibly have been due to dreams, out-of-body experiences of some sort, or perhaps, deep meditation or even aspects of instinct which could well up from the SFU memories of man's distant ancestors. He may have been unintentionally accessing the psi-domain by these means.

More on the Intelligent Universe

In this book, it is proposed that we live in an Intelligent Universe, which was the original source of the initial intelligence in the universe. Over many millions of years, this intelligent capability has been enhanced by the arrival of living organisms with increasing complexity and intelligence. This intelligence has been, in part, distributed to other entities including the evolving domains of the unconscious and conscious and throughout living entities across planet Earth.

Initially, a very limited degree of basic cognition was evolved down to the earliest forms of the species' formative unconscious for the protoid and bacteria and held within their SFUs. Evolution ensured that, over many millennia, intelligence was gradually and increasingly lodged within more advanced life forms' physical architecture, especially as brains, as centres of consciousness and short-term memory evolved more complexity.

As higher animals evolved, they also evolved a more sophisticated degree of intelligence, established both within their brain duads, and their associated SIUs. Every centre of intelligence, whether elementary or sophisticated, provides information that function as "cells" that are elements within the overall "mind" of the Intelligent Universe.

As species evolved more complexity, sophistication and diversity, so the overall net intelligence content of the universe increased; the Intelligent Universe evolved to be increasingly intelligent.

As already described, intelligence can be defined, at least in part, as the capacity to understand and perceive and comprehend meaning. Intelligence is also about solving problems. Nature has had to solve many problems long before man evolved. The problems solved included establishing the rate of expansion of the universe to be at critical rate and, as Hoyle discovered, the establishment of vast quantities of carbon, which was, due to its characteristics, incredibly unlikely.

These were seriously difficult problems to solve. To ensure these events took place, the Intelligent Universe established the tools to do it. This involved forming the domains of the unconscious, organised as defined by the various Matrix Models, and harnessing entities existing in nature, the Effectuators, as tools to be used in a teleological manner.

Creative capability exists within the unconscious and its associated mind array, as shown in Fig. 13; this includes abstract and original thoughts, ideas and concepts which can well out of these domains in great profusion. This creative capability is extended to the universal unconscious within the Intelligent Universe and its associated mind array, but in this case, the original thoughts and ideas lead to new ideations.

The human unconscious and its associated mind domains are modelled on the mind structure of the Intelligent Universe and has evolved to be so; it has come closer in structure over many millions of years. The Intelligent Universe gives evolutionary direction for the cosmos and all living species. Abstract and original thought is capable of imaginings without limit, which has led to millions of species, some arising without fossil evidence of ancestors, with their amazing diversity.

The tools used to move from an Ideation within the Intelligent Universe's mind to establishment of a new species include, mutation, evolution, natural selection and Ideating a completely new species from the existing tool kit; bone structures, tissues, eyes, wings, cardio-vascular system and so on, as appropriate.

As described in earlier chapters, the Ideation leads to the establishment of a new SFU which is instrumental in defining form, (morphogenesis, shape, body structure to a greater or lesser extent) function, (what it does to survive, how it does it, and survival instincts) and behaviour (how it relates to its environment, other members of its species and procreates).

Clearly, if a new species is a small evolution form its ancestor, the changes and contribution of the new SFU will be small since it would inherit most of its DNA coding from its parental genome; if, however, it is the realisation of a completely new species, the SFU contribution will be very considerable

The Intelligent Universe, in a limited form, existed before the Big Bang, and is present everywhere and is common to all living and non-living entities and is active over the entire universe. The Matrix Model for humankind and all living entities are evolutions and permutations constructed by the Intelligent Universe, which is evolving and has been evolving for the last 13.8 billion years.

Humankind as the Next Effectuator

The Effectuators were collectively and sequentially established by the Primary Formative Unconscious, the PFU. They have been described in Chapter 4 as a group of entities that effect the establishment and evolution of the cosmos and eventually, the establishment of life-supporting environments on planet Earth.

Humankind has evolved technologies including pesticides and insecticides. He has also been responsible for atmospheric pollution on a vast scale, deforestation, over-fishing, plastic and other pollution of the oceans and global climate change, which could have dire consequences and could threaten our life-support systems, and indeed, the life-support systems for all oceanic and terrestrial life-forms, many of which are being driven into extinction.

Humankind, as a species, has seriously damaged the planet. All these facts mean that humankind is influencing the future direction of life on Earth. To this extent, man has become an Effectuator, and possibly, a very destructive one.

If humankind changes in ways that respect and protect the planet, the outcome may eventually turn out to be beneficial. Whether humankind can achieve this remains to be seen. Plunging insect populations, including bees and other pollinators due to the use of pesticides (even the name given to these chemicals denotes a negative attitude towards insect life), increasing numbers of animal species that have become extinct or are in danger of extinction or on the "endangered" list does not bode well.

The fact that human population is expected, by some, to double over the next 50 years will put intolerable burdens on the global infrastructure including the provision of all resources including food, essential materials and water for people in some parts of the world. However, in some areas of the planet, human fertility is significantly reducing, which may indicate that nature is intervening in a teleological manner to halt this increase.

It is not clear that technologies can fill the gap between current food supply and future needs. It is to be supposed that man's role as an Effectuator carries huge responsibilities, taking care of the environment, together with a degree of population control, must be among them. But perhaps, an eventual awareness of the role may lead to an excellent outcome.

As our understanding of the cosmos improves, we may be able to predict its final state. Currently, it is thought that Earth will eventually be vaporised by the Sun, as the star expands to become a red giant and consumes parts of the solar system, including Earth, Venus and Mars.

This will result in the extinction of all life on Earth. However, all will not be lost, since man and other animals, will continue in the forms of billions of Monads in the psi-domain. Higher animals will exist as intelligent, conscious entities interacting with one another, and with the psi-environment which will continue.

Regardless of what eventually happens to the physical planet Earth, the psi-domain, with its massively diverse content, will continue as an active vibrant domain.

The Mind Evolution

The human mind has undergone an incredible evolution from the time when man had just learned to use simple stone tools through to the arrival and establishment of the incredible technologies that saw the agricultural revolution, the industrial revolution and the scientific revolution.

These momentous events took place over an extremely short period of time, compared with the time it took to evolve humankind, driven by evolutions in the human mind. We are probably about to enter an environmental revolution at the same time as a revolution in technology, which will cover the fields of artificial intelligence, communications and transport.

The environmental crisis has been much publicised, and some actions are now being taken to stabilise global warming. Much greater urgency is, however, required to reduce carbon dioxide in the atmosphere and eliminate the use of single-use plastics. Man's mind-processes will have to evolve to solve these problems.

In total, the global steps required to help save the planet will probably lower global wealth, which will cause significant economic and, therefore, political problems. In terms of transport, for example, it is entirely possible that, with the advent of driverless cars, private ownership of cars will cease since privately owned vehicles spend over 90% of the time "parked" and are expensive to run.

They will be replaced by a regime where everyone will have an account with a driverless car company, in the same way that we have mobile phone accounts. When someone needs to travel, they will "call up" a car (electric, of course) and "tell it" the required destination. On arrival, the client alights at his destination, and the driverless car returns to its base and awaits the next call. This will result in a cheaper, more efficient, national transport system.

Communications technology will progress exponentially with faster internet, and broadband universally available. Quantum computers, that already can perform simulations and computational feats, that are not feasible with even the most advanced classical digital computers; they will revolutionise new subjects, such as artificial intelligence.

Humankind is in for a roller-coaster ride on many fronts. As robots, advanced computers and AI take over our production and wealth development, few people will have to work. There will always be specialist areas, particularly in the arts, music, the theatre and creative fields and those essential to maintain the robots, but they will be a minority.

Everyone will be paid a "national wage." This will expand leisure activities, creative arts and community activities; the national wage will also reduce, or perhaps, eliminate inequality. These are possible future trends; forecasting the future is always a high-risk activity. Actual outcomes remain to be seen, but there is an irresistible logic to these projections.

The evolution of the mind, according to Matrix Model Theory, implies evolution of the domains of the unconscious and the higher conscious. Historically, evolution of these domains led to associated evolution of many aspects of all species, in terms of form, function and behaviour. The Matrix Model for all species has always evolved and continues to do so.

This evolution is far wider than man's implementation of new technologies, it also encompasses new ways of thinking, understanding our environment and the cosmos around us. It is also possible that some revolutionary ideas or ways of thinking originate in domains of the unconscious and are transported down to the SIUs of individuals.

There may or may not be something in the old concept of the seeding of original thoughts and ideas sourced from the domains of the unconscious; perhaps, due to accessing a multiplicity of other SIUs of other researchers, together with some mechanism for combining these "other ideas" to result in new ideas.

Tesla alluded to this when he described his brain as a receiver which, "collected knowledge and inspiration from the universe". He went on to say that he did not know what the source was, but that he "knew it existed".

As evolution lead to the establishment of more complex life forms, and the plethora of species, more "mind-stuff", intelligence and greater powers of cognition were increasingly imparted to these later life forms via their SFU families.

The eventual evolution of both the SIU and the brain-duads in higher animals accelerated this process: higher animals have complex and sophisticated minds, with Matrix Model structures similar to humankind, but with different content in the domains, as described in chapter 7.

The extremely rapid increase in brain size for Homo sapiens' ancestors over an incredibly short period of time has also been described. This event enabled the evolution and establishment of an advanced version of the higher conscious which was the final element of human-mind architecture (possibly!).

This evolution also greatly increased the complexity and sophistication of the human mind and gave rise to the current structure of the human mind, as depicted in Fig. 13. The greatest creative achievement in the entire history of the cosmos was the evolution of the human mind.

The mind evolved from the total nothingness of the Great Void, which was characterised by a state of a total absence of matter, energy or time, but contained the embryo of the Intelligent Universe, which was key to all that followed. The arising evolution and establishment of the human mind took 13.8 billion years, with countless essential intermediate stages; it was formed by an amazing series of teleological events.

References and Bibliography

1   Singularity is defined as a point in space where matter density is theoretically infinite. Thought to be the point of origin of the Big Bang, but singularities are also thought to occur in black holes. Black holes are regions where the gravity field is so strong that no particle with mass and no light can escape.

2   S Hawking, Lucasian Professor of Mathematics, Clare college, Cambridge.
    Theoretical physicist and Cosmologist.

3   E P Hubble PhD Astronomer. Specialist in extragalactic observation. Revolutionised the field of astrophysics, contributed greatly to work proving that the universe was expanding.

4   Penzias and Wilson Nobel Prize winners for work on microwaves demonstrating an expanding universe.

5   Rupert Sheldrake F R S; Professor of Biology Fellow of Clare's College Cambridge His book "Presence of The Past", Icon Books, covered his theory on morphic resonance

6   Max Velmas. Emeritus-Professor of psychology at Goldsmiths College London. Principally known for his work of consciousness

7   Hawking. His book "A Brief History of Time", Bantam Books covered the start of the universe, the Big Bang and explanations of what happened just after the Big Bang, and aspects of time-space. The book became a best seller

8   Alessandro Morbidelli. Italian Astronomer. His work specialised in solar-system dynamics. Reference here is to "Meteorites and planetary science" 2000.

9   Sir F Hoyle F R S. Professor of Astronomy and Experimental Philosophy, Awarded Belzon Prize for Astrophysics. Formulated theory

of Stellar Nucleosynthesis. Promoted the Panspermia theory on the origin of life.

10 Morowitz. Professor of Molecular Biophysics and Biochemistry, Yale University. Research included work on the origin of life. Studied the application of thermodynamics to living systems. Later, became the Robinson Professor of Biology and Natural science at George Mason University.

11 W A Bonner Research Chemist work on Ion channelling and amorphization. Wrote "Chirality of Life"

12 Bradley and Thaxton. Bradley Professor of Mechanical Engineering, Texas A M University. Harvard.

13 Hoyle: Omni-lecture given at Royd Institute entitled "Evolution from Space."

14 Sir James Jeans. FRS Fellow Trinity College. Professor of Mathematics, Princetown. Researched Stellar Evolution and quantum theory. Author of "The Mysterious Universe"

15 Hoyle's paper on "The Carbon Atom and its unique properties".

16 J Lovelock FRS, visiting fellow Green College Oxford, and Harvard University, wrote "Gaia; a new look at life on Earth" Oxford University Press, describes Lovelock's theory that the evolution of life and the evolution of the Earth are a single tightly coupled process from which self-regulation of the environment emerges

17 Sheldrake. In his book "The Science Delusion", Coronet, he challenges the belief that Science already understands the nature of reality describing how science is constricted by assumptions that have hardened into dogmas. He supports more free thinking and open-minded approach to science.

18 H H Price Philosopher. Fellow of Magdalene College Oxford, Professor of Logic. Wrote "The next world would be realms of real images"

19 Dr D Foster. Cybernetician; International Conference of cybernetics Imperial College, London 1969

20 Carl Jung. His book "The Archetypes and the Collective Unconscious" Routledge and Keegan Paul, describes the personal unconscious which is unique to each person, and a deeper layer which he calls the collective unconscious, which is not unique to any individual person, but is

universal to every human. The contents of this collective unconscious are the source of Archetypes and Instincts.

21 Edmund Solous. Ornithologist and prolific author on birds and natural world. Researched flocking birds sought explanation with the idea of thought transfer. Solous was the author of "Bird Flocks"

22 Eugene Koonin. Biologist. Russian-American, Expert in fields of evolution and computational biology.

23 Lynn Margulis. Environmental theoretician and biologist, University of California. Co-operated with Professor Lovelock on some aspects of the formulation of Gaia Theory.

24 Dr Fritjof Capra. In his book "The Web of Life" Arrow Books, Capra challenges the conventional mechanistic view of the world. He uses several sources including Gaia Theory, chaos Theory, ecosystems and social systems moving closer to answer the question "what is life". He also wrote "The Tao of physics" where he explores the parallels between modern physics and Eastern mysticism Flamingo/ Harper Collins publishers.

25 Dr Werner Gitt German Engineer. Head of Dept. of Information Technology at the German Federal Institute of Physics and Technology.

26 Leslie Orgel. Research Chemist. Fellow Magdalen College Oxford. Known for theories on origins of life. His theory of "Specified Complexity" described the criterion by which living organisms are distinguished from non-living matter. Orgel worked with Crick at the Salk institute for Biological studies.

27 R Carrier "Are Odds Against The Origin Of Life Too Great To Accept" a critique of all non-mechanistic explanations for the origin of life. He is a historian and activist-atheist.

28 F Hoyle "The Universe Past and Present Reflections" Engineering and Science, November 1981

29 Jonathan Wells. American author and advocate of intelligent design.

30 Karl Lashly experimented with attempts to find memory traces in animal brains over a period of 30 years. He trained animals to perform certain tasks then removed ever increasing parts of their brains and was amazed to find they still remembered how to perform the tasks. This work supports the proposal that memory is not stored in the brain. Professor, Chicago university.

31 Rhine and Rhine (1943) Psycho-kinetic effect "Journal of Parapsychology"

32 Nicola Tesla. Physicist, inventor in areas of electrical engineering radio systems and other unique devices

33 Professor Rupert Sheldrake, his book "A New Science for Life" Icon describes his theory of morphic resonance.

34 J B Rhine. American Biologist founded research Parapsychology as a branch of Psychology at Dukes University.

35 Eben Alexander Neurosurgeon. Author of *Map of Heaven* explores the mysteries of afterlife and truth about what lies beyond.

36 W C Harris Experiments on Chirality

37 R Rosenburg. Chemist Argonns National Laboratory, Illinois

38 The Shaman. Macmillan. A book by Piers Vitebsky describes the history and present-day manifestations of Shamanism.

39 Professor Brian Bateman. Wrote "The Real Middle Earth", Sidgwick and Jackson. Brian Bateman is based at Brighton University also wrote "The Way of Wyrd", Arrow Books.

40 Giorgi Parsi. Rome University Theoretical Physicist focusing on Quantum Field Theory and statistical mechanics and complex systems. Also researched flocking birds.

41 Viscount Illya Prigogene. Professor specialising in physical chemistry. Nobel Laureate. Noted for his work on dissipative structures, complex systems and irreversibility.

42 Professor H P Yockey. Work included fields of Physics, Information Theory and Molecular Biology. Studied the application of information theory to problems in biology. Critic of "primordial soup theory" for the origin of life.

43 Sir Alistaire Hardy FRS Marine Biologist specialising in marine eco-systems. He proposed that "something akin to telepathy might influence the processes of evolution"

44 Dr Edgar Mitchell. Lunar module pilot Apollo 14, the 6th person to walk on the Moon. Founding Chairman of the Institute of Noetic Science, which researches consciousness and other related phenomena.

45 Eugene Marais. Naturalist and Entomologist wrote a book entitled "Life of Termites".

46 Lenid Kiuglyac. Professor of Ecology and Evolutionary Biology specialising in Evolutionary Genetics, University of California.

47 Laurence Barron FRS FRSE Professor of Chemistry, University of Glasgow

48 Thomas Lindahl. F Med Sci British Scientist awarded Nobel Prize for Chemistry for mechanistic studies of DNA, especially DNA repair.

49 John D Hawks. Associate Professor of Anthropology, University of Wisconsin-Madison, specialising in Human Evolution and Biological Anthropology.

50 Brian Josephson FRS Theoretical Physicist. Professor Emeritus of Physics, University of Cambridge. Nobel Prize in Physics. Best known for his work on Quantum Tunnelling.

51 Quantum Entanglement-Einstein-Podsky-Rosen 1935. This paper described the EPR paradox, and the concept of non-locality indicates instantaneous transfer of information does appear possible and has been demonstrated experimentally.

52 Christian Anfinsen. "Experimental and theoretical aspects of protein folding". Advances in Protein Chemistry. Won Nobel prize for this field of work.

53 The New Science of the Brain. National Geographic, February 2014.

54 Humberto Maturana. Biologist/philosopher. Cybernics theoretician. Nobel Laureate. Santiago theory of cognition. Also created the term "autopoiesis" referring to self-generating self-maintaining structures in living systems.

55 National Geographic April 2014.

56 Francis Crick OM FRS Nobel Laureate. Molecular Biologist at Cavendish Laboratory, Cambridge and Salk Institute for Biological studies. Developed a model for the helical structure of DNA together with Watson.

57 Eric Kandel. Nobel Prize winner. Medical Doctor, specialising in the fields of psychology and neuroscience. Professor of biochemistry and biophysics, Columbia University.

58 Dr Francis Prior. Specialist in pre-history in the UK Archaeologist. Author of several books including "Britain B C" by Harper Perennial

59 SFU Species Formative Unconscious. Provides part of the coding for RNA. It is a domain of the Matrix Model.

Index